Saved and Sanctified

THE HISTORY OF AFRICAN AMERICAN RELIGIONS

UNIVERSITY PRESS OF FLORIDA

Florida A&M University, Tallahassee
Florida Atlantic University, Boca Raton
Florida Gulf Coast University, Ft. Myers
Florida International University, Miami
Florida State University, Tallahassee
New College of Florida, Sarasota
University of Central Florida, Orlando
University of Florida, Gainesville
University of North Florida, Jacksonville
University of South Florida, Tampa
University of West Florida, Pensacola

SAVED AND SANCTIFIED

The Rise of a Storefront Church
in Great Migration Philadelphia

Deidre Helen Crumbley

UNIVERSITY PRESS OF FLORIDA

Gainesville · Tallahassee · Tampa · Boca Raton
Pensacola · Orlando · Miami · Jacksonville · Ft. Myers · Sarasota

Copyright 2012 by Deidre Helen Crumbley
All rights reserved
Printed in the United States of America on acid-free paper

This book may be available in an electronic edition.

First cloth printing, 2012
First paperback printing, 2013

Library of Congress Cataloging-in-Publication Data
Crumbley, Deidre Helen, 1947–
Saved and sanctified : the rise of a storefront church in Great Migration Philadelphia /
Deidre Helen Crumbley.
p. cm. — (The history of African American religions)
Includes bibliographical references (p.) and index.
ISBN 978-0-8130-3984-8 (cloth: alk. paper)
ISBN 978-0-8130-4900-7 (pbk.)
1. African Americans—Pennsylvania—Philadelphia—Religion. 2. Philadelphia (Pa.)
—Church history. I. Title.
BR563.N4C78 2012
289.9'5—dc23   2012001056

The University Press of Florida is the scholarly publishing agency for the State University System of Florida, comprising Florida A&M University, Florida Atlantic University, Florida Gulf Coast University, Florida International University, Florida State University, New College of Florida, University of Central Florida, University of Florida, University of North Florida, University of South Florida, and University of West Florida.

University Press of Florida
15 Northwest 15th Street
Gainesville, FL 32611-2079
http://www.upf.com

This book is dedicated to The Saints.

. . .

In Memoriam
Beloved Mother: Elder Bernice Nicholson Crumbley
Beloved Father: Elder Joseph Crumbley
Dearest Auntie: Roberta Nicholson Ragan
Sweet Cousin: Eugene Crumbley

CONTENTS

Acknowledgments ix

· · ·

1. Call   1
2. City Tales   29
3. Saints Tales   49
4. Becoming Saints   107
5. Family   139
6. Response   165

· · ·

Notes   175
Bibliography   187
Index   201

ACKNOWLEDGMENTS

There are books that lure you into writing them. They give you no rest until their story is told. This is one of those books. It drew me into the academy to gain the intellectual grounding and professional credentials required to tell the story of The Church in a manner that would command serious scholarly attention. Still, it could never have been written without the generous cooperation of the saints who gave of their time, shared their personal lives, and offered me more hospitality than I will ever be able to reciprocate. Their love and prayers are greatly appreciated.

While the physical act of writing is a solitary act, a book grows out of communications with mentors, colleagues, and the works of intellectual ancestors. Although the work of some ancestral scholars ground this book project, they are yet to enter the canons of anthropological literature. The most notable example is Zora Neale Hurston's *The Sanctified Church* (1981), which has been recognized more for its literary value than as an anthropological study. Happily, still among us is Ira Harrison, author of the first institutional analysis of storefront churches that I encountered; the richness of his archival materials, combined with the intellectual dynamism of Faye Harrison, produced the groundbreaking edited compilation *African American Pioneers in Anthropology* (1999), which reinserted scholars of African descent into the intellectual history of our discipline. Melvin Williams's *Community in a Black Pentecostal Church: An Anthropological Study* (1974) paved the way for my book project, because of his strong message that an urban storefront church of African American "saints" demands the serious intellectual attention that anthropologists have given religious phenomena from around the world since James Frazier's *The Golden Bough*. I am also indebted to Caribbeanist and humanistic anthropologist John O. Stewart for his course African American Anthropology, which he taught at Northwestern University in a way that validated the transnational study of the African

American experience as a theoretically and methodologically grounded field worthy of curricular inclusion in any reputable university.

Finding scholars who appreciated an Africanist anthropologist doing research and writing about African American religion was not easy. Happily, two collaborative groups welcomed me into their circle. At Princeton University's Center for the Study of Religion, a project on Women and Religion in the African Diaspora encouraged such trans-Atlantic intellectual journeys. This Ford Foundation–sponsored project was co-directed by R. Marie Griffith, now at Harvard Divinity School, and Barbara D. Savage of the University of Pennsylvania. The recently formed Black Religious Studies Group initiated by Barbara Savage and Anthea Butler, both at the University of Pennsylvania, grew in part out of the conversations stimulated by the earlier project. The interdisciplinary, cross-cultural, and diasporic orientation of these two groups has been a source of ongoing inspiration.

Whenever my resolve to complete this project faltered or I simply got bogged down in the minutiae of professional and personal life, it seemed that I would run into the indomitable and effervescent Edie Turner at a professional meeting or come across an especially germane article in the *Journal of Anthropology and Humanism*, which she edited, and the writing of this book would reassert its pull on my life. Reading *Transforming Anthropology*, published by the Association of Black Anthropologists, or attending this group's panels at annual meetings of the American Association of Anthropologists, never failed to re-enliven my dedication to this book project.

The support of professional colleagues with whom we work day to day is central to seeing a book to its conclusion. Two heads of Africana Studies at North Carolina State University have helped sustain me through the writing of this book. Dr. Kwesi Brookins, on whose able watch Africana Studies developed both minor and major degree programs, has been my professional rock. Dr. Sheila Smith McKoy, whose research, like mine, spans both African and African American studies, has been an ongoing source of inspiration, perspectives, and sisterly support. The Interdisciplinary Studies Division within North Carolina State University's College of Humanities and Social Sciences has supported my research in both word and deed, with release time and grants so that I could complete this manuscript.

In academic life, it is important to have colleagues who are committed to seeing that a manuscript finds a publisher. Elias Bongmba read the proposal for this book and directed me to Anthony Pinn, his colleague at Rice University. Pinn was then editing a series on the history of African American religions for the University Press of Florida, and he believed in the work's intellectual value. I am also deeply grateful to Amy Gorelick, the press's acquisitions editor, for supporting this project and to Nevil Parker, who saw it to its conclusion. Grey Osterud's intellectual skills as a development editor were, as always, invaluable. I especially appreciate her availability because, during the year I was completing this work, she was also finishing her own book manuscript. I am also thankful for Matt Shipman's professional copyediting and for Grace Jenkins's skills in information graphics; both worked graciously under tight time constraints.

On a more personal note, I wish to express my appreciation for the prayerful support of the laity and clergy of the Episcopal Dioceses of North Carolina, especially St. Ambrose, the historically African American parish established just five years after Emancipation, the Racial Justice and Reconciliation Committee, and Bishop Michael Curry, the first African American bishop in North Carolina. My brother, Dr. Joseph Crumbley, has been an invaluable sounding-board and an ongoing source of intellectual and emotional support. I am profoundly grateful to my mother, who, until her recent death at the age of eighty-six, just as the book was about to be published, never tired of my questions and supported my efforts with her knowledge and prayers. Finally, to those whose names I have inadvertently omitted, my sincere apologies. Know that your contributions were appreciated and not wasted.

·

A portion of the royalties from this book will be donated for scholarships to support the higher education of youth of The Church in gratitude for the loving cooperation that made this book possible.

1

CALL

THERE ARE MANY WAYS OF BEING HUMAN; one is being Black in America. There are many ways of being religious; one is being a Christian. There are many ways of being Christian; one is being saved, sanctified, and full of the Holy Ghost. On one level, this book explores a universal human quest for truth and meaning through faith. On another level, it relates the particular narratives of a group of women and men who established their own faith community and lived by a unique formulation of Christianity configured within the cultural crucible of the African Diaspora in the United States. Because "The Church," as the "saints" or members refer to their faith community, was started by a woman, and women have continued to share leadership with men, this book is about gender, religion, and power. Because The Church has survived the death of its founder, this book is also about institution-building. Because The Church was founded during the Great Migration, this book is about religious innovation during periods of rapid social change and inequitable cultural contact.

This book can be read in several ways. It begins by placing this faith community in the context of African American history and lived religion. Then it relates the life histories of founding members, explores the religious beliefs and practices of The Church, and delineates its organizational structure. Readers who wish to meet the founding saints and learn of their journey from south to north of the Mason-Dixon Line may start with chapter three, "Saints Tales," which focuses on the experiences of founding members, both in Philadelphia and in the southern towns from which they migrated. For readers interested in religious practices and beliefs and their cultural and historical roots, chapter four is the best starting point; "Becoming Saints" offers thick ethnographic description of the congregation's rituals and symbols and situates them within the context of African diasporic religion. Those wanting to understand the social-historical background of storefront Sanctified churches should start with the second chapter, "City Tales," which describes the social and cultural dynamics that shaped the religious landscape of early twentieth-century Philadelphia, within which The Church emerged. Readers seeking insight into institution-building, gendered organizational processes, and innovative strategies for routinizing charisma will find chapter five, "Family," an especially valuable point of departure, as it analyzes the ways in which kinship and marriage, spiritual adoption, gender, and age have informed the social organization of this faith community. This introductory chapter, "Call," situates the story of The Church within germane scholarly literature and analyzes previous research in terms of "calls" for methods, approaches, and interpretive frameworks that better assess faith communities such as The Church. Chapter six, "Response," concludes by addressing ways in which these chapters respond to these calls.

The Church

The Church emerged around a charismatic woman preacher, healer, and pastor whom the saints addressed as "Mother." At the request of the saints, I have used pseudonyms for "Mother Brown" as well as for the names of the saints and their faith community, "The Church of Prayer Seventh Day."[1] Mother Brown was born in Virginia in 1879 just sixteen years after the Emancipation Proclamation and remained "the pastor" until her death on June 10, 1984, at the age of 104 (Crumbley 2000). She settled in North Philadelphia in 1914, the same year that what was then called the Great War began in Europe. The first generation of founding saints, who came mainly from the southeastern states, began arriving in Philadelphia around the start of World War II. The founder and the saints were participants in the mass migration of African Americans from the rural South to urban centers in the Northeast, Midwest, and West Coast, whose two phases were associated with the world wars (Hine 1991; Sernett 1997: 3; Holt and Hudgens 2009). Between 1916 and 1918, nearly five hundred African Americans left the South each day; by 1925 more than one-tenth of African Americans, formerly concentrated "below the Cotton Curtain," had relocated in the North (Dodson and Diouf 2004: 115). Between 1940 and 1960 alone, the South lost three million Blacks (Davis 1991: 11). Over a total of six decades, the South lost six million Blacks "seeking the warmth of other suns," comprising what Isabel Wilkerson calls the biggest underreported story of the twentieth century (Wilkerson 2010: 9–13). Philadelphia, the saints' adopted city, was renowned for its legacy of African American religious, economic, and political self-determination. Its history was marked by paradox: the City of Brotherly Love had been built on slave labor, yet it had generated an assertive, faith-grounded antislavery activism.

Mother Brown was a native of Mecklenburg, Virginia, where the first recorded Black congregation was organized on the plantation of William Byrd in 1758. "Baptist bred and Baptist born," she experienced a divine call to the ministry, but, on reporting it to Baptist church leaders, was advised that "God never called a woman to preach." In Philadelphia, buffered by urban anonymity against the monitoring gaze of family, neighbors, and home-church laity and clergy, she founded her own church and demonstrated organizational forethought not usually associated with charismatic authority. Consequently, the church was spared some of the crises and reversals associated with the quest for enduring institutional structures, a topic that is explored in the chapter on its organization (Turner 1969: 133–39, 153; Weber 1968, vol. 1: 23–28, 215–16, vol. 2: 223–46, 1113–48; Crumbley 2007).

Mother Brown's biblical literalism, emphasis on keeping the commandments, and spirit-privileging vision of being saved shaped the life of this church. The saints' southern cultural roots and mass migration experiences informed both their unique reformulation of Christianity and how they negotiated new urban realities. The Church has been housed within several inner-city structures, including the homes of members. The congregation expanded, mainly along lines of kinship, and has stabilized at approximately one hundred (Crumbley 2000: 7, 13–20).

Although sharing ritual, symbolic, and theological features of twenty-first-century "New Reformation" Pentecostalism, The Church can be understood as distinct from this intentionally evangelizing global phenomenon, which now has more than a hundred million believers in Africa and Latin America (Corten and Marshall-Fratani 2001: 1, 8–9, 82; Kalu 2008: xi, 105–21; Marshall-Fratani 2001: 91–96). The Church, founded a half century earlier, has tended to draw explicit and firm boundaries between itself and other institutions, religious and secular alike. The founding saints did not see themselves as part of a vast evangelizing movement changing the religious topography of the earth, but rather as a "select and chosen few" waiting for the millennial reunion of the saved found on the periphery of institutional Christianity. The saints speak in tongues and keep Sabbath, but they have not self-identified institutionally with a Pentecostal or Sabbatarian denomination.

Approach

Ethnographic Voices in Historic Landscapes

This study sketches an ethnographic portrait of an unaffiliated inner-city storefront church as a window on American social history and African American culture. In this approach, first-person documents, ethnographic descriptions, and social-historical perspectives are all brought to bear on the key questions this book addresses. Central to this endeavor are the saints' personal narratives. As an informant in another study of African American life wisely observed, oral histories help ethnographers "put some meat on the bones" of social-scientific concepts (Martin 1994: 193). In this study, the life stories of founding saints give concreteness and substance to anthropological notions of race, religion, gender, and migration. Their stories communicate what Ronald Fraser, drawing on Pierre Vilar, calls the "atmosphere" or "climate" of lived intangibles—the motivations, frustrations, aspirations, and regrets that ordinary people bring to their experience and recollection of large-scale social events and crises (Fraser 1986: 29–31).

By documenting what it was like "living while Black" both North and South of the Mason-Dixon Line during the first half of the twentieth century, these ethnographic voices offer a valuable alternative to what Cheryl Townsend Gilkes critiques as "flat images" of African Americans by portraying their "nuanced humanity" in three dimensions. In his study of a Black Pentecostal community, Melvin Williams observes that too often "the beauty and the good that reside in the adaptive life styles of poor black people have been overlooked or misinterpreted" by ethnographers who begin with distorted assumptions. Williams calls for "good anthropological ethnography on the behavior of the poor Black man in the United States" (Williams 1974: 3). Gilkes also notes that "writing the culture and its members into existence" can counter the dehumanization that accompanies marginalization (Gilkes 2002: 176). The oral histories documented in this book represent an ethnographic critique of the society that treated the saints as peripheral and silenced their voices and viewpoints. The saints' lived experiences demonstrate what Leonard Barrett has termed the "Soul Force": the worldviews, values, and behaviors that helped New World Africans endure and even flourish under horrors of their diasporic dispersal during and after enslavement, a moral and emotional resiliency that fostered the realistic grasp of their circumstances but at the same time galvanized them to look beyond their present suffering (quoted in Stewart 2005: 18–19).

The founding saints of The Church were not in a position to record their own stories. Stretching the low wages they earned during long hours of labor as domestics and blue-collar workers to pay rent, feed children, support extended family, and save toward a dream of buying a home, they did not enjoy the luxury of journaling or the means to become published academics. Their experiences and perspectives have been absent from the reservoir of information that informs educational curricula and shapes the public policies that have directly affected them and their descendents. This book writes the saints into our common body of knowledge in order to subvert the social practices that have excluded their stories from the human saga. It is, then, an exercise in liberating "subjugated knowledges" (Foucault 2003: 7; 1981: 81–83, 95–98, 101–3, 105), since it takes the saints' interpretations of their experiences and their understandings of the world seriously. As Faye Harrison notes, the ethnography of African American people has generally been relegated to "veiled" and peripheral spaces in the arena of anthropological knowledge (Harrison 2008: 15–19, 69; see also Harrison and Harrison 1999: 1). As the founding saints' labor was subjugated within the inequitable socioeconomic and political structures of the dominant society, so their commentary on the world was subjugated and removed to the outskirts of intellectual discourse, when acknowledged at all. Epistemologically, the saints' recollected lives are treated as valid sources of knowledge about what it means to be human beings who are faithful during trying times. As St. Clair Drake observed, "Some things can be known *only* by those who have experienced them" (Drake 1987: 1–4).

This study, like all ethnography, is undeniably political. Whether serving as "handmaiden to colonialism," "setting the record straight" in the African American tradition of "vindicationist scholarship," or by grounding postmodern critiques of "objective" knowledge, the ethnographic endeavor always entails power dynamics between those who are studied and those doing the studying. The "person" of the ethnographer always has been embedded within the ethnographic process, despite earlier conventions of writing culture that erased any trace of the ethnographer's social positioning and cultural grounding (Harrison 2008: 2–3, 67; Spickard 2002: 249–51; Harrison and Harrison 1999: 1–3; Okely 1992: 5).

The narratives of the founding saints were collected under two different sets of conditions: the first while I was growing up as a "child of The Church," the second formally structured and academic. It is in the intersection of these two vantage points that the story of The Church is written. The formal interviews, conducted when I was a research fellow at Princeton University's Center for the Study of Religion in 2001–2, were based on open-ended questions. While each interview covered the same general topics, the saints were allowed to tell their stories freely. Some, including my mother, spoke at such great length that their narratives comprise a veritable autobiography. Other methods of data collection were also used. Members of each of the major church families were asked to gather information and compile their family histories, and given token compensation for this effort. Short, anonymous surveys were distributed to the adult members as well.

I heard many stories during my childhood and young adulthood. Before the Internet and when television was so new that not every home had one, the human voice was the only vehicle for certain kinds of knowledge, and personal memory its only reservoir. Some of these narratives were told while sitting around after Sabbath lunch and others in the blueberry field, where they broke that special monotony unique to farm labor. My mother was the family *griot*, for like these West African "keepers of history" (popularized in 1976 by Alex Haley's *Roots* and by the "World Music" marketed in the 1980s), she has kept our story alive through oral histories, which have been a crucial medium of knowledge of the world and my place in it. It seems only natural to pass on what was passed on to me and to document it through up-to-date information technologies for the future.

James Clifford wisely notes that ethnographic observations are "inherently partial" (Clifford 1986: 7). If another member of The Church decided to write about it, he or she would select and interpret data differently than I have, because he or she would have access to a different set of stories and be positioned differently within the configuration of church families. There are many stories to be told about the saints, and I wish I could tell them all, but there are always constraints on what one book can cover. The historical focus of this work is on the founding years of The Church during the Great Migration era, and the life stories presented in chapter three, "Saints Tales," are limited to founding members who became elders. Some of these founding-saint elders died before the study was conducted, and three of those interviewed passed on before the manuscript was completed.

I hope that the saints will resonate with the way I have presented The Church's story. The Church is a face-to-face social grouping that includes about one hundred people. Ethnography tends to emphasize the particular over the general, the individual over the universal. Yet, within the "thick description" of this study, it is possible to ascertain patterns, associations, relationships, and trajectories that suggest more general truths about the ways that human beings employ cultural legacies, social ambiguities, and religious faith to negotiate the challenges of rapid social change.

Why construct historically embedded ethnography? Why not just write a simple ethnography of The Church? Without historical context, ethnography runs the risk of rendering a community isolated and static, explaining its ideas and behaviors as little more than vehicles of social cohesion and stability. Setting the present in historical context offsets the conservative tendencies that can follow from uncritical functionalism (Macfarlane 1977). The Church did not emerge fully formed out of a cultural or historical vacuum, and it has not remained frozen in time. Its symbols and modes of worship developed from a dynamic synthesis of the religious legacies that the saints brought with them from the South and the religious options available to them in the urban North.

Indeed, the fact that the saints were in Philadelphia at all is directly related to the acceleration of industrialization during the two world wars, which increased the demand for labor at the same time that many men were entering the armed services. African Americans, who had historically been excluded from industrial employment, enjoyed new opportunities. The Great War dramatically reduced European immigration, and in the 1920s, the United States passed legislation restricting immigration. The prospect of finding decent jobs, coupled with the desire to escape the blatant economic exploitation and violent racial oppression that prevailed in the South, fueled the northward migration of millions of Black people. Until recently, the Great Migration has been studied primarily in socioeconomic terms. The personal narratives of the saints attest to these dynamics, as women recall earning less than three dollars per week, men relate accounts of debt-laden sharecropping, and both men and women describe incidents of violence and murder.

Lynching, the extralegal but semiofficial murder of Black men and women by organized groups of Whites, has marred post-Emancipation American history. Between 1822 and 1930, 1,663 Blacks were lynched in the "Cotton South"—South Carolina, Georgia, Alabama, Mississippi, and Louisiana—alone (Tolnay and Beck 1991: 27; Cohen 1991: 211; Allen, Als, Lewis, and Litwack 2000). After the end of Reconstruction in 1877, southern Whites established laws and social institutions to "redeem" society from the consequences of Emancipation: they seized and monopolized political power by redistricting and imposing poll taxes, literacy tests, and property criteria for voting; they controlled Black labor through sharecropping and furnishing contracts, enacting vagrancy laws, and using chain gangs of prisoners. They imposed White supremacy through social organizations with paramilitary functions, including—in addition to the notorious Ku Klux Klan—"rifle clubs," Red Shirts, and the White League. Lynching flourished in the late-nineteenth century as Whites were erecting the Jim Crow regime; during the four-year period from 1885 to 1889, lynching increased by 63 percent (Cohen 1991: 3–43, 201–47).

While I take seriously the personal and spiritual themes that recur in the saints' narratives as reasons for joining The Church, I do not ignore the material difficulties the saints faced. As John Dollard observed, "Oftentimes, just to go away is one of the most aggressive" actions a person can take (quoted in Wilkerson 2010: 10–11). The founding saints did just this. They fled the South, settled in Philadelphia, and responded to the challenges of urban life by establishing a sustainable institutional arena of meaning, community, and safety in the inner city. Understanding The Church demands more than what George Marcus calls "closely observed cultural worlds" (1986: 165–66). It demands an examination of larger, impersonal processes of change that respects both ethnographic particularity and social-historical breadth (Tweed 2002: 63; Trouillot 1995: 1–4; Comaroff and Comaroff 1993: xiii–xvii, 1992: 7–11; Comaroff 1985: 257–63; Fox 1991: 96).

Elders' interviews addressed personal experiences both in their southern hometowns and in the city of Philadelphia. This approach was inspired by two works. In her novel *Jazz* (1992), Toni Morrison relates an urban tale of infidelity, murder, retribution, and redemption. Set during the Great Migration, the story tracks Black lives back and forth between rural southern worlds and New York City. Allen Ballard's *One More Day's Journey: The Story of a Family and a People* (1984) situates his family's migration from South Carolina to Philadelphia within the histories of both regions. These "back and forth" accounts mirror migrants' lived experiences and put flesh on the telling of the Great Migration. Like Wilkerson's *The Warmth of Other Suns*, with its core of Great Migration narratives, this book is written to relate how African Americans "dared to make the crossing" and do what "human beings looking for freedom, throughout history have often done. They left" (Wilkerson 2010: 540, 15). They went on to build a new place to call home.

Within and Without

How should a scholar approach the study of a faith community when it is his or her own? Should she distance herself, fling herself into the ethnographic moment, or, in the words of Susan Harding, remain standing in the gap? (Harding 1987). In anthropology, dichotomies between "etic" foreign outsiders and "emic" native insiders have given way to critically hybridized categories and intentionally blurred boundaries between these positions. Now scholars emphasize the lived experience of doing fieldwork by adopting ethnographic approaches that sympathize with poetics, politics, and history (Harrison 2008: 17–19; Aguilar 1981; Bakalaki 1997; Clifford 1986; Feleppa 1986; Gwaltney 1976; Halstead 2001; Harris 1976, 1990; Hymes 1990; Jones 1970; Kim 1987; Medicine 2001a, 2001b; Morris, Leung, Ames, and Lickel 1999; Narayan 1993; Pike 1990). Researchers acknowledge "sights and blindnesses," "pitfalls and privileges," and the "data and passion" that accompany this approach (Nason-Clark 2002: 29; Neitz 2002: 33). They also direct scholars to be honest about their *own* "doctrines—both secular and sacred" as these inform the ethnographic endeavor (Adams 1997: 2).

In line with these thinkers, my approach to the insider-outsider conundrum is to be transparent about my own complex location "as a sociologist and a believer" (Milmon Harrison 2005: ix). I begin, then, with a confession: The Church means more to me than an interesting intellectual topic. The Church was the only "really real" world for my first twenty-odd years, and millennial anticipation, being "filled" with the Holy Ghost, keeping Sabbath, eating "clean," and dressing "as becomes holiness" were integral to a constellation of beliefs and actions that shaped my life. Although I attended Philadelphia High School for Girls, a selective and academically rigorous public high school, and regularly visited the city's museums and other cultural institutions, the world constituted by The Church had strong boundaries. Within it, family and religious community were conflated. Most of my mother's siblings and my cousins were members. Maternal kin also constituted many of the founding members and current board of elders.

"Observant participation," rather than the more conventional "participant observation," has informed the collection of research materials. This stance is in line with Bennetta Jules-Rosette's approach to studying the Maranke Church of the Twelve Apostles in southern Africa. As a trained sociologist, she made the epistemological leap of converting to this African Instituted Church (AIC), which privileged the interplay of the trans-human with the personal (Jules-Rosette 1975: 15, 22, 207). Formal education within the Western academy required "conversion" to "faith" in the social-scientific method, which privileges material constraints—often at the expense of human agency—in assessing social reality.

Though initially put off by the reductionism of classical structural-functionalist analyses of religion, in time I came to share Armin Geertz's appreciation of anthropology as salvific (Geertz 2002: 230). The holistic, cross-cultural, critical relativism of anthropology made it possible to situate The Church within the panorama of human institutions, respecting its uniqueness but also recognizing its universalities. This view was in sharp contrast to growing up in The Church, a self-isolating sacred oasis that rigorously distanced itself from a wicked world. Through the macroscopic lens of anthropology, then, I could see that the saints share a human hope for individual and communal flourishing, as well as the wherewithal to confront meaningless suffering and inevitable mortality.

Still, anthropology's gifts of interpretive breadth and cross-cultural comparison have not obliterated the early years of my life in The Church. Because of close ties to both maternal and fictive kin, my connections to this faith community and my commitment to its integrity and dignity remain strong. In this study, I employ my position from within and without the veil of faith to tell the story of the saints in a way that diversifies, deepens, and expands our understanding of how men and women search for meaning through shared faith. This stance introduces the voices of those who are rarely given the opportunity to inform the production of academic knowledge into discourses surrounding religion and gender.

The research approach employed in this exploration is initiated at the nexus of autobiography and "polyocularity," a concept developed by Magoroh Maruyama. A trained mathematician and ethnographer of California prison life, Maruyama foreshadowed Armin Geertz's "ethnohermeneutic" use of models proposed by both scholars and "natives," and it predated James Clifford's decentered dialogical approach (Geertz 2002: 233; Clifford 1986: 25–26). Maruyama's methodological approach highlights "the differential" between the viewpoint of an outsider-researcher and the logic of the group being studied (Maruyama 1974). This book applies this notion by attending to the life histories and theological reflections of the saints as well as to the social and historical contexts within which their personal experiences occurred.

Polyocularity, here, is not synonymous with even-handedness, for my goal is not to present all points of view with equal weight. This book is written in line with Delmos Jones's critique of the "myth of neutrality" and in response to his call for a "decolonized" anthropology that "sets the record straight" (Jones 1970). Before Clifford's observation about the "partial" nature of ethnographic knowledge, St. Clair Drake articulated a philosophy of knowledge that "approximates total knowledge" through the assessment of the "partial perspectives" of those who actually experience the social reality under investigation. The partial truths of the saints' perspectives are presented in the tradition of vindicationist scholarship, which contests the supposedly objective but deeply biased research that has too often misrepresented Black lives (Drake 1987: vxvi–xviii, 1–6, 85–86, 92, 100).[2]

In addition to these social scientific methods and models cited, the humanistic work of two literary figures informs how this book is written. Literary icon James Baldwin wedded the personal, socioreligious, and literary in works such as *Go Tell It on the Mountain* (1953) and *The Amen Corner* (1954). Diane Wilson, a social-justice activist, addresses the Holiness-Pentecostal religious experience in her autobiographical *Holy Roller: Growing up in the Church of Knock Down Drag Out; or, How I Quit Loving a Blue-Eyed Jesus—A Childhood Memoir* (2008). Both model ways of writing with the whole self, in which youth and adulthood, profession and vocation, intellect and passion, aspiration and action, and the sacred and profane are reconciled within both their persons and their writing. Baldwin and Wilson are revisited in the concluding chapter, and the reader is likely to sense their influence throughout the book.

In sum, autobiography, polyocularity, and historically situated ethnographic voices shape the design of this research project. Its major goal is to document a religious tradition that has not been adequately appreciated by the larger religious and intellectual community for its intrinsic worth and for the ways its unique particularities relate another chapter in the story of the quest for meaning and agency within situations of social constraint, political subordination, and rampant inequality.

Interpretation

Exile, Refuge, Reconciliation

Speaking in his native Philadelphia at Temple University shortly after the publication of *One More Day's Journey* (1984), Allen Ballard observed that, of all the people who came to these American shores, only African Americans have never left the land of their oppression. In line with Ballard's observation, The Church is interpreted as a spiritual and social refuge that provided founding saints with religiously forged tools for becoming reconciled not only to their new urban reality but more generally to living while Black in America. Although the United States was the only land they could call home, they also knew it to be so oppressive, hypocritical, and dangerous that they had fled the region of their birth to seek relatively safer spaces elsewhere. As anthropologist Melvin Williams notes, "The history of Black people in the United States has been one of constant geographical movement . . . [as they] have seldom discovered . . . the combination of ethnic, economic, social, and political factors that create and maintain community" (Williams 1974: 5–6). Indeed, Milton Sernett's history of religion in the Great Migration describes this mass movement as a "second exodus" from the shadow of slavery to what they hoped would be a promised land but found to be "but one more chapter in the odyssey of a pilgrim people" (Sernett 1997: 85).

Daniel Sayers draws on Edward Said's notion of exile as an imposed state of being perpetually foreign, uprooted, and never at ease in another's land. Sayers argues that the experience of Black people is that of economic and political exile as a minoritized and marginalized group throughout American history. Yet, such experiences of displacement can elicit "contrapuntal" creative cultural reformulations among the exiled (Sayers 2006: 16–17; Said 1990: 361–66). Cheryl Sanders, wedding history, theology, and ethics, proposes that Sanctified churches not only carry a dialectic of refuge and reconciliation within their ethos but also, especially for rural migrants settling in urban Washington, D.C., serve as arenas of self-determination that counter the historical onslaught on Black families and communities (Sanders 1996: ix, 36–39). In line with Sanders's interpretation, my study explores The Church as both a fortress against an alien social setting and a reservoir of divinely empowered beliefs and practices for negotiating it.

This study also draws on biblical themes of exile articulated by the saints. They speak of having "no continuing city" in this world, but looking to "one to come" (Hebrews 13:14 KJV). As the adopted seed of Abraham, the saints, like the Jews, "sojourn in a strange land" (Acts 7:6 KJV), confident "that if our earthly house of this tabernacle were dissolved, we have a building of God, a house not made with hands, eternal in the heavens" (2 Corinthians 5:1 KJV). In this light, The Church represents an attempt to come to terms with exile as a lived experience both as a minoritized people within a racist nation-state and as spiritual exiles in a sinful world.

African Diaspora Religion and World Christianity

This study views The Church as a religious expression of people of African descent in the Diaspora, where the beliefs and practices of their ancestors interacted with those they encountered as enslaved people in the New World. This Diaspora is ongoing: a half-million Africans came to the United States between 1992 and 2002. The assumption that they left voluntarily must be tempered by the recognition of the dire conditions in their homeland, including civil war, religious persecution, and impoverishment so severe that people die of deprivation (Dodson and Diouf 2004; Crumbley 2008a: 3–4). Still, these conditions contrast sharply with the forced migration of millions of enslaved Africans to the Americas, transformed from persons who belonged to various ethnocultural groups into chattel property and forced laborers, Black commodities without legal personhood or human rights. Furthermore, their peregrinations did not end with the Middle Passage, for the history of Black people throughout enslavement entailed continued relocations, most of which were involuntary.[3]

During the military confrontation of the Civil War, tens of thousands fled their masters and crossed Union Army lines to such an extent that, as historians such as Steven Hahn have argued, this mass movement transformed a political war to preserve the Union into an ethical one that abolished slavery (Hahn 2009: 55–114). After Emancipation, the voluntary migration of African Americans accelerated as Blacks exercised their new mobility and traveled near and far to find mothers, fathers, children, spouses, and other loved ones from whom they had been so pitilessly torn. Others carved out new geographies of life and opportunity, including Benjamin "Pap" Singleton, who in 1877 led recently freed Blacks who were discouraged and terrorized by Whites intent on regaining control of Black labor to the West, where the "Exodusters" established Nicodemus and other all-Black towns in Oklahoma and Kansas (Dick 1970: 157; Dodson and Diouf 2004: 97–111; Painter 1977: 3–34, 108–17). Thus, the founding saints' participation in the twentieth-century Great Migration, like the relocation of Haitians to Montreal and of Jamaicans and other West Indians to London (Gomez 2005: 164–66, 199), stands in the tradition of identifying and exploiting "diasporic switching points" to find more salubrious conditions in which human beings with black bodies and African legacies might flourish (Appadurai 1996: 171).

The notion of the African Diaspora means more, however, than mere physical dispersal of people, applied loosely to any and all types of displacement. This study respects the importance of power relations as well as historical and cultural particularities of migrants and their hosts (Braziel and Mannur 2003: 12). This investigation situates The Church, both historically and culturally, within the global landscape of African diasporic formation, rather than limiting its interpretation to the boundaries of the American nation-state and its religious landscape. For example, in "Becoming Saints" the saints are represented as culture-bearers of a religious tradition that reflects selectively institutionalized features of African-derived religion, bolstered and legitimated by American revivalism. Similar processes of religious change took place in western Africa in situations of inequitable contact associated with the rise of "independent church movements" (ICMs). I suggest that Afro-Atlantic peoples have reworked Christianity in ways that reflect comparable cultural legacies as well as hybridization within contexts of domination by, and resistance to, expanding empires (Gordon and Anderson

1999). This interpretive framework, in keeping with current trends in African Diaspora studies, proposes ways of looking at people in Africa and its Diaspora that transcend institutionalized academic conventions of territorial boundedness or static analytical categories (Harrison 2008: 82–83; Matory 2005: 263, 274, 285; Alpers and Roberts 2003: 13–14; Yelvington 2001: 237, 240, 248–49; Byfield 2000: 3–4, 7–8; Gilroy 1993). In the ritual and symbol chapter, with what Faye Harrison calls "bifocal vision," I employ the same interpretive and analytical purview for both The Church in this study and African Instituted Churches (AICs), about which I have written elsewhere (Harrison 2008: 101; Crumbley 2008a; Crumbley 2008c; Crumbley 2008d: 126–27; Crumbley 2010).

Locating The Church within global configurations of Diaspora also provides a window on "World Christianity"—that is, an interdisciplinary interpretation of Christianity that explores continuities and discontinuities in the ways people who self-identify as Christians configure, institutionalize, and live out their lives as believers. While a World Christianity interpretation may focus on a particular community, findings are reported in ways that interpret their significance for cross-cultural comparative analysis. Critiques of World Christianity range from the vastness of the subject matter and a dread of essentialism to the "repugnance" elicited by the study of a religious tradition that is simultaneously too familiar and too different from that of the West (Robbins 2003a, 2003b; Frankiel 2003). Rather than waiting until World Christianity has become better established and more theoretically sophisticated, I have chosen to get on with the business of producing research findings as intellectual fodder for what Joel Robbins calls "good comparative conversation" within a community of like-minded academics (Robbins 2003a: 194). Thus, this study investigates ways in which this little storefront Sanctified church connects, and does not connect, with the variety of lived experiences that have constituted Christianity over its two-thousand-year history of reformulations across cultures.

Religious Transformations during the Great Migration

The Great Migration is the context within which the rise of The Church is historically situated. The Great Migration is interpreted not only as a "watershed in African American religious history" but also as a "second emancipation" from southern economic exploitation and racial violence, a "second exodus" pilgrimage to a promised land beyond the "Egyptland" of the American South (Sernett 1997: 27, 55–56). As the saints' narratives attest, they had fled the raw violence of southern racism, but in Philadelphia they encountered new racial practices structured by impersonal socioeconomic hierarchies embedded within global contingencies.

Some participants in the Great Migration reconstituted their southern home churches in the urban North. Others, like the saints, established new religious institutions housed in affordable storefront rental property. They brought with them spiritual traditions and ritual legacies that tended to be more demonstrative, revival-oriented, and preacher-centered than established Black independent churches in the North. Although these practices were initially regarded with disdain, the migrants' churches eventually influenced northern churches. As the theologian and scholar Robert Franklin notes, southern migrants may have been economically poor, but they were spiritually rich (Franklin 1989: 17; Sernett 1997: 3–4, 7, 179–80, 182; Kostarelos 1995: 11).

In his in-depth study of religious groups that arose from the Great Migration in Chicago, Wallace Best rightly describes storefront churches as the "least understood expression of African American urban Christianity of that time" (Best 2004: 302). Biased scholars have not only reduced these churches to sociological epiphenomena of mass migration but also stigmatized them as "lower class," "escapist," "other-worldly" in orientation, socially irresponsible, and rooted in rural antimodern "backwardness" (Sernett 1997: 5, 8; Best 2004: 303–12). James Weldon Johnson (1871–1938), renowned Harlem Renaissance author, early civil rights activist, and author of the lyrics to "Lift Every Voice and Sing," the "Negro National Anthem," saw their proliferation as diverting funds from more worthy endeavors, such as building hospitals, old folks' homes, and orphan asylums (Sernett 1997: 135). Additionally, many leaders of established Black churches distanced themselves from the discomfiting "African survivals" of "slave religion" and characterized the more spirited southern forms of religious expression as theologically immature, mere vehicles of stress release (Gregg 1993: 76–77, 130–31, 181–82; Sernett 1997: 183; Best 2004: 319–20; Frazier 1963: 59).

Despite these elitist, condescending, and hostile attitudes, storefront churches flourished. During the influx of southern migrants in the 1920s, over half of the Black churches in Harlem were housed in storefronts. Over time, some of their musical and homiletic styles reshaped modes of worship in urban Black churches across denominations. In cities that seemed "cold and impersonal," storefront churches served as a refuge from a "hostile white world" in which most of their members were "common laborers and in domestic and personal service" (Frazier 1963: 54–60, 71).

During the Great Migration, storefront churches filled the "gap between the South and the city" and carved out sacred space along sinful avenues of urban commerce and vice. Black migrants gathered there to meet God and other Christians, worship in culturally familiar ways, and rehearse liturgies of hope for the future. Compared to the long-established Black churches in the North, their worship experiences gave greater room to what Milton Sernett calls the Black "southern praise legacy" while northern Black churches, which had greater material resources, were more explicitly involved in political protest and social outreach. The interaction between these two orientations would transform the Black church in America profoundly (Sernett 1997: 248–49; Best 2004: 302, 308–10, 316; Gregg 1993: 194).

This project explores The Church as a case study in Great Migration religion, for it offered people who had recently arrived from the South worship spaces infused with familiar ways of being human. These common practices included patterns of speech, childrearing, music, cuisine and commensality as well as shared experiences of being Black at this particular juncture in American social history. As indicated in their narratives, most of the founding saints had been Baptists in the South, but after settling in Philadelphia, they "found salvation," "got saved," and lived "sanctified" lives as "born again" saints in The Church. Their decision to get saved was not a knee-jerk reaction to social rejection or alienation from long-established Black Philadelphians, but rather a proactive pursuit of religious experience that these older churches simply did not provide them.

The Church also provided founding saints with experiences of agency unconstrained by racism or classism. Despite good minds, firm determination, and a strong work ethic, members of the founding generation encountered racial discrimination in the job market. Because they had been excluded from public schooling or relegated to inferior segregated schools in the South, they were stigmatized as uneducated. Determined to make the most of the situation for themselves and their children, they took whatever jobs they could obtain and struggled to ensure that their children had as much formal schooling as possible. Ironically, in so doing, they participated in and contributed to the very capitalist structures that constrained their racialized lives in the city. In their religious lives, by contrast, they found arenas of leadership, dignity, and spiritual sustenance, for on Sabbath the saints, who during the week toiled in a racially segregated world that excluded all aspects of their Blackness except their labor, enjoyed respect and holiness as interpreters of tongues, healers of the sick, and evangelists of The Word. Within The Church, these founding saints also found well-deserved respite from White faces reminding them of the color-coded hierarchies that they, as minoritized people, had been forced to negotiate daily, both north and south of the Mason-Dixon Line.

Storefront Churches

Storefront churches are small faith communities housed within humble structures, including rented storefronts, refurbished residential properties, and warehouses. The Church was founded in a room above a horse stable and, as membership grew, it relocated into renovated residential corner properties. Such venues have been used by the established denominations, including Baptists, Methodists, and Church of God in Christ (COGIC), to pioneer churches in the inner city, but these have tended to be temporary and used only until the congregation has stabilized (Best 2004: 305; Butler 2007: 64–70, 100; Sernett 1997: 157, 160–61; Williams 1974: 18). In this study, I use the term "storefront" to refer to faith communities such as The Church, which emerged as independent congregations and remain unaffiliated with larger denominations, and whose spiritual and symbolic content stand in the tradition of the Sanctified Church.

Their distinctive mode of worship privileges embodied spirit and the wedding of movement and music in an interactive style that blurs boundaries between audience and podium. Laity and clergy tend to be drawn from the working poor, lacking the material resources required to pursue the formal education that access to the professions requires. Women predominate among the laity (Sernett 1997: 188–97). Storefront churches also dot the contemporary urban religious landscape, as indicated by a February 5, 2011, want ad posted at *ChicagoSuperAds.com*: "Looking to rent a storefront or church on the southside to minister to that community. Seat at least 150 people w/dining area/2 washrooms and office and parking space."[4] Storefront churches, then, continue to provide alternative spaces of sacredness and social healing for diverse inner-city residents, including African and Caribbean immigrants, as they confront inequality and marginalization in their lives (Harvell 2010; Smith-Brown 2010; Abrums 2009: ix–xxvii; Cnaan 2006: 28–29; Vergara 2000; Grant 2002; Dehavneon 1995).

Until recently, storefront churches have fallen by the wayside in the academic study, too often marginalized as otherworldly cults whose clergy are "exploiters and charlatans" (Sernett 1997: 188–98; Haynes 1978: 59; Collins 1970: 65, 66; Frazier 1963: 59). By contrast, as I grew up in a storefront church I experienced this faith community as the place where truth and salvation triumphed over the lies of a sinful world. In The Church, I became persuaded that, as a Sabbath-keeping saint, I was "head and not the tail, above only and not beneath" (Deuteronomy 28:13), which forcefully contradicted prevalent notions of White racial supremacy and conventions of racial exclusion. Yet, I was not unmoved by the derogatory label "holy rollers," and it angered me when people paused below the church window and danced to the Holy Ghost–filled music that overflowed from our devotional service. But then, I consoled myself, they were sinners; like most of us living in North Philly, they had little formal education; and what they thought of us mattered only to them.

It was not so easy, however, to dismiss such misguided assessments by people whose privileged backgrounds afforded them access to higher education, power, and the means to transform their misapprehension into published scholarship for the entire literate world to read for the foreseeable future. Some of their pronouncements marginalized, sexualized, and entirely misrepresented us. They reduced our worship to the emotion-laden release of psychological stress and belittled our theology and approach to biblical interpretation. They ridiculed our gender practices and organizational styles while refusing to acknowledge the humanity and dignity that we believed Jesus had died for, making these misrepresentations not only arrogantly inaccurate but also ungodly.

Illustrating these general misconceptions, a 1959 article titled "Store-Front Religion" (Eddy 1958–59: 68–85) asserts that these churches represent "marked deviation" from established religious institutions. The singing is described as "noisy," preaching as "raucous," the theology as "bizarre," the preachers' call is attributed to "egoistic desire," and the religious experience is described in sexual terms. In recounting the worship service, the article describes a "fat woman" of about thirty who "threw back her head convulsively, screeched 'Halleluiah!'" and, with feet "moving faster and faster in these moments of religious ecstasy," suddenly "reached a climax and fell to the floor" (Eddy 1958–59: 73).

Norman Eddy also found sermons and official statements "baffling to the serious inquirer" and asserted that the "psychopathic emotionalism" of some storefront churches provided the psychoneurotic and psychotic with a safe "place for haven." He described worshippers as children who "are not socially constructive" and their faith as an attempt "to leave the hostile world far behind." Their carefully balanced structures are explained away as "ridiculously over-organized" compensation for social marginalization. Women church leaders are the objects of special censure: "For instance, one of the older women in churches of this type is often selected as *Church Mother*. During the service, she will sit just below the pulpit where she will face the congregation from her honored position. During the testimony period, each member of the group will begin by giving thanks for his church, his pastor and his church mother. I was told that her primary role was that of counselor. Young people may take their problems to her and she will reward them with her sage advice. . . . The office of Church Mother is but one of a great variety of obscure offices within such groups" (Eddy 1958–59: 72). This observation not only disparages Church Mothers as one of many "obscure offices" but completely ignores the power that they and other women wield in these churches (Eddy 1958–59: 68–74, 77, 83–85; Gilkes 1986, 1987, 1994).

Taking a different tone, William Willoughby commended the clergy and teachings of storefront churches as "the policeman's best friends," especially during the "long hot summers" of urban uprisings in Black sections of major American cities in the 1960s. According to Willoughby, the 105 storefront churches in Washington, D.C.'s Second Precinct Clergymen's Association were free from anti-white "militants," making storefronts "one of America's best stabilizing forces." "Ask the ghetto policeman," he said rhetorically (Willoughby 1969). Whether pathologizing these churches or praising them as instruments of social control, this approach refused to treat storefront churches as serious religious institutions worthy of respectful academic attention.

Ethnographies

Ira Harrison introduced the study of storefront churches as a valid and significant anthropological topic in "The Storefront Church as a Revitalization Movement" (Harrison 1966). Harrison's non-reductionist, non-moralistic, non-elitist, and historically situated analysis paved the way for subsequent ethnographies. In this study, he explores the structure and organizational processes of sixteen storefront churches in Syracuse, New York, founded by southern migrants, many of whom were employed in a defense plant during the 1940s. Members self-identified as "sanctified and saved" servants of a "living God," who "shout" during worship and "wouldn't give two cents for a religion that wouldn't make me move." Applying Anthony Wallace's concept of religious revitalization movements, Harrison analyzes storefront churches as deliberate, conscious, organized efforts of migrants to create a more satisfying mode of existence. The Bible serves as their "code" and preaching as the normative communication vehicle. Harrison argues that these churches' formal organization, underpinned by biblically sanctioned beliefs and practices, routinizes charisma into enduring structures that facilitate the saints' transition from southern rural to northern urban lifestyles. Harrison ends by calling for more anthropological research on storefront churches because they shed light on the process of routinization, a classical concern in western sociology (Harrison 1966: 163). This book is a direct response to this call, especially chapter five, "Family," which analyzes gender, age, kinship, and institutional processes.

The first ethnography of storefront Sanctified churches that I encountered was Melvin Williams's *Community in a Black Pentecostal Church: An Anthropological Study* (1974). The church he studied is headed by a man and is affiliated with an established denomination, The Church of God in Christ (COGIC), which stands in the Sanctified Church tradition. Williams's work is an important point of departure for analyzing The Church, because it focuses on "the cohesive nature of the social relations and behavior" of this faith community by documenting the history, organization, activities, symbolic expression, and physical setting of "The Zion Holiness Church" (pseudonym) (Williams 1974: 5). Like The Church, Zion started in a "horse stable which they had converted into a church, and prior to that it had met in members' homes" (Sernett 1997: 200; Williams 1974: 18). Zion also shared social dynamics of "the church as family."

While Williams focused on conflict, cohesion, and community, Frances Kostarelos's 1995 ethnography, *Feeling the Spirit: Faith and Hope in an Evangelical Black Storefront Church*, focuses on the shared "religious cosmos" of "First Corinthians Missionary Baptist Church" (pseudonym) located on the West Side of Chicago. Like Williams, Kostarelos explores the church's social-historical context, structure, activities, and organizational processes. Although the church is affiliated with an established denomination and the congregation is male-headed, her study is methodologically and interpretively germane to my study (Kostarelos 1995: xiii, xvi, 1). First, Kostarelos describes her work as a "historical ethnography" comprised of both ethnographic description and analysis of the historical processes that have given rise to and sustained this congregation. Second, she did not regard her intimate engagement with the faith community as a deterrent to serious anthropological inquiry; though racialized as "a young white woman" in the larger society, Kostarelos became so fully immersed in the beliefs, values, and lives of the saints that they saw her as "sent" by God to communicate to others the faith that enables them to flourish in the face of personal suffering and social injustice (Kostarelos 1995: xi, xvii). Third, she explores the storefront church as a locus of empowering theological reformulation. She attends to "the role of their sacred vision in constructing their social world" and takes seriously the congregation's interpretation of scripture, showing how it gives meaning to members' lives in ways that promote social solidarity in the face of the oppressive racist and capitalist structures that shape inner-city Black life. In contrast to Willoughby, Kostarelos argues that storefront churches, far from accommodating to White-dominated power structures, "define a worldview that withstands the self-interested principles defined in the American mainstream" by standing in a three-century-long tradition of Black resistance and self-determination (Kostarelos 1995: 1–2, 4).

In *Moving the Rock: Poverty and Faith in a Black Storefront Church* (2010), Mary Abrums, writing as both anthropologist and nurse, focuses on the effects of poverty and race on the health and well-being of female storefront church members and their families. She squarely situates these stories within the social-historical context of the Great Migration and subsequent economic dynamics of urban Seattle, and she provides statistical data that documents "the realities of poor people's lives" (Abrums 2009: ix–xi, xvii–xxiv). Modestly, Abrums states that the scope of her book does not extend to an in-depth analysis of the church, yet the women's voices that speak so eloquently in this work provide invaluable knowledge about, and insight into, the importance of Black church communities in negotiating the material consequences of structural racism. Like Kostarelos, Abrums became close to the members of this Baptist storefront church at formal services as well as in their homes. She is keenly aware of the privileges that she as a White woman and ethnographer enjoys and, to offset possible biases, she relates the stories of members in their own voices. Although Abrums is well grounded in Black feminist theory and reflexive feminist anthropology, she intentionally avoids academic jargon lest these interpretive frames interfere with relating members' views (Abrums 2009: x–xv, xxviii; 186–92). Like the faith communities studied by Williams and Kostarelos, but unlike the storefront in this study, this faith community is affiliated with an established Black denomination.

In line with Kostarelos, I explore the beliefs and practices of The Church as religious responses to the larger society and reject the notion that storefront churches are too otherworldly to serve constructive ends. The Church, I argue, does not reject social responsibility; it serves as the crucible within which social responsibility is acted out in concrete, everyday ways. In line with Abrums's focus on the socioeconomic dimensions of storefront religion, this book addresses how the saints negotiate poverty and marginalization through a redistributive network of resources, including interest-free loans, the laying on of hands, traditional healing remedies, carpooling, and sharing employment opportunities.

This work builds on the ethnographies of earlier anthropologists by interpreting The Church as an organized effort by recently transplanted, economically exploited, and socially marginalized Blacks to establish an empowering religious institutional space of their own making, thereby offsetting experiences in White-controlled, secular institutions where their needs and aspirations were mere afterthoughts, if they were considered at all. This book adds to earlier ethnographies of storefront churches because it focuses on a church that is not affiliated with an established denomination; its institutional processes provide a living example of grassroots institution-building. This exploration also situates the particularity of a storefront church within larger cultural contexts of the African Diaspora, World Christianity, and the human saga of religious reformulation. Finally, this ethnography is written from the vantage point of one raised within this faith community.

Sanctified Roots

Storefront churches house religious and cultural legacies. The saints are culture-bearers of the Sanctified Church tradition that institutionalized African-derived spiritualities legitimated by the fruits of Great Awakening revivalism (Raboteau 1978: 149; Sanders 1996: 3–5; Hurston 1981: 101–5; Gilkes 1990: 228; MacRobert 1988, 1997). Just as southern migrants did not arrive in the North as religious *tabula rasa*, their enslaved African ancestors brought a rich mix of religious beliefs and practices with them to these North American shores. Despite rich cultural diversity, faith traditions of Western African peoples exhibit certain symbolic and ritual commonalities: belief in a community of ritually accessible deities who include a Supreme Being; communal worship that entails religious dance and music; the intimacy of embodying divinity through spiritual possession; notions of spiritual power as both neutral and malleable; evil as a concrete reality expressed through people's behavior as opposed to a purely abstract notion of wickedness; ancestor veneration; belief in individual existence beyond death, incorporating notions of both ancestors and reincarnation; well-being that is simultaneously spiritual and physical and is restored through both pharmacopoeic expertise and rituals of healing; and access to esoteric knowledge through rituals of divination (Olupona 2000: xv–xix; Zahan 2000; Dodson and Gilkes 1995: 527–28; Austin-Broos 1997: 5–6; Margaret Drewal 1989: 206–10, 231; Henry Drewal 1989: 247; Opoku 1978; Mbiti 1969: 168–69; Parrinder 1949: 80–94; Murphy 1988: 14; Ray 2000: 42–44; Besson and Chevannes 1996). Although these elements were affected by the religious milieu into which their culture-bearers were thrust, some persisted and were varyingly reconfigured, most specifically religious dance in the form of the "shout" and possession by Spirit. From the early seventeenth to the late-eighteenth centuries, the majority of enslaved Black people were "only minimally touched by Christianity" (Raboteau 1978: 149). My argument, then, is this: as Africans were initially not the object of systematic Christianization, African religious traditions and spiritualities were able to flourish in secret reformulated expressions, selectively reinforced by the continual arrival of newly enslaved Africans and by the spirit-privileging features of Euro-Christianity.[5]

During the enslavement, exposure to White Christianity occurred in services closely monitored by armed slave patrollers where White ministers' sermons articulated a theology of social control that stressed the virtue of submissiveness (Graebner 2009). Enslaved Blacks reworked Christianity into new formulations that drew on their religious legacies during clandestine worship that, according to the oral histories passed down by my elders, included upturning a pot "to catch the noise" so that the masters would not hear and punish those gathered to pray (see also Wiencek 1999: 34–35).

The roots of the Sanctified tradition are to be found in this culturally expressed resistance to the distortion of Christian ideals for racialized subjugation. Practiced secretly, in contrast to the public institutional self-determination of the Black church in the North, southern slave religion harbored elements of West African traditions that included conjure, divining esoteric knowledge, working spells, herbalism, and a cosmos predicated on accessible, imminent, and intervening spiritual power experienced during divine possession. Selected African practices were sustained long enough for spirit-privileging Protestantism to legitimate them. The resonance between the two is pneumatological—that is, the wedding of "psyche and soma" in the embodiment of spirit (Smith 1997: xviii; Austin-Broos 1997: 6–7, 13; Stewart 2005: 160, 198).

This creative fusion occurred in the wake of a Christian revival movement that swept through Scotland, Wales, and England and then invaded North America in two waves, now known as the First (1720–1770s) and Second (1795–1815) Great Awakenings. The Second Great Awakening was accompanied by outreach to Black people and gave birth to the Holiness movement among Methodist evangelicals, who met for the first time in an 1886 revival in the region of eastern Tennessee and western North Carolina. In the aftermath of the Civil War, Holiness attracted displaced Whites and Blacks (Synan 1971: 35, 46, 52–53, 165–66). The Holiness religious experience is characterized by instantaneous conversion, emphasis on personal moral perfection, physically manifested Spirit, and Biblical literalism.

Pentecostalism, which emerged later, added to these features glossolalia, or speaking in unknown holy tongues (Synan 1971: 23, 34–35; Washington 1984: 36–41, 59, 63). Although recent research documents the independent outpouring of the spirit around 1906 in India, Korea, China, Côte d'Ivoire, Nigeria, and Wales, Pentecostals around the world trace their lineage directly or indirectly to the Azusa Street Mission in Los Angeles founded by African American evangelist W. J. Seymour in 1906, which attracted interracial though predominantly African American followers (Anderson 2006a: 37–43, 46–47; Anderson 2005: 179–80, 182–83; Hollenweger 1970: 22–24, 43; Synan 1971: 114, 117, 121, 168; Llewellyn 1997: 7–9). The Azusa Street revival represents more than a "charter myth for black Pentecostals, who deploy it as a statement of the spiritual ascendance over Whites" (Austin-Broos 1997: 99); Azusa Street was a historical event recognized as "the beginning of classical Pentecostalism as an international movement in modern times," with at least twenty-six denominations tracing their origins to the Azusa Street revival by 1911 (Anderson 2006b: 111). Allan Anderson discusses the Azusa Street revival as "rooted in the African American culture of the nineteenth century" and argues that Pentecostal "manifestations" "were also found in the religious expressions of the African religious culture from which slaves had been abducted" (Anderson 2005: 180).

In addition to being a consequence of reinforcing spirit-privileging in both African and European American religious traditions, the Sanctified Church tradition can be understood as a response of Black Christians to changes that were occurring in established Black independent churches. By World War I, these churches were being perceived by some as digression from the spiritually grounded early Christianity; they were also seen as intentional distancing from the spirituality of slave religion (Giggie 2008: 21, 179; Washington 1984: 58). The Azusa Street revival produced Charles Harrison Mason, who founded the first incorporated Pentecostal church in America, the Church of God in Christ (COGIC), in Nashville, Tennessee, in 1897. Under Bishop Mason's leadership, COGIC ordained scores of White ministers who pioneered other COGIC congregations. Within fifteen years, however, most of these White clerics left COGIC, some to establish the historically White Assemblies of God in 1914. Although these White breakaway churches continued to privilege spirit, their departure marked the triumph of American Jim and Jane Crow until the dramatic reconciliation service that occurred in 1994 at the Memphis Miracle (Rosenior 2009; Sanders 1996: 4, 19–20, 29–32; Tinney 1971: 4; Lincoln and Mamiya 1990; 78–81; MacRobert 1997: 295–309).[6] The remaining Black churches are referred to generically as "Sanctified" churches, and although they share spirit-privileging elements with White Holiness Pentecostalism, the two have different cultural roots, historical trajectories, and ontologies of worship (Hurston 1981: 103–7; Llewellyn 1997: 1–5).[7] The two largest are the Church of God in Christ (COGIC), which was incorporated as a denomination in 1906, and Pentecostal Assemblies of the World (PAW), founded in 1916, although in 1924 White PAW members broke off to form the United Pentecostal Church International (Daniels 2003: 167). At the other end of institutional scale and organizational complexity are unaffiliated storefront Sanctified churches.

The spirituality of Sanctified churches entails the ability to "move between worlds simultaneously without conflating, integrating, or blending them," holding human agency and divine intervention in tandem (Daniels 2003: 176–77). For example, the seemingly otherworldly millennial anticipation of the saints coexists with notions of "chosenness" and "commandment-keeping" that promote success in "The World." In this light, Sanctified churches share the more general disposition of the Black church as a religious institution in which "the secular and spiritual realms are united as both sources and goals of power," which galvanize and support "holy communities" that put Christian teachings to their own special uses (Washington 1984: 1, 13, 17).

Gender, Charisma, and Institution-Building

As Cheryl Gilkes notes, even after storefront churches began to command the attention of scholars, those led by women continued to be ignored. Gilkes observes, "Sociologists who have studied organizations and structures within urban ghetto communities have confessed . . . that they ignore small churches pastored by women precisely *because* they were pastored by women" (Gilkes 1986: 34). Except for the African Methodist Episcopal Zion (AMEZ) Church, which ordained women as early as 1884, Sanctified churches have offered greater ministerial opportunities for women than older Black independent churches (Carpenter 1989–90: 12, 18; Best 1998: 153).[8] Holiness, Pentecostal, and Sanctified churches have tended to privilege divine call over formal educational credentials, reflecting not only the value placed on spiritual gifts but the reality of the social constraints placed on their members' access to educational opportunities (Best 1998: 153). Still, women encountered conventions of patriarchy in Sanctified churches, which some women chose to negotiate and others rejected outright.

Gender practices of Sanctified churches are connected to those in the larger society. According to Patricia Hill Collins's Black feminist analysis of "intersecting dominations," these gender practices are the product of complex cultural legacies, historical processes, and the laws and conventions of the nation-state (Collins 1990: 229–30). In this study, gendered dynamics of the Sanctified tradition in general, and of The Church in particular, are interpreted within the framework of African gender practices, selectively reinforced within "matrices of domination" effected by chattel slavery and Jim and Jane Crow and then sustained by racialized social hierarchies that structure American society. I also draw upon Bennetta Jules-Rosette's analysis of gender and power in African Instituted Churches (AICs), using but also complicating her heuristic distinction between ritual and political leadership (Jules-Rosette 1979, 1981, 1987).

Additionally, the works of three West Africanist scholars inform my interpretation of gender in The Church. Nkiru Nzegwu, philosopher and author of *Family Matters: Feminist Concepts in African Philosophy of Culture* (2006), cautions against uncritically employing a "mono-sex" model of power, which makes what men do the touchstone of "real power" (Nzegwu 2006: 196, 199). She proposes a "dual-sex" model of gender as a more accurate and productive framework for assessing gender among non-western and minoritized ethnic groups within western nation-states, such as the United States and Canada. Nzegwu's dual-sex model assesses women's and men's roles as different in content but equal in their importance to social process (Nzegwu 1994: 84, 91–95; Nzegwu 2006: 196, 199–233).

I take seriously the intersection of gender with other organizing principles, such as age, as analyzed in the works of social anthropologist Ifi Amadiume, author of *Male Daughters, Female Husbands: Gender and Sex in an African Society* (1987), and sociologist Oyeronke Oyewumi, author of *Invention of Women: Making an African Sense of Western Gender Discourses* (Amadiume 1987: 15, 28–29, 31–68, 89; Amadiume 1997: 110, 119, 123–30, 191–92; Oyewumi 1997: ix–xiii, 13–15, 29, 31, 46–49, 58–62). This study analyzes gender in The Church along with seniority and relative family status, since gender works with and through other forms of difference and hierarchy.

The framework employed here draws heavily on Gilkes's critical application of the dual-sex model in the African Diaspora context of the Sanctified Church. Gilkes argues that enslaved African Americans retained a West Africa-derived dual-sex model in which both women and men hold positions of authority across society, and even when duties and responsibilities vary, they are equally valued. This legacy was reinforced by American slavery, when Black women labored alongside men in the field, and both were victimized by discriminatory post-Emancipation laws and conventions that compelled Black men and women to work in tandem for their families to survive and flourish. Gilkes argues that this tradition of common disfranchisement and shared leadership has tempered Black male patriarchy, although keeping it at bay requires keen vigilance and determined agency (Gilkes 1994: 90–94). It is in this tradition of vigilantly exercised agency that Mother Brown answered her call even after being informed that "God never called a woman to preach."

Mother Brown and the founding saints were institution-builders. Unaffiliated with older institutional churches, they inherited neither written bylaws for decision-making nor organizational structures. The Church offers a window into grassroots institution-building and the routinization of charisma—that is, the transformation of an informal group into an enduring formal structure. Classic analyses of routinization have focused on the rise of the movement around a powerfully charismatic individual, after whose death bureaucratically inclined surviving members establish explicit organizational structures, which ironically reaffirm the hierarchical structures of institutions from which the founder had intentionally departed. This "structuration" includes the return of gendered hierarchies (Turner 1969: 133–39, 153; Weber 1968, vol. 1: 23–28, 215–16, vol. 2: 223–46, 1113–48).

This research goes beyond sociological models by documenting routinization as a process in which the charismatic founder shared the institution-building task with founding members, whose narratives lie at the core of this book. The Church also diverges from standard models of routinization because it adopted a creative strategy for extending the leadership of women beyond the death of the female founder.

·

In sum, this book is about a quest for meaning and community that has spanned social space and historical time. This quest is particularized through the story of a handful of women and men of African descent who created a sustainable community of faith, even while negotiating mass migration amid a highly racialized society. To explain the rise and development of The Church, I argue in the following chapters that its religious content, gender practices, and institutional survival into the twenty-first century are informed by: (1) the institutionalization of African-derived religion selectively legitimated and reinforced by spirit-privileging American revivalism; (2) African gender legacies buttressed and expanded by racial practices of chattel slavery and post-Emancipation Jim and Jane Crow; (3) human agency exercised by the saints to determine their individual and collective lives.

Two central questions shaped this investigation. How did the saints' religious heritage and their experiences as migrants from the rural South to the urban North inform the organizational structures and spiritual practices of their faith community? What insights do gender relations within this female-founded faith community provide into the process of creating and sustaining leadership structures within which both men and women share the highest levels of power?

The research materials for this study were collected both from within and without the veil of faith. I employ a polyocular perspective by viewing The Church through the macroscopic lenses of a trained anthropologist as well as the microscopic lenses of a "child of The Church." The Church is interpreted within de-territorialized and re-territorialized diasporic contexts and is situated within a trans-Atlantic framework of independent church movements among Africans and people of African descent. Additionally, The Church is a case study in World Christianity, in that its beliefs, practices, and gendered institutional processes provide insight into how Christianity can be reconfigured within a particular social-historical and cultural constellation.

Finally, the reader will come to realize that this book is a serious intellectual work that is just as seriously political and personal. It documents and preserves the life stories of the saints as a critique of a society that silences those who are not positioned to write the books, own the publishing houses, or set school curricula that shape their representation in scholarly literature. This book also represents the happy fulfillment of my duty and honor to record the narratives of lives that have given so much direction and meaning to my life.

2

CITY TALES

MOTHER BROWN EXPERIENCED a divine call to preach in Virginia. Similarly, many founding saints reported life-changing spiritual experiences that they had while still in their southern hometowns. However, it was in the northern urban center of Philadelphia that they answered their call to a life of holiness and, together, established an enduring religious institution. The story of The Church, then, is intimately bound up with the story of Philadelphia—its racial history, immigrant legacies, and unique place in the social history of the Black religious experience in America. Indeed, were this a drama rather than an academic study, Philadelphia would be listed among the *dramatis personae*, not merely as the setting.

This chapter relates the story of the city in terms of encounters, moving chronologically from encounters between African religious expression and European American Christianity to encounters between northern Black churches and the spirituality brought by southern Black migrants. It recounts Black citizens' struggles with segregation in both employment and housing and their encounters with hostile White mobs, as well as interethnic encounters between Blacks and Jews. The social history of religious and community life in Philadelphia grounds and complements the life histories of founding saints told in "Saints Tales," the chapter that follows this one.

Religious Encounters: African Spirituality, European American Christianity, and Black Independent Churches

The racial history of Pennsylvania, particularly Philadelphia, is characterized by irony and contradiction. Pennsylvania was a slaveholding colony, but was also the home of Quaker-inspired antislavery activism. Philadelphia's wealth was built upon trading in slave-produced commodities, and in 1700 one in ten residents was a slaveholder. William Penn, who gave the city its Greek-derived name, "City of Brotherly Love," held slaves who toiled on his estate at the same time that he aggressively pursued and secured religious freedom for his fellow English Quakers by founding the chartered colony of Pennsylvania (Ballard 1984: 19–20, 27). Philadelphia Quakers were teaching Blacks to read as early as 1750, but slavery was not legally extinguished until 1847 (Ballard 1984: 52, 59).

During the Great Awakening, revivalism reached out to Black people in Philadelphia, which had one of the largest concentrations of free Blacks in America (Hopper 2008: 1–3). Much scholarly attention has been given to the socio-historical significance of Philadelphia as the locus of the first independent Black church, Mother Bethel African Methodist Episcopal Church (George 1973: 10–48; Gregg 1993: 2; Hopper 2008: 6–7).[1] However, too little attention has been paid to the cultural significance of Philadelphia in the study of Black religion.

Historical records include evidence of African forms of spiritual expression in the city, such as observations of Africans "dancing in numerous little squads," singing "each in their own tongue accompanied by homemade guitars and instruments made of our gourds" (Ballard 1984: 28–29). Philadelphia annalist John Fanning Watson collected oral histories and documented the presence of African cultural practices before and after the American Revolution and noted that African languages were heard in the city as late as 1800. Watson observed that Black Methodists had a different and, in his eyes, suspect way of expressing their Christianity, and he recalled that when enslaved Blacks had been "allowed the last days of the fairs for their jubilee," they danced "lightheartedly" for long periods of time in the Washington Square burial ground (Stuckey 1987: 22–24, 75; Nash 2006: 40–41).[2] Following historian Sterling Stuckey, I believe that what Watson observed conforms to the West Africa–derived traditions of religious dance known as the "ring shout," which celebrates the presence of spirit in the gathering and in the bodies of the faithful. This early documentation of the shout adds a cultural dimension to the political tradition of protest and self-determination in the religious history of Black Philadelphia.

While Watson recalled with dread the contagious enthusiasm of the Black Methodists in Philadelphia, they appear to have become more liturgically staid by the time the African Methodist Episcopal (AME) Church founded branches in the South. Indeed, some Black northern clergy battled relentlessly with the "incurable disease" of impassioned and physically engaged worship in their southern congregations, where the fusion of religious fervor and political engagement had powerful consequences. Bishop Daniel Payne encouraged AME clergy to make members "stop their dancing," cease singing "corn-field ditties," and not feature "the ring" as an essential part of camp meetings. Not only did these practices continue, but they were constantly reinforced by southern Blacks who migrated to Philadelphia from Emancipation through the Great Migration (Stuckey 1987: 22–23, 75, 92, 95; Nash 2006: 40–41).

In the nineteenth century, Black independent churches in the city multiplied, each with distinctive demographic markers of migrant members' origin and employment strategies. By the turn of the twentieth century, many members of AME churches had come from Georgia and South Carolina. North Carolinians were found in AME Zion congregations, and Maryland natives predominated in the Colored (now Christian) Methodist Episcopal (CME) Church. Black Methodists tended to belong to the "middling group" of Blacks working in the building trades and as servants for Philadelphia's White elite. The leading caterers, barbers, and business proprietors joined Black Episcopal and Presbyterian congregations. The poorest Blacks toiled as day laborers and domestic servants or were unemployed and gravitated to the storefront churches that were founded during the Great Migration (Gregg 1993: 3).

W.E.B. Du Bois's 1899 study of Black churches in Philadelphia reports fifty-five African American churches, with 12,845 members, whose church property was valued at $907,729 and whose annual income was at least $94,968. Du Bois analyzed the church membership of the 2,441 Black families who resided in the historically African American Seventh Ward, listing (in descending order of the number of affiliated families) Methodist, Baptist, Episcopalian, Presbyterian, Catholic, and Shaker institutions. Fully 30 percent (721 families) attended church regularly, but they were not formal church members or their affiliation was "unknown." Some of them no doubt attended the "host of little noisy missions" that, according to Du Bois, represented "an older and more demonstrative worship." He quotes a description of a service in one of these churches located "in the slums of the 5th Ward" where, after the sermon was preached, the worshippers "formed a ring" and clapped and sang loudly "for hours" (Du Bois 1899: 197–221). Milton Sernett observes that U.S. religious censuses conducted in 1906 and 1916 did not refer specifically to Black Pentecostal and Holiness churches, although storefront churches were present in the urban North and growing in numbers along with the Black population. Especially between the two world wars, southern migrants brought with them a unique legacy of worship (Sernett 1997: 95, 180, 182, 188).

Violent Encounters: Black Residents Confront White Mobs

In 1810, Blacks accounted for 10 percent of Philadelphia's population (Ballard 1984: 29). The number of Black residents almost doubled in the forty years before the Civil War, from about 12,000 in 1820 to 23,000 in 1860 (Hopper 2008: 8). White mobs attacked Black neighborhoods, motivated by fear of economic competition combined with resentment toward educated and "prideful" Blacks, especially after the Haitian revolution against the French empire (Hopper 2008: 5,10).

Numerous incidents occurred before the Civil War. Three weeks in August 1829 were marked by White violence: Whites entered a Black home and tossed the corpse of a Black baby onto the floor and burned two Black churches.[3] The perpetrators were mainly young Irish men manipulated by Democratic Party politicians and resentful about competing with free Blacks in the labor market. During White race riots in 1835 and 1838, orphanages and churches were burned and, in 1842, Whites destroyed the newly erected African Hall along with the homes of Black citizens. In 1849, Irish gangs attacked a Black hotel owner married to a White woman, and in the 1860s, White men murdered James W. Purnell, who was en route to the Black Episcopal Church of the Crucifixion with his light-skinned, straight-haired wife, whom the murderers mistook for White (Ballard 1984: 75, 77, 78; Hopper 2008: 8–10, 15).

During the Civil War, Philadelphia's mayor stated publicly that he would not let his family ride on a trolley car with Blacks, and outraged Whites physically removed Black soldiers serving in the Union Army from Philadelphia streetcars (Ballard 1984: 83). After the Civil War, the year after the Fifteenth Amendment had granted Black citizens the right to vote on the same terms as Whites, federal armed forces had to be brought to Philadelphia to protect Blacks voting in the 1871 election. That same year O. V. Catto, a thirty-two-year-old Black voting-rights activist, was shot and killed by White Philadelphian Frank Kelly, who was apprehended but later released (Ballard 1984: 80–82). As Black participation in the economic, social, and political life of Philadelphia increased over the next four decades, so did White supremacist ideology and mob violence. It permeated American life between Emancipation and World War I. For example, before the famous boxing match between the reigning heavyweight, African American Jack Johnson, and James Jefferies, the "Hope of the White Race," Jeffries said of the competition, "I am going into this fight for the sole purpose of proving that a White man is better than a Negro" (Bederman 1995: xi–xii, 1–4, 12–15, 17, 20, 25).[4]

By 1890 the Black population in Philadelphia had reached 39,371; over the next decade, it rose to 62,213. Most Black city dwellers worked in the service sector, as household domestics, launderers, horse drivers, and caterers. They lived mainly in the Seventh Ward, bounded by Spruce Street on the north, South Street on the south, Seventh Street on the east, and the Schuylkill River on the west (Hopper 2008: 18). Black workers were paid lower wages for less desirable work, lived in poorer housing, and paid higher rents than Whites (Du Bois 1899: 295–97; Hopper 2008: 17). Black neighborhoods emerged in Germantown, Frankford, West Philadelphia, and North Philadelphia (Hopper 2008: 17). Mother Brown, like many Blacks, arrived in North Philly in 1914, when the Great War began in Europe. Black churches, including storefront churches, could be found along Ridge Avenue. By 1950 there were 257 storefront churches throughout the city (Hopper 2008: 20; Levenstein 2009: 21).

Blacks were leaving the South in response to White supremacist violence and the boll weevil infestation's devastating impact on the Cotton Kingdom; they were drawn to the North by the prospect of urban employment in a less racially violent social climate, as wartime demand for labor accelerated the mass migration.[5] Each year between 1922 and 1924, twenty thousand Blacks arrived in Philadelphia. By 1930 the city had 219,599 Black residents, comprising 11.3 percent of the population (Hopper 2008: 29; Gregg 1993: 13; Sernett 1997: 40). The vast majority of Black migrants came from the same southern states where the founding saints were born and raised: Virginia, the home state of Mother Brown and Elder April; South Carolina, the home state of Elder Stables and the many family members she brought into The Church; and Georgia, the home state of Elders Hannah and Esther.

As founding saints relate in their narratives in the next chapter, the possibility of finding more gainful employment and a less oppressive society motivated their flight from the South. Their narratives corroborate scholarly observations that Black women in the South averaged $2.75 per week for domestic work, but up North they could earn about that much in a single day. Wages for Black men in northern factories and railroads averaged $3 to $4 per day, compared to 75 cents per day for farm labor in the South (Sernett 1997: 45).

Mother Brown settled in Philadelphia at a time when racial tension was intensifying across the country. Protests against lynching were unavailing, as the federal government refused to intervene. In Philadelphia, Black clergy organized meetings denouncing the inflammatory White supremacist message of D. W. Griffith's 1915 film *The Birth of a Nation*, which President Wilson allowed to be screened in the White House. Set in the South during

Reconstruction, it was filled with blatantly racist images of Black rapists and "scalawag" politicians and presented the Ku Klux Klan as redeemers of southern civilization and national honor. Protests led by the National Association for the Advancement of Colored People (NAACP) occurred across the nation, but the film was a box-office hit. In Philadelphia, a protest demonstration involving about five hundred Black men and women began peacefully, but ended with 150 police charging the demonstrators, injuring many, sending some to the hospital, and arresting Black doctors, lawyers, and educators (Sernett 1997: 23; Stokes 2007: 129–62, 154–55).

White violence against Blacks in Philadelphia escalated at the end of World War I, as it did across the country. For example, near the University of Pennsylvania, about one hundred "little white boys from about six to fourteen years of age disabled and halted a trolley, and then beat the Black riders who included six women" (Ballard 1984: 84). Black veterans and other citizens responded by defending themselves. In 1918, when a Black female probation officer moved into a White neighborhood and was attacked by Whites, she fired her pistol in self-defense. Fighting ensued for several days in South and West Philadelphia, resulting in numerous injuries and arrests (Hopper 2008: 29). Black Philadelphians were aware that lynching cast its malevolent shadow even in Pennsylvania: just seven years earlier and thirty-seven miles away in the steelmaking town of Coatesville, African American Zachariah Walker had been thrown into a fire before being burned to death by a mob of several thousand Whites. Ironically, this mob included Eastern European immigrants, who recently had been the object of disdain by longtime White residents (Downey and Hyser 1991: 7–9, 13–43, 125–26, 130–31, 141).

Black-Jewish Encounters in Strawberry Mansion

Many Black women, including founding members of The Church, were employed as day workers who cleaned the homes of White Philadelphians. Some of these were Jewish homes located in the Strawberry Mansion neighborhood of North Philadelphia near Fairmount Park. Regarding this gendered, interracial interaction, Allen Meyers notes: "As Jewish families worked harder and earned a better living, the need to have a domestic clean the house, store, or help raise children became a regular part of life. In Strawberry Mansion, Jewish housewives traveled to specific corners, where the trolleys let off black women (Thirty-third and Norris or Thirty-first and York streets) to hire a domestic. The salary included their carfare, lunch, and 25 cents per hour in the late 1940s" (Meyers 1999: 53). Elder Hannah recounted what it felt like to be one of these Black women. Many Black women, including founding saints of The Church, worked five days a week, one day for each family, and their accounts suggest that the relationship between Black domestic workers and the Jewish women who hired them was simultaneously intimate, interdependent, and inequitable.

Founding saints say that they had White neighbors and that North Philly was racially mixed until World War II. North Philly had been a White residential area, and Strawberry Mansion's historical connections to Jewish Americans went back to the Revolutionary era.[6] Strawberry Mansion did not become a Jewish neighborhood until the early 1900s, when upwardly mobile German and Irish immigrants moved out of this area into newer neighborhoods. In 1898, just two years after the U.S. Supreme Court ruling in the case of *Plessy v. Ferguson* declared racial segregation legal, Nathan Weinstein emigrated from Russia and settled in Strawberry Mansion, where he and his wife raised eight children. Many Eastern European Jews who arrived in Philadelphia at the turn of the century settled in the vicinity, and the Mansion became a prosperous community that boasted five synagogue buildings and forty-five kosher butchers among two hundred other businesses, including pharmacies, doctors, "mom and pop" stores, a poolroom, and ice cream parlors where you could purchase "yum yums," a unique cross between sherbet and water ice. An effective trolley service connected this neighborhood with other Jewish communities throughout Philadelphia (Meyers 1999: 8, 9, 13, 16, 23–28, 33, 51, 53; also see Meyers 2002).

By 1920 Black children constituted 8 percent of students in the city's public schools, and by 1940 they represented 23 percent. Most were children of recent southern migrants, and African American faces began to appear in class photos of the neighborhood's elementary schools. While the appearance of both Blacks and Jews varied widely enough that it is not always possible to distinguish them in photographs, seven of forty-seven students appear obviously Black in the 1941 class of Walton Elementary School, located at Twenty-eighth and Huntingdon Street. At least ten out of about ninety students at Blaine Elementary School, located at Thirteenth and Norris Street, appear to be Black. The 1939 class photograph of Fitz Simon, located at Twenty-sixth and Cumberland, includes at least eighteen Black children out of approximately 114 students.

The youth of the Mansion could walk to Dobbins High School at Twenty-second and Leigh Avenue for vocational education, but for an academically oriented high school education they had to leave their neighborhood. They traveled to the southeastern edge of North Philadelphia near Center City to attend Central High School for Boys (Central), at Broad Street and Spring Garden, and Philadelphia High School for Girls (Girls' High) nearby at Seventeenth and Spring Garden. By the 1950s, however, both schools had been relocated to the Broad and Olney area. Similarly, Northeast High School for Boys, which Elder Cromwell recounts attending, originally located in North Philly at Eighth and Lehigh Avenue, was moved to 1601 Cottman Avenue in all-White Northeast Philadelphia in 1954 at a cost of $7 million (Meyers 1999: 37–44; Levenstein 2009: 130). These three excellent schools were removed from increasingly Black neighborhoods to newer, all-White neighborhoods in Overbrook, Mount Airy, West Oak Lane, and Oxford Circle (Meyers 1999: 8, 9). As Meyers points out, "many Jewish families migrated to new neighborhoods and three urban high schools moved more than 5 miles to new locations" (Meyers 1999: 42; also see Levenstein 2009: 121–55).

Black migrants settled in North Philadelphia, especially around Ridge Avenue, and in parts of West Philadelphia that had been exclusively White. During the 1920s, Philadelphia realtors, like realtors in other American cities at that time, seeing an opportunity to turn a quick profit, purchased at low prices the property of Whites desperate to flee the increasing number of Black neighbors. The realtors then rented or sold to Blacks at inflated prices, making huge profits at the expense of both Blacks and Whites. Simultaneously, White communities' racially restrictive covenants and public protests limited where Blacks could hope to rent or own homes (Hopper 2008: 29; Gregg 1993: 27, 29; Sernett 1997: 122). As Elder Beverly relates so movingly in her narrative and as I recall from my youth, realtors working closely with White residents prevented Black families from even viewing homes that were for sale. In the city's poorly funded and segregated public housing, efforts at racial integration were accompanied by bitter protests in which "White women often took the lead" (Levenstein 2009: 101).

Although what was commonly called "White flight" was the predominant pattern in Strawberry Mansion, as in other neighborhoods across the city, no group is homogenous. In their narrative, Elders Ronald and Esther Wilson speak of their caring Jewish next-door neighbors who did not abandon the Mansion when their neighbors did. Meyers documents the activism of Hanna Silver, a Holocaust survivor who settled in Strawberry Mansion in the 1950s: "'White flight' did not stop Hanna in her fight to bring justice and action in building a sense of pride and purpose for the next inhabitants of the Mansion. She protested taprooms and her group stopped 21 out of 23 attempts to open them in the area. Hanna, with the help of several agencies and the school board secured one school bus to take 600 children to Smith's playground in the summer on a daily basis" (Meyers 1999: 55). In protesting the granting of liquor licenses to taprooms, bars that attracted disorderly gatherings of idle men on street corners, Silver joined Black women in other city neighborhoods who were attempting to protect children on the way to and from school and young women running errands from a potent combination of temptation and insult (Levenstein 2009: 155).

Black-Jewish encounters in domestic workplaces and mixed neighborhoods are important to this investigation for at least two reasons. The founding saints recount their interactions with Jewish employers and neighbors, which in some cases differed from the interactions with White Christians. Secondly, what Christians call the Old Testament and Jews call the Torah informs the saints' beliefs and practices, ranging from "keeping Sabbath" to "eating clean" (Crumbley 2000). The saints kept Sabbath from sunset Friday until sunset Saturday, as Jews do. Although the cost in money, time, and space may have prevented them from keeping kosher, founding saints were meticulous in their avoidance of pork, and they ate out only rarely and with great care.[7]

Encountering the Un-Promised Land

By 1930 over two-thirds of Black Philadelphians had been born in the southern states of Virginia, North Carolina, South Carolina, and Georgia; one in every ten was from South Carolina. Migrants often lived near others from their home state (Ballard 1984: 8, 13). The Philadelphia they encountered fell woefully short of the Promised Land they had hoped for, as the prospect of economic success and social well-being was constantly undermined by discrimination in the housing and labor markets. The Great Depression hit Black people with doubled force. According to a 1933 survey, 60 percent of Black fathers in North Philadelphia were out of work (Ballard 1984: 211, 231). Major industries left the city, where most Blacks lived, and by World War II had relocated to suburbs where Blacks were excluded from buying homes (Gregg 1993: 220; Hershberg et al. 1979: 68–70, 73, 78–80; Ballard 1984: 231). The removal of industrial workplaces from the inner city to the racially exclusive White suburbs of Philadelphia sheds light on the male saints' stories of carpooling to work at Strick's truck and trailer factories.

During the Great Migration, Black women swelled the ranks of domestic service workers in metropolitan areas; in Philadelphia, three-fourths of employed Black women toiled as domestics. White women, particularly those who were Irish, were leaving this low-paid and physically demanding line of work for clerical positions in offices and stores, while Black women were excluded from office and sales positions that required a high school education and involved interacting with White customers (Collier-Thomas 2010: 281).[8] The experiences of Black domestic workers differed significantly from those of their White counterparts. White women were usually paid more, and domestic service was often their stepping stone to better jobs in factories, stores, or offices. Because Black men encountered job discrimination, which was supported both by employers and by labor unions, and were confined to the least stable and well-paid jobs, married women, including the mothers of young children, found it necessary to earn money in order to make ends meet (Clark-Lewis 1994: vii–viii; Dill 1994: 142).

The influx of Black women precipitated anxiety in Whites and even on the part of some middle-class Blacks. This attitude was expressed in fear-laced language and acts of moral condescension. The Philadelphia branch of the National League for the Protection of Colored Women was established in 1905 by Sarah Willie Layten. Layten, a Black Baptist leader, public schoolteacher, and a founder of Black women's clubs in California, worked closely with White social worker Frances Kellor on issues regarding recently arrived southern Black women in major urban centers. Layten's goal was to train uneducated Black women so that they might not fall into the "story of failure, of want, of crime, of poverty, of disease that might be avoided had the girl only been safeguarded" (quoted in Gregg 1993: 37–39; see also Smith 1996: 403–6; Higginbotham 1993: 157–58). Similar institutions were established in other northern urban centers, expressing "moral panic" over the plight of "colored women," whose presence was problematized, sexualized, and surrounded with an aura of pathology and danger (Carby 1992: 730, 747, 751, 753).[9]

Black migrants encountered racialized hiring practices almost everywhere, even in municipal employment. Several founding saints recount their experiences of a dramatic confrontation that occurred four years into World War II. Racial tensions in Philadelphia had intensified as Black workers were hired by defense plants and moved into previously all-White neighborhoods. Approximately thirty-six thousand African Americans settled in Philadelphia between 1940 and 1945; the three hundred thousand Black citizens in a city of two million amounted to approximately 15 percent of the population. The employment of Black labor in war industries was a national necessity, and civil rights groups led by A. Philip Randolph seized the moment to demand that Blacks be hired in plants that held defense contracts. President Franklin Delano Roosevelt issued Executive Order 8802, desegregating war plants and establishing the Fair Employment Practices Commission (FEPC) to enforce it. This federal policy set the stage for a major racial confrontation in the City of Brotherly Love.

On August 1, 1944, ten thousand White Philadelphia Transit Company (PTC) workers and Rapid Transit Union (RTU) members walked off their jobs rather than comply with the FEPC's order to open the position of trolley driver to African Americans; Black PTC workers previously had been restricted to lower-ranking positions. African Americans organized around the NAACP and combined their efforts with those of the Transport Workers Union, an affiliate of the activist Congress of Industrial Organizations (CIO). On August 6, federal troops arrived in Philadelphia, in line with the 1943 Smith-Connally Anti-Strike/War Labor Disputes Act, which authorized the federal government to seize and operate businesses threatened by strikes that could interrupt war production. The strike was peppered by incidents of violence, including three "White motorists" who drove through a Black neighborhood and shot a fifteen-year-old Black male. As saints recall, Blacks "tore up" Ridge Avenue, sparing those White- and Asian-owned business they deemed good and fair. After a week of conflict, four strike leaders were arrested and striking White workers signed pledge cards and returned to work alongside Black trolley drivers (Winkler 1972: 73–74, 85–87; Wolfinger 2005).

Police brutality toward Black citizens was endemic, even normative, in the city (Levenstein 2009: 186). The Philadelphia school system practiced racial segregation, underfunded majority-Black schools, and steered Black students away from academic tracks into vocational education (Levenstein 2009: 121, 130, 132, 134). Elder Jerald relates the consequences of these discriminatory policies for his own education. Black teachers were not allowed to instruct White children until the 1930s, which helps explain why Elder Beverly's mentor, Philadelphia-born Temple University graduate Mr. Bowman, taught her at Bettis Academy in Trenton, South Carolina.[10] As renowned African American urban anthropologist Arthur Huss Fauset recalled, even with a master's degree from the University of Pennsylvania, the city's elite postsecondary institution, Fauset was prohibited from teaching in a White junior high school; eventually he was appointed principal of a Black school (Ballard 1984: 83–85, 77, 52–54, 59, 211).

Blacks faced poor health, including an infant mortality rate that was twice as high for Blacks as Whites. The death rate from tuberculosis (TB) was four times higher for Blacks than for Whites; Elder Jerald's family was deeply affected by this scourge. While White physicians argued that persons of African descent were innately predisposed to TB, African American Charles

Lewis, a 1912 graduate of the University of Pennsylvania medical school, rejected this unscientific notion. Dr. Lewis established a research program at Mercy Hospital, a historically Black institution where I was born the year before it merged with the other African American medical center, Douglas Hospital. Lewis demonstrated that high Black TB rates were due not to inherent racial weakness, but rather to inadequate nourishment because of poverty and poor, crowded housing. Population density averaged 28.2 per acre for Whites but 111 per acre in Black neighborhoods, promoting the spread of this contagious disease (Ballard 1984: 240, 251).

Black southern migrants encountered constrained leisure and entertainment opportunities, including exclusion from eating establishments and recreational facilities. In 1930, Blacks had to sue to gain entry into the Horn and Hardart cafeteria chain (Ballard 1984: 85), where Elder Ronald recalls working as a youth. In North Philly, which was fast becoming known as a little South Carolina, many of the Black churches were located in "pitifully small and antiquated structures" and "there was no YMCA, recreation center, no public library, no municipal betterment center" (Ballard 1984: 8, 85, 188).

Black Northerners' Racial Uplift Work and Southern Migrants' Response

In the spirit of "racial uplift," established Black churches in Philadelphia shifted their priorities to the material needs of southern migrants flooding the African American community. The notion and practice of uplift entailed taking measures to improve the material circumstances and moral values and practices of poorer, less-educated Black people so that they might be more successful in middle-class White America, as the long-established Black Philadelphians had already done (Hopper 2008: 27, 31; Gregg 1993: 5, 69–86, 111, 210). Black independent churches worked both through denominational and nondenominational organizations to address issues ranging from child welfare, education, and housing to employment and entrepreneurship.[11]

The Northeast Federation of Colored Women's Clubs, which held its 1915 meeting at Allen AME Church in Philadelphia, passed resolutions supporting women's suffrage and pressing for a private interview with President Woodrow Wilson to urge the passage of an anti-lynching law. Anne Biddle Sterling, from a prominent and wealthy White Philadelphia family whose philanthropy touched the life of Elder Beverly, directed the Inter-Racial Committee's Anti-lynching Committee in the mid-1920s, with African American scholar Arthur Huff Fauset and Methodist leader Rev. Dr. Charles

A. Tindley as participating members (Ballard 1984: 242). The Philadelphia chapter of the NAACP regularly held meetings about racial discrimination in the city's school system in Black churches (Hopper 2008: 32). Cooperation between the two groups became a force to be reckoned with. Around 1933, Black Baptist Rev. James E. Kirkland, other church leaders, and NAACP lawyer Raymond Pace Alexander worked with Black parents when nearby Montgomery County tried to prohibit Black children from enrolling in a new school. In an especially offensive expression of the dominant ideology, the head of the local school board, Norman Greene, declared, "Niggers are like parrots, and they have to be led, and we are only striving to make better citizens of them by keeping them segregated and together" (Hopper 2008: 35; Canton 2008).

Older Black churches interacted with newly arrived Black southerners culturally and were soon influenced by Black southern preaching and musical styles. Rev. Tindley, who founded one of the largest Black Methodist churches in the eastern United States, pioneered a radio ministry that featured his "gospel" musical compositions (Hopper 2008: 36; Southern 1997: 457).[12] Rev. Tindley's gospels were less likely to be sung by his fellow Black Methodists than by Baptists, who had already embraced Thomas A. Dorsey as their "Prince of Gospel," and were even more likely to be sung in storefront churches. Similarly, the southern revival style of preaching began to affect the older Black churches when pastors realized that their restrained preaching style was no longer attracting new members (Gregg 1993: 25, 70, 77, 131; Southern 1997: 458).

The relationship between Black northern church folk and those recently arrived from the South was not always strained. Indeed, Rev. Robert J. Williams, the pastor of Mother Bethel, who had been raised in the South, sent out leaflets encouraging southern AME members to move to Philadelphia and make Bethel their new home church (Gregg 1993: 181, 191; Hopper 2008: 30). In time, however, the increasing numbers who joined Bethel made enough older members uncomfortable that this congregation became divided (Gregg 1993: 191–92, 182–88). In part, these conflicts are related to wartime migration of Blacks to Philadelphia in larger numbers and from different parts of the South: forty thousand had arrived during and just after the war, and most hailed not from the urban upper South, such as Baltimore, Maryland, Richmond, Virginia, and Washington, D.C., but from more rural southern states, including the Carolinas, Georgia, and Florida. The migrants from these regions brought with them ways of singing and preaching that were not readily accepted in the older and more established northern Black churches (Gregg 1993: 24, 131, 213–16, 219).

The notion of racial uplift was grounded in collectivity and service. The slogan of the national Black women's club movement, "Lifting as *we* climb," underlines these women's sense of obligation to improve the conditions of Black men, women, and children of all classes and thereby to "advance the race." Some Black scholars have argued that by World War I, northern-born members of older Black independent churches, despite a commendable tradition of uplift and protest, "had waxed fat and stuffy" and "disdained their own" (Washington 1984: 58; Ballard 1984: 9). In some cases, uplift was conflated with elitism and "colorism"—that is, the practice of granting higher status to light-skinned African Americans who could claim descent from Whites and from Blacks who were free before the Civil War (Hunter 2002: 177). Photographs of AME church leaders in Philadelphia between 1890 and 1940 suggest that colorism flourished as visible White ancestry was conflated with status; leadership positions were held by light-skinned persons, called "toasties," who sat in prominent pews, relegating darker-skinned members to the back and balcony (Gregg 1993: 208–9).

This conflation of skin tone with status, although lamentable, follows rather logically from associating the physical features of the dominant group with access to the resources the group enjoys and avoiding the violent oppression it exercises. Looking more like White people has improved the life chances of some African Americans. During the early twentieth century, my maternal grandmother's first cousin migrated to Chicago, where she engaged in strategic "passing" by day so she could work at the I. Miller department store and returned at the end of the day to her African American family and community on the South Side. Even today, as Matthew Harrison's research has demonstrated, a lighter-skinned Black would be recommended for a job over a darker-skinned Black, even when the résumé of the darker person indicated greater competency (Harrison 2005: 1–28). In this light, I agree with Allen Ballard that the uplift-oriented Blacks who could "pass" but chose not to do so are to be commended for identifying with and working toward the advancement of Black people rather than pursuing individual aggrandizement beyond the pale of race in America (Ballard 1984: 121).[13]

Some critics have argued that the uplift strategy espoused by the Black elite, including church women's organizations, critically accepted capitalist economic structures and bourgeois values (Gaines 1996: 3, 20, 27, 113, 257–58). Nevertheless, aspiring to and achieving bourgeois respectability can also be understood as lived contestation of stereotypes of Blacks as lazy, innately inferior beings ill-equipped to achieve, let alone aspire to a serious work ethic. While "beating them at their own game" may lack the critical edge of a carefully articulated anti-hegemonic ideology, Black achievement in a capitalist society demonstrates lived rejection of oppressive social structures.

How did Black southern migrants respond to the attitudes, social positioning, and cultural aspirations of the Black establishment they encountered in the North? These recent arrivals were not entirely cowed. Rising to the occasion, they helped to infuse revitalizing energy into the Black community. As one migrant observed, "Those Old Philadelphians . . . couldn't snub me in the first place. I made my own society. . . . When I came home from college, I made my own social order through the church, my college fraternity, and business connections." Another critically commented that "The Old Philadelphians were not intellectuals. They were caterers, barbers, butlers, cooks. They worked for these rich White people. But the others, they had to make it. And they became more versatile, smarter, more competitive, tougher. . . . They were dark and brown and could not lay claim to the kind of life that these people had here." Arthur Huff Fauset remarked that the Old Black Philadelphians "depended on their rank, tradition and pedigree," while the "shrewd" southerners who arrived in Philly "had their eyes out for something" and "went after it." A successful Black politician concluded that the "Old Philadelphians were so busy being Old Philadelphians that they missed out" (Ballard 1984: 202–3).

Fauset's "Cults" and Ida Robinson's "Church"

With the "New Philadelphians" came an array of religious expressions that dramatically diversified the city's Black religious landscape. New institutions included Father Divine's Peace Mission Movement and Daddy Grace's United House of Prayer for All People, as well as two groups of "Black Jews": the Church of God and Saints of Christ, founded by William S. Crowdy, born into southern slavery in 1847, and the Church of the Living God Pillar and Ground of Truth for all Nations, founded by Prophet F. S. Cherry. Their doctrines drew selectively on Hebrew law, and they tended to identify themselves as "true" Jews compared to the "White Jews" (Chireau 2000: 30–31; Fauset 2002: 13–21, 31–40; Glazier 2001: 53; Hopper 2008: 38–40; Miller 1995; Pinn 2006: 78–87; Singer 2000). Bishop Mary Magdalena Tate established a branch of her Church of the Living God Pillar and Ground of Truth Without Controversy in the city. Bishop Ida Robinson's Mount Sinai flourished and spread, and Bishop Sherrod Johnson, leader of the Church of the Lord Jesus Christ of the Apostolic Faith, became a media fixture by broadcasting his sermons on Philadelphia's Black-owned WDAS and seventy radio stations around the world.

At the time, scholars regarded these religious phenomena as distinctive because of the central role their charismatic founder-leaders played, the striking degree to which their beliefs and practices diverged from mainstream American religion, both Black and White, and the spiritual and social distance members placed between themselves and nonbelievers. Finding an effective descriptor for them was (and continues to be) a problem, not least because most descriptive terms imply a judgment about them. Drawing on Raymond Julius's notion of "cult" and his typology of its varied expressions, Arthur Huff Fauset used this term in his *Black Gods of the Metropolis: Negro Religious Cults of the Urban North* (1944). Calling these groups "cults" is jarring and especially off-putting when he applied it to Bishop Ida Robinson's Mount Sinai, which stands in the tradition of the Sanctified Church and was well institutionalized during the lifetime of its founder. Fauset's other four case studies are Daddy Grace's House of Prayer for All People, Drew Ali's Moorish Temple, Father Divine's Peace Mission Movement, and Bishop Cherry's Church of the Living God Pillar and Ground of Truth for All Nations. Indeed, it is not clear what these religious institutions shared that justified their identification as "cults," as they varied dramatically in size, scale, institutional structure, and the historical sources of their beliefs and practices. Still, unlike other scholars of the time, Fauset refused to diminish the social and cultural significance of these religious movements; instead, he called on scholars to give them serious attention. His study explores the work of storefront churches in helping members make the transition from rural southern to inner-city lifeways (Carpenter 1999: 228; Fauset 2002: 78–80). He also used the ethnographic forum of his study to reflect on the key debates in African American history and cultural studies. Like the research and writing of many African American and other minoritized academics as well as that of women scholars, Fauset's work has "been disappeared" from the intellectual canon of anthropology, and the importance of his work to the study of Black religions in America has only recently been recognized. His political activism has tended to take precedence in how he is remembered in academic circles (Curtis and Sigler 2009: 1–2; Savage 2002: x–xi; Harrison and Harrison 1999). Nevertheless, *Black Gods of the Metropolis* addressed an issue that has endured into twenty-first-century scholarly debates—namely, the origins and distinctive characteristics of African American religion. Fauset balanced the differing opinions of Jewish American anthropologist Melville J. Herskovits, who argued for African sources, and E. Franklin Frazier, a Black American scholar who emphasized New World religious encounters. Fauset concludes: "Common sense required us to believe that everything cultural which the Negro brought over with him from Africa could not have been eradicated from his heritage. . . . Nevertheless, if we do not go all the way with Frazier and Park in their almost wholesale assertions that there are no African religious survival[s] to speak of neither can we accept every chance correspondence which might appear to indicate survival" (Fauset 2002: 101).[14] Fauset also took exception to Herskovits's assertion that a "deep religious bent" makes Blacks "turn to religion rather than to political action or other outlets for their frustration" (quoted in Fauset 2002: 4, 96). Fauset argued that, rather than fostering political passivity, Black religious institutions function as "mechanisms" for African American economic, political, and social development (Fauset 2002: 100).

Black Gods of the Metropolis was one of the first published urban ethnographies (Szwed 2002: xvii). Although the research was conducted more than fifty years ago, Fauset's fieldwork approach and his style of ethnographic writing are compatible with recent methodological concerns with ethnographic voice, positioning, and reflexivity (Savage 2002: x–xiii; Carpenter 1999: 230; Fauset 2002: 9–12). Fauset had personal ties to the Black church and Black Philadelphia. His father was an AME minister from an old Black Philadelphia family that went back two hundred years, and his mother, though born a Jew, converted to Christianity (Carpenter 1999: 217–21; Savage 2002: vii, viii; Harrison and Harrison 1999). Fauset was keenly aware that his ethnographic focus on alternative religious groups, rather than large churches, limited his ability to identify general patterns or establish strong correlations (Fauset 2002: 10). However, his in-depth, thick description of these religious movements' origins, organization, financial strategies, sacred texts, beliefs, and rituals documents what Barbara Savage has aptly described as "the adventuresome range of religious ideas and practices that appealed to disparate groups of African Americans in the 1930s and 1940s" (Savage 2002: x, xvi).

Gendered Encounters: Women, Respectability, and Sanctified Churches

The experience of living in a large urban center expanded the religious options southern migrants might exercise, and some of these offered more expansive notions of what it meant to be Black, female, and churched. Demonstrating how urban anonymity influences religious affiliation, a woman from

Virginia who embraced a life of holiness in Philadelphia reported that she had not dared to attend a Sanctified church back home because "The people in the little towns down there all know each other and this makes them afraid to be different. But we were in Philadelphia now, and in this big city, we didn't have to worry what our friends might think" (quoted in Hardy 2009: 23).

Some women not only joined Sanctified churches, but actually founded them. The Church of God in Christ (COGIC) did not, and still does not, ordain women. Yet women stood out in the expansion of this denomination as its members traveled north. Lillian Brooks Coffey pioneered the first COGIC congregation in the North, and a central figure in establishing COGIC in Philadelphia was "Mother" Juanita Elizabeth Dabney (1890–1967). With the blessing of COGIC founder Bishop C. H. Mason and working hand in hand with her COGIC-ordained husband, she answered a divine call to a ministry of prayer and healing. Her work as a missionary to new urban communities and as an evangelist and teacher attracted many Philadelphians seeking a "life of holiness" (Haney 1995; Butler 2007: 41, 52–53, 59–63; Curtis and Sigler 2009).

Mother Dabney inspired other women to find salvation and answer their call to the ministry, and she did so in ways that transcended the color line.[15] According to some of the saints' narratives, the land on which Mother Dabney's Garden of Prayer expanded was a gift from a White woman whose son Mother Dabney had healed. I heard about another White woman whose life was deeply touched by Mother Dabney from my colleague Walter Wolfram, Professor of English at North Carolina State University. When I was telling him about this research project, Walt excitedly recalled that his wife's mother "was healed of asthma by Mother Dabney." He described Mother Dabney as his mother-in-law's spiritual "mentor" and said that it was at the Garden of Prayer that she "found the Holy Spirit." Out of the interaction between this Black woman and this White woman came an expression regularly used in his family: "You're the child of the King."[16]

In *Women in the Church of God in Christ: Making a Sanctified World* (2007), Anthea Butler explores the creative skill with which women evangelists, teachers, and missionaries were able to "wield power through a traditional office in subversive yet spiritual ways." The Women's Department of COGIC exercised economic power in fundraising and directly influenced succession. COGIC women set the denomination's cultural and behavioral norms. Their civic outreach has extended even to the White House. They were able to accomplish all this while complying with scripturally grounded beliefs and gender practices of COGIC that exclude them from ordination (Butler 2007: 1–5, 7, 117–34).

Some sanctified women headed churches as ordained ministers, even though the larger society regarded them as "extremist because of their religion, lower class because they were Black, and subservient because they were female" (Best 1998: 154). Bishop Mary Magdalena Tate, with the help of her son, established a branch of her Church of the Living God Pillar and Ground of Truth Without Controversy (COLG) in Philadelphia, along with congregations in Hartford, Connecticut, and Orlando, Florida. Mother Tate's COLG had several schisms, and in one of these she was succeeded by a male bishop, Archibald White, who disapproved of female bishops because he felt that women were the source of "too many problems." According to Felton Best, women are still ordained in this branch of COLG, but they have not predominated on the Board of Bishops. At the 1981 COLG general conference, two female elders demanded to be made bishops or they would leave the church with several female pastors and their loyal laity (Best 1998: 164–65; Alexander 2008: 62, 66, 107).

Ida Bell Robinson established a more stable, enduring, and gender-inclusive Sanctified institution in Philadelphia, and her Mount Sinai is considered the largest denomination founded and led by an African American woman. Born in Hazlehurst, Georgia, in 1891, Robinson followed her sister to Philadelphia in 1917 just three years after Mother Brown had arrived in the city. Her religious affiliations before starting Mount Sinai included the Church of God (Tennessee), which had prohibited women's ordination by 1919, and Elder Henry Fisher's United Holy Church, which in 1924 decided not to ordain women. So disturbed was Robinson by the imposition of restrictions on women's religious leadership that she went on a ten-day fast seeking spiritual guidance, and at its end she reported that she had been instructed to "Come out on Mt. Sinai and loose the women." Robinson would affirm, "If Mary the mother of Jesus could carry the word of God in her womb, why can't women carry the word of God in their mouth?" With this rhetorical question, she claimed her place in the long tradition of Black women preachers who argued similarly (Andrews 1986: 36; Haywood 2003: 82–83, 87; Alexander 2008: 119–23, 136).

Wise administrator that she was, Bishop Robinson consulted a lawyer on the most effective way to establish a stable and enduring new church. She ordained women not only as ministers but also as elders and bishops, and she instituted a Monday evening "Women Preacher's Night" when she listened to their sermons and provided constructive criticism. She also ordained men and, as Estrelda Alexander notes in *Limited Liberty: The Legacy of Four Pentecostal Women Pioneers*, Mount Sinai was and continues to be a female-led but not a female-dominated religious institution. Mount Sinai has enjoyed greater institutional stability than Bishop Mary Magdalena Tate's COLG. There was only one schism during Bishop Robinson's lifetime, and between 1924 and 1946 she established 84 churches in the United States with foreign missions in Guyana and Cuba. She ordained 125 females out of 140 church elders, and at the end of the twentieth century, equal numbers of male and female pastors led the denomination's 156 congregations. Mount Sinai's bishop has always been female (Best 1998: 158–61, 168; Alexander 2008: 119–27, 135–47).

Theologically and culturally, Bishop Robinson's teachings are conservative, but she took courageous public stands on controversial issues of the day. Her congregation was interracial, which itself was remarkable. Mount Sinai's newsletter, "The Latter Day Messenger," critically addressed racial and economic discrimination. Like COGIC founder Bishop Mason, she was an open pacifist. Expressing this theologically grounded but unpopular position at a time even when the United States was at war, she was listed among agitators in FBI files in 1942. Additionally, Bishop Robinson's home and the apartment above the New York church served as what Fauset called a "hospice" for the respite and rejuvenation of the women of Mount Sinai (Alexander 2008: 128–34; Fauset 2002: 34, 89; Dupree and Dupree 1993: 53).

As Clarence Hardy notes, Sanctified women, whether in male- or female-led churches, lived by a set of values that went beyond middle-class White norms. Reflecting on Evelyn Brooks Higginbotham's important assessment of gender, religion, and interracial reform, Hardy accurately observes that Sanctified churches broadened the norms of acceptable comportment for women beyond the version of middle-class respectability promoted by the long-established Black churches, which more closely resembled the norms of the dominant White culture. Sanctified congregations offered ways of being Black and female that were grounded in sacred rituals, values, and modes of conduct developed through the experience of moving between the rural South and the urban North (Hardy 2009: 23; Higginbotham 1993).

The founding saints of The Church were active participants in the Great Migration to Philadelphia. With their female pastor Mother Brown at the helm, they carved out a culturally and spiritually satisfying space within the religious landscape of the city. In The Church, they came to terms with the reality of Philadelphia as considerably less than the Promised Land they had hoped for, yet as a refuge offering greater possibilities than anything they had ever known "down South." The next chapter relates their testimonies.

3

SAINTS TALES

ALMOST ALL OF THE FOUNDING SAINTS migrated to Philadelphia from the South. When they were interviewed for this research project, they had risen to the office of elder, serving as the spiritual leaders of The Church, and ranged in age from seventy-six to ninety-eight. Some elders were talkative and others were laconic; some stayed on point, while others pursued lines of thought that produced rich and germane information. In presenting their stories, I have focused both on common experiences and on individual insights that illuminate the trajectory of lives marked by struggle and by faith.

The first narrative is that of the oldest elder interviewed for this work, who died before its publication; the last narrative is that of the oldest living elder. Because members of the Nichols family predominate in this group, narratives of elders who do not belong to this extended family are interspersed among them. The narrative of Elder Holly Nichols Stables appears before those of her siblings because her story grounds theirs. A recurring theme in the Nichols narratives concerns the interweaving of Black and White family histories in their southern hometown. All the elders' narratives discuss the processes of chain migration to the North and of the spiritual journeys that led them to The Church. The chapter ends with an exploration of recurrent themes that "enflesh" the social-historical information about the Great Migration in the previous chapter.

Elder Hannah Pope Nichols (1915–2007)
"Honey, you don't know the half!"

"Sturdy Welsh" and "Negro Scalawags"

In the middle of our interview, tears began to roll down Elder Hannah's face. She explained that earlier that day she had seen a television spot for the Christian Children's Fund. The pitiful conditions of these poor children, she explained, had "brought back so much" about how she had "come up" as a child in South Carolina.

Hannah was born in 1915 in Blenheim, a small town in Marlboro County. Located on the North Carolina border, the county had a history of sustained and concentrated slaveholding. Here, according to the 1860 U.S. Census Slave Schedules, 6,893 Blacks were held in slavery, with forty-nine slaveholders owning close to half of them.[1] Some enslaved Blacks had worked side by side with Whites in cotton mills, but a century later job discrimination excluded African Americans from the textile mills (Lander 1953: 165, 172). A 1927 document prepared by the South Carolina Department of Agriculture, Commerce, and Industries and Clemson College, refers to the Reconstruction period in Blenheim as "the days of negro scalawag government"; it describes when "one negro mysteriously disappeared" as "the nearest approach to a lynching in the county's history." The same document reports that in 1785 the area was settled by "sturdy Welsh Baptists and reinforced a little later by numbers of hardy ... Scots." Blenheim, renowned for its mineral springs, had a population of 234 in the early 1900s, when Hannah was growing up, and has remained a small town into the twenty-first century.[2] In 2000, this town of 0.6 square miles had a population of 130, and just over half of its residents were of African descent.[3] Elder Hannah described Blenheim as an isolated town with a substantial Black population who enjoyed very few opportunities for economic improvement and where an indiscretion—or even the perception of a possible indiscretion—could be dangerous for Black people.

Hannah was one of twelve siblings. Her father was a sharecropper who worked on "thirds": "When you picked three bales of cotton, the third one would be yours," she explained. Like her mother, she married a sharecropper. Elder Hannah reflected that if she, like her parents, had had more than two children, and if she and her husband had owned more farm animals and equipment, she might not have seen so little for her years of hard work. Hard labor, minimal fruits, and times of scant food were recurrent themes in her recollections of childhood and young adulthood in Blenheim. She talked of picking cotton as a child and "not seeing a nickel"; after working all day, they went to the creek to "catch our supper." At times they only had what they grew in their garden. At this point in the interview, Elder Hannah's eyes began to tear up as she recalled the Christian Children's Fund TV spot.

Hannah had the good fortune to attend a school set up and supervised by the Black Baptist church that she and her family attended. She could have continued her education, as people were willing to pay for her to attend high school at a time when there were no free public high schools for Blacks. But at nineteen she fell in love and married. She said she regretted this decision all her life, especially because her parents, who had had no formal education, had taught her to value it. "I messed up. I didn't get there. I went ahead and got the husband first." Still, Elder Hannah placed a high value on education, and when I remarked that some "saved" people believe that education interferes with your salvation, her shocked admonition was that education is "the best thing you can get!"

Run Out of Blenheim, Lined Up Like Horses in Philadelphia

In Hannah's experience growing up in South Carolina, Blacks and Whites got along fine as long as Black people "stayed in their place" and said "yes, sir; no, sir." When they were not deferential, the cost was high. For example, one day when Hannah was working as a live-in domestic worker for the family of a White preacher, assisting his wife and caring for their two children, a young Black boy named J. Moses was speaking to the preacher's wife. The preacher thought that this youth had addressed his wife by her first name, and the preacher "went off that morning." In truth, the preacher had "misheard" the youth, but as she explained, "I couldn't say that to him.... I'd have been treated just like J. Moses." Reports of the incident "flew around town," and J. Moses was in danger. "By the weekend, J. Moses was in Philadelphia," she concluded. When I expressed sympathy regarding the terrible way she and her Black neighbors were forced to live, she laughingly replied, "Honey, you don't know the half!"

Elder Hannah recalled that in South Carolina during the early 1930s she received 50 cents for a day's work as a domestic, which usually included cooking; it rose to 70 cents before she left for Philadelphia. She reflected on doing domestic work for a White woman: "You could go up in her house and clean it, and cook her food, but you couldn't use the front door." When asked to recall "good" interactions with Whites in the South, she could not. Her relationships with Whites in the North seemed neither positive nor negative, to the degree that they existed at all. Arriving in Philadelphia around 1940, she observed that northern Whites "mostly kept to themselves" and that "you couldn't go to the White parts" of town or participate in public events as Whites did.

Interactions with White Philadelphians occurred mainly around work and were generally impersonal and distant. Elder Hannah recalls going to a street corner in the Strawberry Mansion area of North Philadelphia where Black women seeking work would stand in line and the White women would pick out the Black woman they wanted to work for them that day "like we were a horse or something." She was paid $1.75 for cleaning on her first day job; that was more than twice as much as she had made down South, and it did not include cooking. After this, "I found work in Jew-town." Hannah never worked in a factory and mainly secured her domestic work through friends and family.

    Hannah had separated from her husband after about three years and had been living with her mother before leaving the South and relocating to West Philadelphia. Her friend Molly had convinced her to "take a chance and try" Philly, and after careful thought Hannah arranged for her mother to care for her two sons for a year while she went North. Hannah initially lived with Molly's sister; she soon moved into her own room, then an apartment, and eventually bought a home in North Philadelphia. She worked hard and saved enough money to pay for her two sons, her mother, and her younger sister to join her in Philadelphia. She sent her boys to public school as soon as possible. When asked if she had ever considered going back, she explained that in the 1990s her son suggested they relocate to the South. Her subtle but firm response was "I'm used to here."

Baptist Benefactor, Holiness Mentor

In the South, where she experienced a call to preach, Hannah had been Baptist. She also attended a Baptist church when she first arrived in Philadelphia. In fact, it was through a Baptist pastor that Hannah met Mother Brown. Pastor Dudley "thought that I had a talent," but "he didn't have a free hand," for in those days "women weren't allowed too much." The pastor, who had met Mother Brown, felt that Hannah would better develop her spiritual gifts under the older woman's guidance. Pastor Dudley, who died shortly afterward, introduced Hannah to Mother Brown, who not only took her under her wing but "helped me with my children and all."

    Sharing family responsibilities was in line with Elder Hannah's understanding of what it means to be saved; as she put it, you know that you are "saved" by "the love you have for everyone and anyone." When asked if a person has to speak in tongues to be saved, she said yes but returned to her point that saints must "love thy neighbor as thyself." Regarding the changes that have occurred in the church since the pastor, Mother Brown, died, she welcomed the young people's presence, adding that it was good that "God had sent young people . . . because my mind is old." Besides, each person has something special to offer, as "things that God put in you, I'll never know."

    Elder Hannah was a stalwart of the Church of Prayer Seventh Day for most of her adult life, devoting over fifty years to The Church. She brought her mother into The Church and as a mature woman married Jonathan Nichols, a younger brother of Holly Nichols. She served The Church as an elder until her death in 2007 at the age of ninety-two.

Elder April Peters Nichols (1924–2006)

"I didn't find comfort in the Baptist church.... I was looking for some people that were solid.... I mean sincere toward God."

Pittsylvania, Judge Coles, and the Lynching of George Towler

Elder April Peters Nichols always valued education. Her father tried his best to realize his dream of sending all his children to college, but the financial resources required were not available to Black people in Hurt, Virginia. April was born in 1924 in Pittsylvania County, in the south-central Piedmont region of Virginia bordering North Carolina. In this county, according to the U.S. Census of 1860, 1,413 Whites held 14,340 Blacks in slavery. After the Civil War, the Pittsylvania County Courthouse became the testing ground for the Civil Rights Act of 1875, which had been passed to enforce the rights of emancipation, citizenship, and voting that had been declared by the Thirteenth (1864), Fourteenth (1868), and Fifteenth (1870) amendments, respectively. When, in 1879, Judge J. Doddridge Coles denied Blacks the right to serve as jurors, he was duly arrested at the Pittsylvania courthouse for violating the Civil Rights Act of 1875. Furthermore, his petitions to drop the charges and release him from prison were denied.

It was not long, however, before Democrats throughout the South took steps to restore White rule by undermining the equitable policies put in place by the Republican coalition of reform-oriented Black freedmen and Whites. The Hurt, Virginia, into which April was born had been shaped both by constrained interpretations of Blacks' constitutional rights and by policies promoting White supremacy in southern political, social, and economic institutions (Butowsky 2008). Legal strategies used to "redeem" the South after Reconstruction were supplemented by terrorist threats and actual violence against Blacks, including lynching.

Southern lynching, though predominantly a White male affair, also drew White women and children as spectators.[4] Family members of the "offended party" often took the "first shot" at the supposed perpetrator. Variously interpreted in terms of a southern code of "honor" into which Whites were socialized, as the expression of a deviant psychosexual desire to impose racialized hegemony, or as a deliberate effort to exert control over Black labor, lynching has involved mobs of both poor Whites and Bourbon elites (Allen, Als, Lewis, and Litwack 2000; Apel and Smith 2008: 51–52; Apel 2004: 97; Brundage 1993: 6–14, 37–38, 140–43; Kahn and Perez 2002: 51, 97, 99, 121).[5] In 1889, just seven years after Judge Coles was arrested for not protecting the rights of Black citizens and only seven years before the U.S. Supreme Court upheld racial segregation in *Plessy v. Ferguson*, George Fowler, a "black youth," was lynched for rape in Pittsylvania County. It was locally known that George Fowler and the White woman had been lovers for some time (Brundage 1993: 66). Elder April recalled that around 1943 in Hurt, a Black man had killed a White man in self-defense, but after a lengthy trial, protests, and pleading, "they lynched him anyway." Her point was that lynching in mid-twentieth-century Hurt was no longer performed by lawless White mobs but done legally by White-controlled courts.

Colorism, Schooling, and "One-Fourth Cropping" in Tobacco Country

Elder April recalled growing up in "tobacco country" as the oldest of eight children. Her paternal great-grandfather was a "slave hand" who toiled in the fields, while his wife, Amanda, was a "house slave." April's great-grandparents' master left over a hundred acres of land to the family, and it is still in the family today, though parceled out among descendents over the next three generations. Intimacy between the slave owner and his female slaves is suggested by the fact that reddish hair, light eyes, and freckles are common among Elder April's family. She spoke of having the "honor" of visiting the old plantation's slave quarters during her family reunion. She also met the granddaughter of the slave owner who had left the land to her family; the White woman seemed "cordial." When I asked Elder April how the White descendents felt about losing over a hundred acres of land to slaves, she said she suspected that they had not really missed it since they owned so much more.

Elder April recalled that her maternal grandmother, Lucy, always wore a bonnet and old-fashioned clothes from "slavery times." Lucy had arrived on a boat "the year that the slaves were freed." She had no idea where she came from, as she was a young parentless child when she and other Black people were put on a boat and told "they were free to go, but when they left they had nothing, you know." Grandmother Lucy outlived her daughter; April's mother died when she was just forty years old, because "of having eight children, which was too much." She became paralyzed and died when her last child was about a month old. During her lifetime, April's mother had mainly cared for the children and the home, hardly working in the field. "We were tobacco farmers" who "sharecropped"; because the family did not own any mules, wagons, or other equipment, "we only got a fourth, and the landlord got three fourths." The landlord, she added, was a Black man who was darker-skinned than April's family. Her father, realizing that he "could never make it there," moved the entire family to Washington, D.C., where "he found work" around 1941.

In Hurt, April attended a "primer" (primary school) up to seventh grade, which was the only public education available to African Americans in the town. However, a distant maternal relative paid "out of his own pocket" for a bus so that the Black youth in the community could ride to Gretna to attend its high school. It only went through the eleventh grade, which April completed before she moved to Washington. There she attended a trade school, but she longed to complete her secondary education, in large part because of the value her parents placed on it. Although her parents had little formal education, her father was a "self-educated man" who "learned from other people" and wanted to send all his children to college.

Her father taught her that education was the way to overcome the White racism they encountered in Virginia, where, Elder April remarked, she had never observed school vaccination programs for Black children. Her father also taught her that education would help her overcome the internalized racism of colorism. To make this point he directed her attention to two sisters who taught at Gretna High, one of whom was "black with short hair and the other light with long hair, but they both were teachers and earned the same salary." Elder April notes that in Philadelphia color differences did not seem to matter as much among Black people as they did in Virginia.

War, Work, and Higher Education up North

In Washington, D.C., April attended "one of those schools Roosevelt had set up for Black people," where she was taught a trade and, along with other graduates of the program, was placed in a job at the federal Navy Yard. There she "fashioned" ammunition according to specifications, because, as she laughingly added, "they weren't looking for too much from Black people to do except for some labor—things that you work with your hands. . . . they didn't expect you to do too much with your head." She worked in the Navy Yard until 1944, when she married Frank Nichols at the age of nineteen. The next day, they moved to Philadelphia where his family lived; she lost her naval shipyard job on relocating to Philadelphia.

April lived first near downtown, in what is now Philadelphia's gentrified and mainly White Center City. At the time she moved there, poorer Blacks lived along Lombard, Locust, and Pine streets. She then joined her father's brother and his wife in the Chestnut Hill area of Northwest Philadelphia, in a small section "where Black people could live." Still, she continued to "want the same things my father wanted for us," especially a college education. In Philadelphia she realized that dream after she had raised her children. "I kept dreaming that I was at school. . . . I heard a voice say, 'Get up and go to school.'" But she wondered how to do this while she was working two jobs to make ends meet, as a domestic worker and as a nursing assistant. Undeterred, she had her Virginia transcripts sent to the diploma program at the Franklin Institute and earned a high school degree there.

Next she attended community college in the evening and earned a certificate in gerontology. April then secured a bachelor's degree in human services from Antioch College and a certificate in special education from Cheyney State University, a historically Black institution. Responding to the comment that some "saved" people believe that education hinders salvation, she asserted, "It is good to know the Word, but there is still a lot more to know and learn in life." Laughingly yet lovingly, she spoke of the disciple Peter, who although he was a close follower of Jesus was not very learned and often "spoke out of turn." Education humbles you, she asserted, because "once you learn some things, you know you don't know nothing!"

Elder April worked as a substitute teacher in the Philadelphia school system from the 1980s until she retired. When she first arrived in Philly without a degree, however, she, like many other Black migrants, did "day's work" in White households. For a time, she took the ferry across the Schuylkill River to Camden, New Jersey, to work at the Campbell's Soup factory, and had her first extended encounter with Hispanics. Later she was employed at a Philadelphia cigar factory, where Black women constituted 22 percent of the employees, working at the "stripping machine." White managers believed that Black women from tobacco-growing backgrounds like Elder April were suited to this work, which was the dirtiest and lowest-paid task. Jobs within the plant were segregated, so Black women had no chance for advancement, and in the 1940s cigar workers' unions were disbanded (Porter 1943: 22–23). Black men like her husband worked at the Navy Yard during World War II. Then they went to work for manufacturing firms such as the Strick Trailer Corporation, which made heavy-duty trailers for commercial trucks, until it closed and "left them stranded."

North-South, Black-White, Jew-Gentile

Comparing Black-White interactions in the North and the South, Elder April described societies that were racially separate, but in different ways. For example, in Hurt, her father was friendly with, and fond of, Mr. Finch, a Jewish man who sold shoes to the family. When Mr. Finch died, Elder April recalled her father and other Black adults sadly looking in the window from outside the building where funeral services were being held. She also spoke of her father as a man "who didn't stand back for the other race of people." He would go into White people's homes and sit down at the same table with them.

Her father modeled dignity for April, which she embraced wholeheartedly. One day, while preparing a meal for a White family in her own home, April ran out of fuel. So she entered the White family's home, using the front door, and finished preparing the meal on the White woman's stove. She was "advised" to use the back door in the future. Instead, she stopped preparing food for that family altogether, since "it was her bread I was trying to get done!"

When asked about her interactions with Whites in the North, she said, "I worked for Jews and that was more or less the contact." She added that some of the women she worked for referred to her and other Black women they employed "as their friends, but . . ." Elder April finished the sentence with laughter, suggesting that actions speak louder than words.

Comparing the quality of her life in the North and the South, she recalled that life in the South was hard, both physically and financially. She recounted walking to school with freezing feet. There were few conveniences, and money was always "a concern." Most Blacks made a living mainly through sharecropping tobacco, although some people, like her maternal uncle, worked at the Lane cedar chest mill. Still, life in Hurt could be "pleasurable," in that you could raise food in your own garden and enjoy eating fruit from your own trees. But, when asked if she would consider moving back to the South, her unhesitating response was emphatically negative. She and her family "kept up" their property in Hurt, but Philly was home.

Discomforting Baptists and Solid Saints

In Virginia, April attended New Bethel Baptist Church, which her great-grandfather founded "back in slavery times." He could not read or write, but he said that the Holy Ghost had taught him the Bible. "I was always looking for something," she explained, and "I didn't find comfort in the Baptist church, and so I was looking for some people that were solid. . . . I mean sincere toward God." Her search ended when she found The Church in Philadelphia. She and her husband had attended Tenth Memorial Baptist Church when she first arrived in Philadelphia, because "relatives were going there." She had been raised to believe in "Love thy neighbor as thyself," but she did not see this principle put into practice in this congregation. Instead, she witnessed "people abusing people." For example, when the presiding pastor went away on a vacation, his members treated the assistant pastor disgracefully. For a while she and her husband, Frank, decided not to attend any church at all. Still, she kept on "looking for something." She often listened to Mother Dabney's radio broadcasts and occasionally attended services at the Garden of Prayer in North Philly, where April's husband's family had settled.

Events converged to draw her to The Church. At that time, Mother Brown was holding services in the room over the horse stable in North Philly not far from where her husband's family lived. April began to notice a "change" in Frank's older sister, Holly, after she had begun to go to Mother Brown's church. The change was radical, sincere, and unwavering. Since Holly, like April, had been "looking for something," April decided to visit Mother Brown's church. She especially loved to hear the pastor's daughter, Ruby, play piano. She was very impressed with the way Mother Brown "knew" and taught the Word during Tuesday evening Bible studies.

Around the time she noticed the change in Holly, April had become very sick, to the point that she was ready to "give up." She decided that she needed "something else beside just me" to continue living. She continued "following afar off," attending services at The Church occasionally, still impressed with Holly's transformation. She had also become close to Beverly Nichols Cornwall, another of her husband's sisters. Beverly was about April's age and, like her, a new mother. Beverly followed her sister Holly into The Church, and April began attending regularly with Beverly. In time, April "took a stand" and "came into the church."

Four Gospels and Millennial Reprieve

Taking a stand was "more than a notion." On the one hand, family and friends who kept Sunday "scorned" the rigors of Sabbath keeping; on the other hand, Mother Brown taught that saints should not be "unevenly yoked together with unbelievers." This "dividing line" led the founding generation of saints to break intimate ties with other family members. As painful as this was, April chose salvation because she was, as she put it, "fighting for my life." She added that later, with time and spiritual maturity, she came to understand that being saved does not require saints to "withdraw yourself from people." Indeed, at the time I interviewed her, Elder April regularly attended annual homecoming services at her family's home church in Virginia and had reestablished close family ties. At The Church, she had initiated an "annual fellowship day" in which nonmembers were invited to worship with the saints, and she supported inter-church activities with a Sabbath-keeping church in New Jersey that one of the younger deacons had initiated through exchanged choir performances.

Elder April had a clear idea of her place in the larger society. She spoke of her "duty" to vote in light of the price that had been paid for Black people to vote in this country. Mother Brown had taught that saints should not vote, since politics was part of "the World." Although respectful of the pastor-founder, Elder April held strongly to the notion that the "scripture is of no private interpretation" (2 Peter 1:20). In a similar vein, one Sabbath, Elder April introduced a different interpretation of a biblical passage by pointing out that there are four gospels, and although each one tells a somewhat different version of Jesus's life and ministry, all four are included in the New Testament.

Although April appreciated the title of elder, she said that she has always understood her life's calling to be that of an "evangelist," a servant of God and of humanity, that is, whose twofold mission is to care for the needy and to "carry the word of the gospel." She was twenty-four when she came into The Church, and she has faithfully paid tithes ever since. For her, being saved means that "you are not your own anymore"; an "inner peace" that comes from "passing from death unto life" makes you truly "love the brethren" and makes it impossible to hate.

When Elder April came into The Church, the millennium and imminent return of Christ were central teachings, and the date that Mother Brown projected from the study of biblical prophecy was in the 1960s. When asked to comment on the fact that the date had come and gone without the millennium, she responded that the saints "don't even bring it up" and that an exact calculation is impossible because "one day is with the Lord as a thousand years, and a thousand years as one day" (2 Peter 3:8). Accompanied by her distinctive laughter, Elder April added that she certainly hoped 1968 wasn't "the end" since "we all had a lot more to set right!"

Elder Holly Nichols Stables (1914–2011)
"Isn't it beautiful!"

The Philadelphia "Snowman"

The flakes fell large and heavy on the City of Brotherly Love as Holly Nichols Stables waited for the bus. It had never snowed like this "down home" in South Carolina. Bursting with awe, she spontaneously turned to a White man standing next to her and exclaimed, "Isn't it beautiful!" He made no reply. He did not look at her, but remained frozen like a snowman. For him, Holly did not exist. Forty years of living in Philadelphia had not erased the pain that her voice held as she related her invisibility in that early encounter.

This vulnerability was in sharp contrast to the Elder Holly I knew as my aunt and godmother, for she was indomitable. After conducting this research, I see her strong, no-nonsense demeanor as less a matter of idiosyncratic personality than an adaptive strategy for growing up Black and female during the first half of the twentieth century in her southern hometown. Elder Holly's story begins in Edgefield, South Carolina.

Edgefield, Bloody Edgefield

Holly, the fifth girl of six sisters and nine brothers, two of whom died in infancy, was born in 1914 to Lilly Adamson Nichols, a former schoolteacher whose grandfather had been a successful White planter in the county. She married Gordon Nichols, a farmer who had worked for her father. The old folks said little to Holly about slavery, referring to the general "suffering" and an upturned pot used to "catch the noise" during secret worship so that the White slave owner would not whip them the next day. However, his response may have had less to do with fear of African rituals than concern about his loss of labor from slaves who had not rested well the previous night (Pitts 1993: 36–37).

Public Schools and Family Feuds

Holly was born in 1914, thirty-seven years after federal troops were removed from Edgefield and nineteen years after South Carolina's 1895 constitution reinstated White supremacy by requiring a literacy test and poll tax six months prior to elections and by prohibiting both interracial marriage and racially integrated schools. When she was not "picking cotton and plowing fields," she attended Edgefield County's only publicly funded school for Black children, a one-room schoolhouse that went up to the fifth grade. She was able to attend for about three months a year, since during planting and harvest seasons she had to assist her parents with farm work. Walking several miles to the schoolhouse for Black children, she was regularly passed by the bus that transported White students to their school. The Tompkins School, at the fork of Lone Cane Road and Highway 438, is where the infamous Sue Logue had a brief and disputed career as a public schoolteacher. Sue Logue was at the heart of a notorious case of collusion and murder that destroyed Black and White families and lives in Edgefield.

Because it runs through the Nicholses' narrative, the story is worth summarizing here. At the heart of the tale is a feud between two landed White families, the Logues and the Timmermans. Sue Logue, reportedly quite attractive and determined, was married to John "Wallace" Logue, although the oral history asserts that George, her brother-in-law, was also her lover. The animus between the two families was so great that when Davis Timmerman's mule kicked Wallace Logue's calf, which died, the confrontation between the two men ended in fatal violence. Davis Timmerman shot and killed Wallace, who had threatened to kill Timmerman. The judge decided that the killing was committed in self-defense, and Davis Timmerman was acquitted. Later, Sue and George, enraged by Timmerman's acquittal, arranged for their nephew Joe Frank, a policeman, to hire Clarence Bagwell to kill Davis Timmerman for five hundred dollars. When news of the assassination eventually reached lawmakers and enforcement agencies outside Edgefield, "the law" was sent in to arrest the Logues. A legendary shootout on Meeting Street followed, which Elder Beverly's oral history passed on to her children and is corroborated in T. Felder Dorn's *The Guns of Meeting Street* (Dorn 2006: 65–80, 83–144).

The revenge killing of Timmerman was not the first to be perpetrated by the Logues. Earlier in Logue family history, Wallace and George's brother, Frank, "on a big drunk" at the time, violently confronted his brother-in-law Clifford Owdom, who shot and killed Frank. The judge ruled that Owdom had killed Frank Logue in self-defense. Incensed, Wallace and George threatened to kill Owdom, but they did not. They also restrained Frank's grieving son, Joe Frank, from avenging his father's death. George and Wallace took an interest in their nephew, supporting his secondary and junior-college education; Joe Frank eventually joined the Spartanburg police. While Wallace and George did not kill Clifford Owdom to avenge their brother Frank's death, they murdered Will Jones, whose testimony they believed had led to the acquittal of Owdom (Dorn 2006: 42–45). Will Jones, a Black man, is said to have been "shot down like a dog" on church property near Willow Springs Baptist Church, which Holly had grown up attending on Sundays.

Elder Holly's recollections of public education in Edgefield are corroborated by an August 1929 issue of the *Edgefield Advertiser*, published when she was fifteen. It celebrates the fact that Edgefield's children were transported from widely separated farms to the schoolhouse "in less time than it took their father to walk a mile," but it does not identify these children as White or say that Black children were relegated to an inferior school to which they had to walk (Dorn 1994: 41n105). Whites took segregation and racial disparities in education for granted. Five years earlier, when Holly was ten years old, the South Carolina legislature finally established a statewide educational system. The law standardized a seven-month school term and levied taxes on the wealthy to educate poorer children and "future citizens of the State." In this way, legislators argued, "The wee mites of humanity living out there in the great open spaces and helping to clothe and feed the world should not be penalized, and this law removes any such penalty that might ever have existed" (Dorn 1994: 9). Sadly for Holly and Black children throughout the state, adequate provisions for African American children were conspicuously absent from this system, even though Black "wee mites" also labored "to clothe and feed" others.

Willow Springs, her family's home church, offered primary schooling. The public schools for Black children went to the seventh grade, and girls were more likely to attend than boys, who usually were incorporated into the family's fieldwork at a younger age than their sisters. If and when children completed the seventh grade, it was the end of their schooling unless their family could afford to send them to a private school, such as nearby Bettis Academy, established and sustained by Black Baptists and assisted by generous and committed northern philanthropists. Elder Holly's parents were not in a position to keep her out of the labor force, much less pay for her education. Unskilled and without access to a regular job, she did domestic work for White families, earning $2.75 per week for cleaning, cooking, and childcare. Holly later took a domestic job in nearby Johnston, where events precipitated her circuitous migration to Philadelphia.

The KKK and a Big Black Dog

When asked to talk about her interactions with Whites, Elder Holly described a nuanced intimate civility that coexisted uneasily with an ever-present potential for racial violence. Trouble was kept at bay as long as "you stayed in your place." As a teenager living and working in Johnston, Holly was accused of striking the child of a "poor white" family who employed her in their home. "Word came" that the Klan would be coming for her.

Holly collected her few personal effects and started walking to Augusta, which was just on the other side of the state line that Edgefield County shared with Georgia, where she had neither friends nor family waiting for her.

This was not the first time Holly had to deal with White violence. Whites had tried to drive her family off their land by attacking their home one night—a rather foolish thing to do as her father was known to carry a gun at all times. His children remember him walking around the farm with a pistol slung in the pocket of his overalls and with a shotgun under the seat of his buckboard when he traveled. That night, he and his sons used arms to run off the would-be land grabbers. Elder Holly remarked, "There was no trouble with those White folks after that." But in Johnston she had no family to protect her, and the Klan was involved. So in 1929, when she was just fifteen, Holly took to the road.

The night was dark in the way only rural country roads can be. Her mind was heavy with fear, and all she could think about was outrunning the Klan. When a big black dog crossed the road in front of her, she absentmindedly shooed it away and kept up her steady pace. She had gone some distance down the road before she realized that its feet had barely touched the ground, its steps had made no noise, and it had moved in slow motion. Stopping briefly, she recalled that there had been a cemetery at that crossroads. But, with neither time nor energy to waste, she continued to make her way to Augusta.

A Death in Augusta and a Strike in Philadelphia

In Augusta Holly found work easily and earned $3.25 per week working as a domestic cook. She had arrived in the city on her own, so there was no one to turn to when a man took an improper interest in her. She was not interested in him, but he refused to accept her rejection. One night he came to her home and became aggressive, and in the ensuing struggle a gun went off, shooting and killing him. Alone and terrified, she waited for the police to come and arrest her, but "they took their time coming." When the White sheriff finally arrived, his was more of a social visit than a crime scene investigation. He asked her what happened and if she was all right, and then he left. "That was the end of that." As Elder Holly explained, "the law" was not concerned about Black crime as long as Blacks were killing each other. "Now if that had been a White man . . ." she reflected, leaving the dire consequences unsaid.

Holly continued to work and save money, and in 1938 she married James

Stables, also a native of Edgefield, although they had not known each other there. Together they worked and saved. In 1941 they migrated to Philadelphia, where they joined his brothers and father. One of her husband's brothers, who was a presser in a Jewish-owned dry-cleaning business, helped her husband get a job as a presser. They lived in racially mixed North Philadelphia at Twentieth and Diamond Street, where she, and later her siblings, rented the first two floors of a three-story apartment building, with seven rooms and a bathroom on each floor. During and briefly after World War II, she worked at Stadham's, a Jewish-owned factory that produced uniforms and other war-related items. When the work began to "fall off," she did "day's work," most often in the homes of Jewish women, and she helped her sisters and sisters-in-law find work and "day ladies" as well.

Elder Holly reported good working relationships with her Jewish male and female employers, though generally she found northern Whites more "standoffish," more often "keeping to them[selves]" than southern Whites. When asked about race relations in the North, she recalled the 1944 strike during World War II when "Black people tore up Ridge Avenue" because "Whites didn't want the Blacks to drive the trolleys." This conflict occurred when ten thousand White employees of the Philadelphia Transit Company (PTC) walked off their jobs rather than comply with new federal regulations that gave Black PTC employees the right to hold more than menial jobs. Elder Holly and other founding saints recall this event with a degree of relish, especially as some of the armed soldiers brought in to enforce the 1943 Smith-Connally Anti-Strike/War Labor Disputes Act were Black. Although race relations were far from congenial in the North, Elder Holly never regretted leaving Edgefield. Besides, there was "nothing there" now, as so many people, White and Black alike, relocated elsewhere, and the formerly abundant farmland is now abandoned or used to grow timber.

Eventually, Holly and her husband bought their own home within walking distance of both her sister Beverly Nichols Cromwell and her brother Frank Nichols. Not long after the 1964 Civil Rights Act outlawed segregation in schools, hiring, and housing, Holly and her husband moved from North Philadelphia into a lovely, tree-shaded home on Johnson Street in the Germantown/Mount Airy neighborhood. She and her husband downsized when they were older and bought a smaller home in lower Germantown on Coulter Street. A lover of beautiful things, she always drove a fine car, wore quality clothes, and furnished her home stylishly and tastefully: a deep blue velvet–covered love seat graced her living room, and an elegant triptych-mirrored vanity enhanced her bedroom.

From Baptist to "Saved"

Although Holly had grown up attending Willow Springs Baptist Church in Edgefield, she also had visited the Lone Cane Holiness Church. When she first arrived in Philadelphia, she attended Tenth Memorial Baptist Church, but she stopped after a choir rehearsal conflict convinced her that "those people needed to be saved." For a while she attended the Garden of Prayer at Twenty-ninth and Susquehanna because of Mother Dabney's ability to heal and preach. Holly eventually left over issues of doctrine, but recalled that a White woman whose son had been healed after Mother Dabney prayed for him gave a plot of land to Mother Dabney to expand her mission.[6]

Holly still longed to be saved and live a life of holiness. One day the Holy Ghost told her to "go to Vanpelt Street." She recalls passing five churches between Diamond and Norris streets and on Vanpelt before coming to "the horse stable" and hearing music coming from the upper room where Mother Brown was leading the service. That night, Mother Brown read from Genesis chapter six about Noah's ark resting on Mount Ararat. As Elder Holly put it, it was the "knowledge" with which Mother Brown taught "the Word" that "caught me." She eventually received the Holy Ghost, not at the church, but one day while working in the kitchen, when the spirit fell on her and she began speaking in tongues.

Elder Holly was the first member of the Nichols family to join The Church. She "brought" most of her family into the church, including her mother and most of her siblings. Elder Holly was probably the most powerful and charismatic woman in The Church next to the founder. She "bowed down to no man," including Mother Brown, though she was the pastor's "right arm." She served the congregation for many years as its secretary. She played piano by ear for devotional service and evidenced the gift of tongues, healing, and preaching. She had the gift of dreams and could "see" when awake. She and her late husband were both founding members and were ordained as elders in the 1980s. Elder Holly continued to hold that office until her death, even after age-related health problems required her to move to a special care facility. The saints visited her there and provided transportation to services and to church activities. When it was her turn in the rotation, she served as presiding elder.

Elder Jerald Cromwell (1924–2003)

"Wait, it's me, Whitefolks!"

The Blacksmith and "the Village"

Born in Philadelphia in 1924, Jerald Cromwell Jr. was a first-generation Philadelphian. His father migrated there from Augusta, Georgia, around 1919, and a year later sent for his fiancée, Leena Blunt, then a teenager living in Valdosta, Georgia.[7] Leena's father was the son of a White man from a "big" undertaker family in Augusta; her maternal grandmother was a Creek Indian who "could sit on her hair . . . it was so long."

Jerald's paternal great-great grandfather, Ed Cromwell, was the son of the White owner of the Cromwell plantation and an enslaved Black woman. Like some enslaved Blacks, he was allowed to learn a skilled trade; he became a blacksmith. After "hiring out" his time, he used his hard-earned money to purchase his freedom and that of his wife and child. Ed was buried at Noah's Ark Church, a Baptist congregation that he founded a year after Emancipation, near Gough in Burke County, about twenty-five miles south of Augusta, Georgia. Ed went on to found two other Baptist congregations in the county. Elder Jerald's father said that Ed Cromwell was so light-skinned he could have passed for White; he married a dark-skinned woman.

Jerald grew up in what locals called "the Village," a North Philadelphia neighborhood roughly bounded on the north and south by Twenty-third and Twenty-seventh streets and on the east and west by Dauphin and Cumberland streets. Jerald's mother said that this neighborhood was one of the first places that Blacks could own a home; during the Depression they could buy a house there for five hundred dollars, often from Jewish owners. Before entering factory work, Jerald's father worked for the Kaufmans, who owned a laundry. The Kaufmans, a Jewish family, were very fond of their employee's son, Jerald, and wrote to him when he was in the service overseas during World War II.

Most of the Black men in the neighborhood worked in manual or blue-collar jobs, and Black women did domestic work. Jerald had a paper route from the time he was a young boy. He attended Philadelphia's Northeast High School for Boys. He was a good student, loved learning, and wanted very much to attend college but, in line with Philadelphia's racialized education practices, the school counselor tried to discourage him, saying Jerald was not "college material." As he related this event over fifty years later, Elder Jerald expressed sad dismay that this racist advice came from an African American school counselor. After graduation and before enlisting in the Army, Jerald was employed in the registration office of Dobbins Vocational High School, attended by Black and White students from all over Philadelphia.

"Whitefolks," Combat, and a Colored Honeymoon

Elder Jerald said that there were no serious racial conflicts in Philadelphia—as long as you stayed in your "pocket" of town and went into White sections only to go to school or work. Northeast High School for Boys was racially mixed, but the majority of students were White and, as a matter of course, Black and White boys regularly had fights after school. One day, in the heat of battle, Jerald heard a voice cry out, "Hey! Wait, man! It's me, Whitefolks!" "Whitefolks" was the nickname Jerald and his friends had given one of their African American schoolmates who looked White. His appearance created confusion during these racially defined melees, so it became necessary for "Whitefolks" to identify himself. Elder Jerald always laughed when he told this story, as did I, his daughter, when I heard it.

Elder Jerald referred to Frank Rizzo, Philadelphia's notorious police commissioner and mayor, as "Hopalong" after the television cowboy character Hopalong Cassidy because of Rizzo's readiness to use force from the time he entered the Philadelphia Police Department in the 1940s, when Jerald was a young man, through his final term as commissioner. In the 1960s and 1970s, Rizzo's violent and draconian repression of the Black Panther Party put Philadelphia in the national news. So did his 1985 aerial assault on the MOVE community in West Philadelphia, resulting in the deaths of six adults and five children and the fiery destruction of an entire African American residential block, documented in the film *The Bombing of Osage Avenue*, narrated by Toni Cade Bambara. These incidents not only were sources of antagonism between Rizzo and Black Philadelphians, but were in keeping with a sustained conflict between the Black community and the police department, which was generally perceived as perpetrating legalized White-on-Black brutality.

Before enlisting in the Army (probably inflating his age to meet the age requirement), Jerald met Beverly Nichols, who "brought him into The Church." They met when they were teenagers and she was visiting her paternal uncle's home across the street from where Jerald lived. Jerald wrote to Beverly and his parents regularly between 1943 and 1945 from the European front. The letters to his parents were often limited by what he could squeeze onto a V-Mail postcard and the constraints of combat. Using the vernacular of the time, he asked his dad, "How are tricks?" and reported that, after only one day of seasickness during the voyage to England, the food was "swell." He provided his mother a brief lexicon of the "different English" spoken in Britain, such as tram for trolley and bobby for policeman, and noted that the U.S. dollar was considerably more valuable than the British pound. He particularly enjoyed reading by sunlight late in the evening during the northern summer.

According to his 1943 allotment authorization slip, which his mother had kept along with V-Mail correspondence, in 1943 he was sending his mother twenty-five dollars each month. In his March 27, 1943, letter, he alerted her to expect documentation of the ten-thousand-dollar insurance policy of which she and his father would be beneficiaries, as well as war bonds. Two years later, he wrote his mother that he would be sending fifty dollars monthly for his sister's stay in the Pocono Mountains to treat her tuberculosis, a condition his mother had also suffered. His sister Roxy died from TB when she was twenty-one, just three years before Filipino Dr. Abelardo Aguilar sent his employer, Eli Lilly, soil samples that led to the isolation of the mycin drug which cured tuberculosis and might have saved her life. Tragic deaths like Roxy's were all too common in Philadelphia's African American community.

On June 27, 1945, just over five weeks after V-E Day, when the armed forces of Nazi Germany surrendered unconditionally to the Allies, Jerald wrote from Leipzig: "Dear Dad, Your letter was received last evening. Mighty glad to hear from you once more. It found me in good health, but mighty home sick. I just returned from a two week tour of duty and didn't have time to write while away. Although the war is over there is still a great deal of work to be done." All of his letters were written in this somewhat formal yet engagingly crafted English, which so captivated Beverly that she shared them with her girlfriends at school. In turn, they showed them to their teacher, who praised his skilled use of English in front of the class. This thrilled Beverly.

Jerald fought with the troops that landed on the beaches of Normandy on D-Day. In France some civilians had insisted to him and his Black buddies that Blacks had tails; finally, to settle the matter, one of Jerald's frustrated army buddies stood up on a table and pulled down his pants! Jerald was wounded during battle and worked hard to earn promotion to sergeant, the highest rank that an enlisted man or draftee could attain as a noncommissioned officer.[8] After fighting for democracy and freedom and helping to defeat Nazi racism abroad, Jerald returned to a racially segregated America. He soon married Beverly Nichols and they honeymooned for a week in South Jersey's Comfort Hotel, "Ocean City's Newest Colored Hotel." Proprietor Thomas H. Gumby's handbill promised lovely seaside accommodations and excellent fare for a mere six dollars per day! Though well spoken, Jerald was a man of few words, and these had to be carefully elicited, making them especially precious. When I asked him for his thoughts on America as a land of opportunity, he agreed that it was just that—for everybody except Blacks. He stated his opinion simply, without rancor, and with only a hint of emotion in his eyes.

Family Rock and Churchman

While Beverly has a charismatic and lively personality, Elder Jerald was the quiet rock of the family. A hard worker, he focused on making a better life for his wife and children. For most of his working life, he worked nights at the Thirtieth Street post office. During the day, he helped with childcare and drove the children to school during the years of "voluntary" racial integration. Jerald rarely slept uninterrupted for eight hours during the day, and after working all night he could be heard going downstairs to study for the examination to qualify for a promotion in the postal service. His eyes always looked red and tired.

In the 1960s, after his older children had grown up, Jerald completed a business degree at Adelphia Business College. With degree in hand, he eventually rose from "throwing mail at night" to a daytime position in regional post office administration. After only a few years, he had to retire because of his occupation-related physical disabilities, although he did not receive full compensation for them. All of Jerald's four children attended college. The older two hold doctorates, the third is a nationally known media figure in radio programming, and the youngest holds a bachelor's in psychology.

Jerald was raised in his mother's AME church in North Philly and probably would never have heard of The Church had he not met and married Beverly. Interestingly, his mother also joined a female-headed Gospel Light Holiness Church congregation led by Elder Mader, a White woman described as "German," who presided at the funerals for both of Elder Jerald's parents. Jerald followed Beverly into The Church shortly after they married. Valued for his ability to express himself well both orally and in writing, he served as a liaison between The Church and other institutions, including the municipal government and the church's lawyer, Mr. Buchman, who was Jewish. As one of the first "head deacons," he assumed the duties of church treasurer after Sister Laura Mae Smythe stepped down. Sister Laura Mae, a founding saint and eventual elder who died before these narratives were collected, is reported to have happily turned over the job to Jerald when her family duties began to compete with requirements of the post.

Elder Jerald was one of the first deacons in The Church and served as chair of the deacon board. In the first generation of The Church, ritual duties were primarily in the hands of the women. However, he did have a ritual duty that only males filled: in a flat glass bottle held in a neatly pressed white handkerchief, he bore the olive oil used to anoint those who came to the altar for prayer; when he was not present, another deacon filled in for him. As an elder of The Church he took on more ritual duties, including preaching, and until his death he faithfully served as a source of spiritual guidance. After he and his wife had relocated to Virginia, they made special trips back to Philadelphia to fulfill their responsibilities to The Church.

Elder Beverly Nichols Cromwell (1924–2011)
"Think of all we could have had . . ."

Segregated Schools, Integrated Families

As a small child, Beverly Nichols used to hide in the top of her favorite tree with a book in hand and lose herself in a world of possibilities free from the all-too-real constraints of Edgefield County where she was born. Beverly was the middle child of fifteen children; her sister Holly was ten years older. Learning was her passion, but Edgefield's public school facilities for Black children were no better when she was born than they had been for Holly. She and her siblings walked to the same one-room schoolhouse. The White children regularly threw stones from the bus that carried them to the Tompkins School, and one day a stone struck her brother Frank. Her father, who never suffered fools gladly, confronted the schoolmistress about Tompkins students "throwing stones at my chaps," insisting "I won't tolerate it." Elder Beverly recalled her father as the only Black man in the area who wore a gun, and he was wearing it at the time he made this passionate pronouncement.

Taking the matter to heart, the schoolmistress firmly assured him that this would never happen again. The parents of Beverly's White maternal cousins, who had been on the bus, also expressed their concern and assured her father that their children would never participate in such behavior. Beverly's parents accepted this reassurance. The Black and White sides of her mother's family recognized each other to the point that a White family member expressed hurt when Elder Beverly did not immediately bring her child to visit them during her trip "back home" from Philadelphia. She also related how embarrassed her mother had been when her White cousins came to the train station with a parting gift of a recently slaughtered chicken. When

I inquired how these White relatives could acknowledge and respect their Black cousins, yet ride past them on the bus while their White schoolmates threw stones at them and other Black children, Elder Beverly answered that they may have been kin, but they were still White.

She told about stopping by to say hello to Cornelia Timmerman, wife of Davis Timmerman, when she and her mother were walking by their house; Miss Cornelia gave them water and cake, and they sat awhile before going on. Informal contact across racial lines was not limited to women: Steve Cogburn, who married into the Logue family, "used to come by our house," sometimes to ask her father to do things for him, but sometimes just to "visit."

White Brides, Black Maids, and Educational Opportunity

Although Beverly was bright and highly motivated, her educational future in Edgefield looked bleak. Around the time a Black girl had completed the seventh grade or was considered old enough to leave school, Elder Beverly recalled, White parents would stop by Black homes, approach the parents, and "ask for their daughters" to work for their White daughters, who usually had just graduated high school, married, and "needed help" setting up their home. Sometimes children's earnings were a Black family's only cash income, and when Whites offered $2.75 per week for cooking, cleaning, and childcare, "they were happy to get it."

The only way a Black student could continue her education was by attending a private secondary school. Bettis Academy in Trenton, Edgefield County, was founded in 1881 by Rev. Alexander Bettis, a former slave and Baptist minister. He negotiated the dangerous waters of Black self-determination by building sustainable religious institutions and schools, while acting as an intermediary in conflicts that otherwise might have ended in lynching (Burton 1978: 45–47). Bettis bought twenty-seven acres of land at three dollars an acre and built a one-room structure to start a school where Black parents could pay for their children's education with a combination of cash and a "commodity card" stipulating the kinds and amounts of farm-raised produce parents could provide in lieu of cash payment.[9] Beverly's maternal aunt Julia, who later joined her briefly in Philadelphia, was married to Reverend Blocker, pastor of Mount Canaan Baptist Church and president of the association of twenty-four Black Baptist congregations that sponsored Bettis Academy. Beverly's Uncle Blocker was taken with Beverly's quick-wittedness and respectful manner, and he and his wife arranged for her to live with them while attending Bettis Academy.

Beverly's parents, with the help of her aunt and uncle, paid for her room, board, and tuition with a monthly fee of seven dollars in cash and seven dollars' worth of food items. She did well at Bettis, graduating as valedictorian in 1944, although she had spent her junior year at Philadelphia's Gratz High School while living with her sister Holly. Fondly recalling her days at Bettis, where all the teachers and staff were Black, Elder Beverly speaks of making lifelong friends and learning habits of thrift and self-discipline. Bettis also developed "character," because there, unlike White society, Black youths were treated with respect. For example, Beverly recalled a firm but fair teacher who always addressed his students by their last name. The academy attracted Blacks from beyond South Carolina as students, faculty, and benefactors. Beverly's favorite teacher, Mr. Bowman, had grown up in Bryn Mawr, a suburb of Philadelphia, and graduated from Temple University. In those days, Black recent college graduates from the North often went south to teach in schools for Black youth. Mr. Bowman became a great inspiration to her, leading her to decide to attend Temple University and become a teacher. Many of the students were from the North, which had few Black institutions. Some had roots in other parts of the African Diaspora; she recalled one student whose father was from Puerto Rico and another from the West Indies.

The academy received philanthropic support from Philadelphia's Supplee Dairy Company and from the prominent Biddle family, which also supported uplift efforts directed toward Black southern migrants. Ms. Biddle, whom Beverly remembered as a "fair and kind" lady, visited Bettis Academy. She decided to reside on campus during her visit, but the White citizens insisted that she conform to southern practices of racial segregation and stay at White-owned accommodations in town. She resisted at first, but on learning that Whites were threatening to attack the school and kill its president if she persisted in her "northern ways," she complied.

Edgefield's "Shotgun Plan"

"Bloody Edgefield" has a long history of White violence, beginning with the decimation of native peoples and vigilantism in the wake of the American Revolution. A culture that privileged male honor, pursued clan vendettas, and was riddled with fear of racial equality and the loss of White supremacy produced an environment in which threats of violence readily translated into murder.[10] After Reconstruction, the "Edgefield Plan" effectively reversed federal mandates for public education, fair labor laws, and Black citizenship rights (Burton 1978: 39). In response to Blacks' political self-assertion, each

White man was supposed to "control the vote of at least one negro by intimidation, purchase, keeping him away, or as each individual may determine." Edgefield's rifle and saber club members accused a Black man of making a speech about Blacks fighting for their rights and shot him dead while he was on his knees because his final prayer was taking too long (Burton 1978: 31–32, 39; Butterfield 1995: 40–42; Kantrowitz 1998). Governor Chamberlain disbanded all Black militias in 1875, and the next year, seven hundred armed members of thirty Democratic clubs wearing "red shirts" paraded into town (Burton 1978: 42–43; Butterfield 1995: 42; Kantrowitz 1998).

By the 1890s, lynchings actually outnumbered legal executions in Edgefield County (Kantrowitz 1998: 223). In 1892, South Carolina governor "Pitchfork" Ben Tillman, an Edgefield native and opportunistic former Populist, conflated White male honor, White female virtue, and the subjugation of dangerous Black men when he stated publicly that he would "willingly lead a mob in lynching a negro who had committed an assault upon a white woman." Tillman's supporters raised a banner that read: "Champion of White Men's Rule and Woman's Virtue" (Kantrowitz 1998: 213–14, 224). Edgefield County was also a major site for organizing the emigration of African Americans to Liberia (Foner 1988: 357, 574–75, 599).

Stolen Youth, Murdered Blacks, and Feuding Whites

Growing up in Edgefield, Beverly saw with her own eyes the impact of this racist ideology on family members. Her cousin James was accused of raping the daughter of his White employer. Beverly's Uncle Ben had done what many Black men in Edgefield did when their sons reached their teens: he found James a job with a White family who paid him for his labor around their farm. Things went well until another White man offered to pay him more money. Shortly after learning of this competing offer, the White employer noticed some blood on the thigh of his seven-year-old daughter after she had come in from outdoors where Uncle Ben's son had been working. He presented this as "proof" to the sheriff that his child had been raped by a Black boy. That night, a White mob took James from his parents' home, tied him to a tree "with his feet off the ground," and beat him until he "confessed." He was fourteen at the time and was sentenced to prison until the age of twenty-one.

When he was allowed to speak with his father in private, James explained what really happened. The little girl had been climbing a tree but climbed too high, so he helped her down, and while doing so she scratched her thigh on a nail and it bled. When her father noticed the blood and brought it to the attention of his wife, she told him the same thing that James told his father. The girl's father nevertheless insisted that something worse had happened and took the matter to the sheriff. (Later, people in Edgefield said that the girl's mother, who had tried to convince her husband that their daughter had not been raped, eventually "lost her mind.") James told his father that they had beaten him mercilessly, but promised to spare his life if he confessed. He told them what they wanted to hear and went to jail instead of being murdered on the spot. His father, Ben, was run out of town and fled to Philadelphia, where his brothers had already gone. James joined him there after serving the full sentence. Although his relatives say he tried to pursue a normal family life, he died from complications of high blood pressure in his forties. Truly, a crime had been committed in Edgefield, but it was not rape, and it was not committed by James. His father dared to behave in a way that would have been admired and encouraged in his White counterpart: he was negotiating a better wage to advance the economic well-being of his family. The White man who took offense at this challenge to his control over the young Black laborer responded by furiously charging the youth with rape—despite the costs to his young daughter and his wife—and provoking a lynch mob that coerced a false confession from the Black youth.

In other incidents, Blacks were terrorized because they were caught in a conflict between competing Whites. When Beverly was around sixteen, a family friend, Clarence Gilliam, was murdered. Beverly grew up calling him "Cousin Clarence," for although he was not a member of the Nichols family, he was addressed as kin. He had worked for the Logues, but decided to leave them and work for Davis Timmerman, who was known for his fairness and the better pay he extended to Blacks. As Elder Beverly used to recount to us while the Cromwells and Nicholses were picking blueberries, Cousin Clarence was riding in a car with another Black man who had left the Logues to work for Timmerman. When they drove by the home of Fred Dorn, a White sharecropper, Dorn shot him with his rifle. The bullet lodged in Cousin Clarence's brain. Nearby neighbors recounted how terrible it was that his mother and father had had to hear him constantly hollering from the pain until he died several weeks later, despite the noble efforts of a White doctor named Nicholson, who gave him nightly injections for the pain.

When asked why he shot Clarence, Fred Dorn is reported to have said that "he was riding too fast in front of my house." According to Elder Beverly, everyone knew that Dorn "was a flunky" for the Logues and shot Gilliam either to curry favor with his boss or because his boss told him to do it. Apparently referring to Clarence Gilliam, but omitting his name and the testimony of

African American voices, Jack Bass and Marilyn Thompson report in their "unauthorized biography" of Strom Thurmond that "a Black hired hand of Timmerman's was killed by a single rifle shot. The killer was never identified, but suspicion centered on the Logues and Fred Dorn" (Bass and Thompson 2005: 59–60).

Will Jones, a member of Willow Springs Baptist Church, which was located less than a mile from the Logues' home, was shamelessly shot and killed near the church after church deacons reported to the magistrate that Jones had been drinking and was "acting out." Magistrate W. S. Logue was the father of George and Wallace Logue, and he deputized his sons to look into the matter. As Elder Beverly observed, the church deacons were well aware that George and Wallace Logue blamed Will Jones for the acquittal of Clifford Owdom for killing their brother Frank, and the deacons must have suspected that violence was likely to ensue with magistrate Logue's legal intervention—and it did. The Logue brothers asserted that they shot and killed Jones in self-defense because he tried to shoot them. Indeed, a pistol was found lying next to Jones's body, but Beverly's Uncle Tommy and most other Blacks were convinced that the brothers had planted the weapon. Judge Thurmond, who tried the case, released the suspects on seven-hundred-dollar bail, and the two brothers were acquitted (Dorn 2006: 48–50). At the scene of the shooting, a light-skinned Black woman known in the community to have been Wallace's "woman" spoke these words: "Wallace Logue, you will die with your shoes on!" Elder Beverly usually added at this point in her narrative, "And he did."

Elder Beverly related the details of these events often over the years, usually when the extended family was gathered. When T. Felder Dorn published *The Guns of Meeting Place* (2006), documenting the violence within and between the Logues and the Timmermans, as well as its impact on the lives and deaths of Clarence Gilliam, Will Jones, and others, Elder Beverly was impressed with Dorn's accuracy and his interviews with surviving Timmerman and Logue family members. She observed, however, that readers might be surprised to learn that Ann Butler, whose photograph appears on page 144, is actually a Black woman who could have passed for White. Both Elder Beverly and her cousin Carrie Lee Adams, who still lives in Edgefield, noted that in the picture "Cousin Ann" was carrying a basket on her arms, just as she did when she brought her niece Maryanne by the Nichols home to play with Beverly's younger sister Roberta.

Like her sister Holly, Elder Beverly recalls the "night riders" who came up to their home, "shot in the air," and told her father to move off the land "or else." When her father took out his "sixteen shooter," he did not shoot in the air but "straight at them," scaring them off. When I expressed my respect for Elder Beverly's ability to survive living while Black in Edgefield, she said, "You have to be taught." Her father told them that they might want to fight back but Whites would kill them and then they would not have a life, and that God would not let any people commit evil forever. Elder Beverly was elated over the election of the United States' first Black president, which seemed to her a realization of her deceased father's words. She was especially happy that "Whites voted him in" since Blacks did not have the numbers. She never thought she would see this day, "but God is able. . . ."

Along with recollections of terrorism and murder at the hands of Whites, Elder Beverly recalls good White neighbors. Davis Timmerman, a large landowner and storekeeper, had the misfortune of being the Logues' enemy but was regarded as a fair-minded man by the Black community. She spoke kindly of a store owner named Timmerman (no relation to Davis Timmerman), who ran interference between her father, a hard taskmaster, and her brothers, whose mischief extended to swiping eggs from under Mr. Timmerman's hens and then selling them back to him! She also recalls the Rubensteins, who allowed Blacks to try on shoes and hats; that was not permitted at Mukashy's, the other Jewish-owned store in Edgefield.[11] The matriarch of the Rubenstein family was kind to Elder Beverly and her siblings and was especially fond of their mother. Elder Beverly had a very realistic, firsthand view of the White-on-Black violence in Edgefield, yet she instilled in her children the importance of viewing all people as created by the same God and Father. Any suggestion that Blacks were inferior was a lie—against God.

Life and Labor in Philadelphia

In 1944, when Beverly left Edgefield with her youngest sister, Roberta, and two youngest brothers, Walter and Alvin, the trains and buses were full of soldiers. Her older sister was waiting for them in Philadelphia. There she met Jerald Cromwell. His parents "favored Lucy," the best friend of Jerald's beloved sister Roxy. Lucy was Philadelphia-born and had light skin, light eyes, and red hair. Beverly, though not particularly dark-skinned, was definitely "from the country." Jerald made it clear, however, that it was the "country girl" he wanted. Elder Beverly noted that his parents, who adored Jerald, quickly "got on [her] side," especially in light of the fact that Jerald was "fighting overseas"; they did not want him to have problems on his mind.

Finding work in Philadelphia was not difficult during the war. During her previous year in the city, Beverly had worked after school as a "mother's helper" for a Jewish family in South Philadelphia, earning twenty-one dollars per week. Later, she worked with other Blacks and Puerto Ricans at the Campbell's Soup factory across the Delaware River in Camden, as did Elder April. After she married, Beverly worked at the U.S. post office during busy holidays. Mr. Tony Lambert, whom her husband had come to know through his involvement with Black workers' rights, encouraged her to take a full-time job at the Thirtieth Street post office. However, as she explained to him, the work schedule would not allow her to be at home early enough to meet her children returning from school. She said, "It shows when children are left to themselves—they don't know how to act." Domestic work accommodated her schedule. So did hairdressing, for which she had trained at the Cartier School of Beauty, graduating in 1946. She also made arrangements with the boss of Stadham's Chemical and Textile plant that allowed her more time with her children, as she left by 2 p.m. When she left Stadham's, Beverly continued to work in ways that did not interfere with her child-rearing activities. She sewed piecework at home on a trestle Singer sewing machine, passing on some of her work to Elder Esther, who had for a while worked at Stadham's with her. As Beverly's sister Holly had been instrumental in helping her find work at Stadham's, so Beverly assisted Esther. Elder Beverly also made dresses for the saints when they needed new attire for church events such as Communion/Passover.

When Beverly began working at the Stadham factory, she earned forty cents per hour and averaged $3.40 per day. This wage, though shockingly low, was more than Black women earned in a week as domestics back in Edgefield. She sought to learn more skilled tasks. Despite being warned of the dangers, she watched her Jewish supervisor cut material and, after becoming his apprentice, she became the first woman cutter in Philadelphia during World War II; she spread materials, made her own patterns, set the cutting knife to the right depth, and cut the cloth with an electrically powered machine. This highly skilled job was crucial to the plant's profitability because a single mistake could be costly, making Beverly's position one of great responsibility. It was almost always reserved for men, and she reported that most cutters were Italians from South Philly who passed the job down from father to son. Elder Beverly recounted the challenge of being a woman with men working under her supervision.

Stadham's owner, Mr. Steinig, was impressed with Beverly's speed and precision, so he paid her good wages and arranged for her to have a flexible work schedule that allowed her to see her children off to school in the morning and meet them at home after school—with the understanding that she would produce the number of pieces needed for the operators to meet the production goals for the day. As a cutter, Beverly did "piecework," so that the more she produced the more money she made. She recalls earning from thirteen dollars to fifteen dollars per hour. But after the war, Elder Beverly explained, the cutters union began to pressure the owners to hire returning veterans, especially those whose fathers had been in the trade and expected to follow them into these well-paid positions. As an employee in a factory with a government contract, Beverly belonged to the AFL-CIO, but not the local cutters union. Mr. Steinig, nicknamed "Steinie" by his employees, fought hard for her right to keep her job, presenting the cutters union with documentation of her efficiency and reliability in meeting the government orders on time and as requested. Elder Beverly said that Mr. Steinig even threatened to close the shop down before replacing her with a male cutter. She continued to work at the plant well after the war ended. However, Stadham's was a small business that had relied on wartime contracts. When "the work began to drop off," she lost her job. So Beverly began doing domestic work on a regular basis, mainly in Jewish homes. Her children helped her clean during the summer months, when they were not in school or picking blueberries on South Jersey farms at piece rates ranging from eight to twelve cents per pint in the 1950s.

Beverly had always aspired to be a teacher. But Temple University remained out of reach, even though it was in nearby North Philadelphia. From the time she first arrived in the city, she had to work to defray the cost of rent, food, and clothing for herself, her younger siblings, and her mother, who was suffering from health problems at the time. There was no money left over for college tuition and fees. So, Elder Beverly said, "I decided that since I couldn't go to college, I'd be the best house cleaner I could be." She had high standards, she was meticulous, and she was remarkably fast.

Elder Beverly confessed one day that she would have preferred to stay home with her children rather than working for pay all her life. But, she explained, "When your husband can't get a good job because he's Black, what else can you do but work to make up the salary that he should have earned if things were fair?" When her older children moved away, she bought and ran her own food cart. She returned to school for training in nursing and worked in health care, but continued to do day's work to provide a better life for her children. Three of Beverly's four children attended Temple University, and one attended Fisk University. Indeed, when I consider Elder Beverly's resiliency in the face of White terrorism in Edgefield and structural racism in Philadelphia, I am convinced that if she had had half the opportunities I have had in my lifetime, she would have become president . . . of the world.

Finding Home in the City of Brother Love

When Beverly settled in North Philly, the neighborhood was over half African American, with the rest of the population consisting largely of Italians and Jews. Most of the businesses were owned by Jews, but there were a few Asian storekeepers in the area as well. Elder Beverly recalled the racial tension associated with the 1944 transportation strike, during which she was seated next to an armed Black soldier "called in to protect" newly hired Black trolley drivers. She also spoke of a "mark" that Blacks put on the buildings of businesses owned by certain Whites and Chinese known to treat their Black customers well; those businesses were spared during the riots around Ridge Avenue.

Elder Beverly was deeply committed to her children's education and the family's quality of life. When Whites fled North Philly, Elder Beverly remarked, "they took everything with them." Better schools were built in new White neighborhoods, and those in Black neighborhoods deteriorated physically and educationally. Good grocery stores departed, leaving behind the corner markets with exorbitant prices, inferior produce, and limited choices. "We stayed broke," she recalled, moving from one neighborhood to another in search of decent schools. When their neighborhood suffered from the consequences of White flight, the family moved again. "Think of all we could have had if we didn't have to move all the time to find better schools for our children," she remarked. Whites could move to a new home on Roosevelt Boulevard in the Northeast or Boxborough, buy a nice place for five thousand dollars, send their children to good schools, and stay in that home and pay it off. The Cromwells, like other African Americans in their situation, spent thousands of dollars on new mortgages, moving expenses, and selling their old home in a neighborhood where real estate values had fallen when its racial makeup had changed.

The Cromwells were well aware of the new neighborhoods being developed on the outskirts of the city. When they phoned the realtors, however, "the minute they got an inkling you were Black," they said that the house was no longer on the market. If Beverly and Jerald wanted to see a house advertised in the Sunday *Inquirer* or *Bulletin*, they drove through the neighborhood that afternoon, but they never got out of the car or approached the house, lest the owner see that they were Black. Elder Beverly explained that realtors worked hand in glove with owners to "keep Blacks out" of new affordable housing. She recalled a block in Roxborough where two Black families lived; they had secured the property through a White intermediary so that the White sellers never knew that the buyers were Black.

Elder Beverly recalled working for a Jewish woman who rather thoughtlessly, if not callously, reported how she had left her North Philadelphia home on Lehigh Avenue when the neighborhood had "changed." Not only had she and her husband purchased a new home, but they were able to "set up" their daughter as well. On relating this, Elder Beverly wondered at how Whites "took care of themselves, and didn't care what it did to us." Still, she concluded, "They did all that, and we still made it." Over the years, she and her husband bought two homes in North Philly, one of which they sold to her younger brother, Elder Walter, and the other to her older sister, Elder Thea, who died before she could be interviewed for this study. The Cromwells bought a lovely home in West Mount Airy when White neighborhoods began to "open up" after the passage of the Civil Rights Act of 1964.

When reflecting comparatively on her experiences of racism in the North and in the South, Elder Beverly said that the racism she met in the North did not surprise her "because they were the same people," namely Whites who had come from Britain and Europe. The only difference between northern and southern racists, she explained, is that in Philly "they just couldn't get by with it," in part because Blacks "wouldn't take it" and in part because "Philadelphia was the Quaker city" with a long tradition of fairness.

Finding Salvation

Like her sisters and brothers, Beverly had grown up in Willow Springs Baptist Church in Edgefield and first attended Tenth Memorial Baptist Church after arriving in Philadelphia. Through her sister Holly, she "came to the truth" by hearing the teachings of Mother Brown, who "taught the Word." Under Mother Brown, she learned "how to pray" and "how to have a relationship to God," and she came to know the "deliverance that only comes through the Word." Elder Beverly has always "taken time" with young people, and they express appreciation of her special and supportive way of interacting with others. Elder Beverly "knows her Bible"; she not only quotes various long passages of scripture but is able to "run references" with alacrity and accuracy in both the Old and New Testaments. Elder Beverly held the important role of interpreter of tongues and was one of the "head saints," assisting the pastor in laying hands on the sick and helping new saints "press through." When she became an elder, the sermons that she and Elder Jerald gave were so highly valued and encouraging that The Church paid for them to fly back to Philadelphia from their home in Virginia when they were scheduled to serve as Presiding Elders. After Elder Jerald Cromwell's death in 2003, Elder Beverly lived in Florida, Georgia, and South Carolina with her children or on her own, but she resettled in Philadelphia to be closer to her siblings and again be a fixture in the life of The Church where, she said, "they pamper me now."

Elder Esther Rogers Wilson (1927–)

"I don't think I could take a separation from God."

A Hard Fight for We

We began our interview on a bus. Elder Esther was just finishing her workday and wanted me to get a sense of what her job entailed. At the age of seventy-five, she takes pride in her work and pursues it with the lively enthusiasm that pervades everything she does. She came to Philadelphia as a teenager from Moncks Corner, South Carolina, located about thirty-five miles from Charleston. Founded in 1728, Moncks Corner was settled by French Protestants fleeing religious persecution in Europe. Here, according to the 1860 census, 2,880 slave owners held 37,290 slaves, making this county the highest-ranking slaveholding county, not only in the state but in the United States.[12]

In Moncks Corner today, a Cistercian Abbey stands on the three-thousand-acre Mepkin Plantation, purchased in 1762 by Henry Laurens, a wealthy slave trader and president of the American Continental Congress (1777–78). The culture and history of Elder Esther's hometown is intimately connected with Henry Laurens's arrangement with British slave trader Richard Oswald to purchase Africans directly from Bance Island off the coast of Sierra Leone and ship them directly to South Carolina for a 10 percent commission. This lucrative enterprise provided Laurens not only with an unlimited supply of unpaid workers but also with the agricultural technology that West African rice producers brought with them. Their skill and toil made Laurens one of the wealthiest men of his time (Opala 1987: 6–14; Fordham 2008: 143–50).

The history of Black people in South Carolina's Low Country, where Esther was born, differs significantly from that of Blacks in other parts of the South. Among these Gullah-Geechee people, a degree of autonomy and distinctive linguistic practices emerged, which were nurtured by the extensive network of vast plantations, a Black demographic majority, geographic isolation, and the direct importation of Africans beyond the end of the legal trans-Atlantic slave trade in 1808 (Jackson 2008; Opala 1987; Mufwene 1997; Creel 1988; Turner 1973). As Leslie Schwalm documents in *A Hard Fight for We: Women's Transition from Slavery to Freedom in South Carolina* (1997), enslaved men and women in the Low Country actively participated in the collapse of slavery, confiscating absentee planters' properties on the heels of Union troops. Freedwomen led protests against Whites' attempts to reassert their privilege and articulated their right to control their working conditions, supervisors, and hours. In Moncks Corner, in particular, an overseer complained that newly freed Blacks were "doing what they pleased and going where they pleased." Even after President Andrew Johnson's 1865 amnesty restored most of the land to former slaveholders and labor contracts were used to maximize Whites' control over Black workers, freedmen and freedwomen negotiated two- to three-day work-rent arrangements in which they received a portion of the profits and land for personal use (Schwalm 1997: 4–8, 116–47, 217–31, 228).

A Man Called Job

This was the legacy of race, labor, and protest into which Esther was born, as one of seven children, to parents who had two and three years of formal education. Esther's Aunt Tora, whom "the family called Nora," possibly in the tradition of Gullah "basket names,"[13] was ten years old when Emancipation came in 1863. Her older relatives rarely spoke to her of slavery times, but said that whatever land they got after the Civil War, the Whites "took back through trickery." Her great-grandmother, who could not read, was deceived into signing papers that relinquished her ownership of the property.

Elder Esther grew up in a Gullah-speaking community but speaks a clearly enunciated American English, although, as a young mother chastising her children, her vowels sometimes became broad and to my child's ears always sounded British. Elder Esther's mother spoke what the adults around me called "Geechee," and as a child I sometimes found her difficult to understand because some words were unknown to me and she used verbs differently. For example, she used the word "go" in the present tense whether she was talking about going somewhere today, yesterday, or tomorrow. Elder Esther describes the area around Moncks Corner as a linguistically and culturally diverse community where she heard Greek, German, Italian, French, Polish, and Yiddish spoken.[14] Her mother, who worked in White homes, mastered both Italian and Jewish cuisine and, according to Elder Esther, her mother's Gullah English was further complicated by the immigrant languages she heard.

When asked about her interactions with non-Blacks in the South, she reported that her personal relations with White neighbors were generally good, but were not like those between equals. The exception was a man they called Job, because before he went to bed at night, he went to the homes of all "his people" and "made sure that they were well fed." He also insisted that they not wear tattered clothes. When Esther and the other children saw Job coming, they would run and hide because he would tear off any well-worn clothing and see that new ones were purchased for them, but the children felt strongly that they should have at least one set of play clothes. Her parents worked for Job and lived on his land throughout Esther's years in Moncks Corner. During all that time, she never entered the back door of his home, and when her mother had to be away, Job's mother would care for Esther and her siblings, who would be tucked into bed with the White children of this man they called Job. As if to distinguish him from the other Whites around them, Elder Esther described him as "English."

Race and Ethnicity, Work and School

Elder Esther said that growing up with Job in her life may have been the reason why she always knew that no one was better than she, despite the racial practices of Moncks Corner. In the late 1930s, the parents of a "dear friend" were beaten up by Whites who then "threw them off the bus" because they refused to "give up their seats." Esther had never been asked to move or give up her seat, but then, she explained, she always wore a white nurse's cap and uniform and accompanied the White children in her charge. She lived near the "Indian reservation" where, she said, the Indian people "kept to themselves," trusting neither Blacks nor Whites. Regarding the attitudes toward Jews that she encountered, she said, "We were all hated—them for being Jewish and us for being Black."

Although Esther's parents had little formal education and separated when she was fourteen years old, they wanted her "to get more than they did." Elder Esther knew of no public schools in Moncks Corner for Blacks: "The church gave us whatever we got," but only provided schooling up to third grade. All her teachers were Black except in first grade, when she had a White teacher. She explained that "we were the testing ground," for White teachers never taught Black children beyond the first grade and "were moved out" to White schools after they had some classroom experience. Black teachers were never promoted to the White school. While most of their teachers were Black southerners, the principals tended to be Black northerners.

When Esther's mother moved to Charleston, she attended its public schools through the seventh grade. When they relocated to Virginia, she attended eighth grade. Determined to earn her high school degree, she completed high school in Philadelphia. When asked what she thought of "saved" people who saw education as an impediment, she disagreed strongly, asserting that it is "the best thing for 'our people,' for even though we are not paid as much as the 'other people' with the same education, they can't deny you." Blacks in Moncks Corner were readily denied equal educational and economic opportunities. A few Black women worked as teachers, but most did domestic work in White homes. Black men sharecropped cotton and some tobacco, or worked in sulfur, asphalt, or paper mills. When asked if she would consider returning to the South, her response was a firm no.

Black Migration, White Flight

Esther moved to Philadelphia in 1942, when she was fifteen years old. She arrived with her mother and joined her mother's sister, Phyllis (though "the family called her Rebecca"), who had already settled in Philadelphia. At night, she attended the racially integrated Barrett High School, then near Fifteenth and Lombard. She started working full-time at sixteen, and because of her age was required to get working papers. During the day, she worked full-time at the True Form corset company, which she described as Jewish-run. She had secured that job through her "mother's newfound friend." She chose not to do domestic day's work, which so many other Black women were doing, because "they wanted too much" labor for the little money they paid—then just over three dollars per day. Esther worked in several factories during and after World War II. When describing the biggest difference between her life in the North and the South she had recently left, she said that in Philadelphia she was not expected to say "yes, sir, and no, ma'am"; she had tended not to do that in the South, which had gotten her in trouble.

Esther lived first at Twenty-fourth and Carpenter and later on Delancey Place, in what is now the upscale Center City area of Philadelphia. When she moved to Delancey Place, it was about half White and half Black, though it soon became an all-Black area. She then moved to North Philadelphia and for a short while lived with Mother Brown, whom she called "Grandma" because the pastor was also her husband's grandmother. His mother, Ruby, had shared Mother Brown's household until her untimely death. Then Esther and her husband moved in with Mother Brown so that she "would not be alone." In 1950 the couple moved to Pennsgrove Street in West Philly, where she still lives today. Hers was the first Black family to move into this White neighborhood; the neighbor on one side was Jewish, and on the other, Italian. When the family left for church on that first Sabbath evening, she and her daughter wearing white dresses and head mantles, the neighbors came out, and one asked, "Are they brides?" Eventually, all the Whites left the neighborhood except for a Jewish couple next door, and they became close friends. When these neighbors grew old, Elder Esther visited and cared for them, and before the husband died, he sold them his home. She remarked, "It needs work, but it's ours."

"Something was missing"

Down South, Esther had been raised in her parents' AME church, and when she arrived in Philadelphia, she first attended her aunt's Baptist church. "I didn't like it," Elder Esther stated, "something was missing." As a child, "God let me know that he had something better for me." She began to experience this improvement when she moved north, finished her degree, and got a better-paying job. She was looking for a more vibrant spiritual life as well and had not found it in the AME or Baptist church in Philadelphia.

She came to know about The Church through her factory coworker Ruby, who was a preacher and musician in her own right as well as the daughter of Mother Brown. She and Ruby became very close, and when Ruby, who was sickly, "had bad days," Esther would carry her home from the factory. Ruby had two sons and was determined that one would marry Esther—she didn't care which one. Elder Esther observed that one son found her "too dark," though I always found her flawless black skin a stunning and perfect accompaniment to the dignity that surrounded her. That son eventually married a Japanese woman, whom he met while serving in the military. Ruby's other son, Ronald, found her more than acceptable and married her. Together, they had six children and remained married until his death.

At The Church, Esther especially loved to hear her mother-in-law Ruby sing and play piano, which she did beautifully. Esther also attended services held in Philadelphia and in New York, where The Church had a sister congregation. "Grandma was the head of them all," she explained, and initially services alternated between the two cities. It was at one of the New York services, while the saints were singing "Lay My Burden Down," that she had a life-changing experience. She said that it was as if she were in a deep dark hole and a piercing light came down like lightning, hit the bottom, and lifted her. At this point, the Holy Ghost hit her so hard that someone had to take the baby from her arms and let the spirit have its way. Before this experience, she had been praying to God for "a purpose" to her life. "In the Baptist [church], there was no purpose. You were just there. The preacher didn't even know your name." After she was saved, her life had a purpose and there was no longer a "block" between her and other people or between her and God. At this point in the narrative, Elder Esther's eyes and voice filled with tears as she confessed, "I don't think I could take a separation from God."

Elder Esther has worked closely with the congregation's young people in Bible study, and as an elder, contributes to the spiritual guidance of the saints. She has always tithed, and recalls the "rallies" that Mother Brown would call from time to time to raise money for major church costs, but which is no longer done.

At the age of eighty-two, Elder Esther continued to work as an employee of the Philadelphia schools, accompanying special-education students on their school bus. After twenty years in this position, she is planning to retire. Previously, Elder Esther served on a federally funded volunteer project designed to collect the views of parents and other citizens on public education. This entailed extensive travel, which she found enlightening, and led to her being hired by the school district. Elder Esther is strongly committed to the development of public schools, especially in light of the cost in human suffering that people, both "Black and White," had to endure for Black people to gain access to all levels of public education denied to her generation in Moncks Corner, South Carolina.

Elder Frank Nichols (1923–)

"You learn as you go on, and you grow as you go on."

Schools and Stones

Elder Frank Nichols, younger brother of Elder Holly Nichols Stables, was born in 1923 in Edgefield, South Carolina, into a society where Blacks and Whites lived in separate, though overlapping, worlds. Elder Frank said that he loved learning but could only complete third grade, and he was "in and out" of school since he had to work in the fields to help the family survive. The Roberson School he attended had one room "with a potbelly stove." He recalls walking there and remembers White students throwing rocks at the Black children from their school bus; one day he was struck and injured, and his father intervened.

Public schools were segregated and blatantly unequal. The schoolhouse the Nicholses attended with other Black children held a maximum of twenty-five students, but there were very few desks, so most of them sat on benches and wrote on their laps. In contrast, according to the floor plan provided in T. Felder Dorn's history of the Tompkins School, the White children had four classrooms, two cloakrooms, a stage, and a main hall, as well as back and front porches. In what Dorn calls a "stark reminder" of the racism that pervaded Edgefield, "minstrel shows, both local and travelling, were common entertainment for a long period at Tompkins" (Dorn 1994: 83). Elder Frank reported that some years later he attended a new consolidated school, Roberson, built for Black children, which had the same floor plan as the Tompkins School. One cannot help but wonder about the level of development the South might have enjoyed had the money spent on maintaining racially separate schools, bathrooms, drinking fountains, and other public facilities been spent on infrastructure that was available to everyone.

Although his father had little formal education, Frank's mother, Lilly Adamson Nichols, had been a teacher, educated at the Schofield Normal and Industrial School established by Martha Schofield, a Quaker teacher from Pennsylvania. Mainly because of her influence, Frank grew up valuing education. When told that some saved people regarded education as a hindrance to salvation, Elder Frank responded that it actually "helped a person in their spiritual journey."

Running Blacks Off and Shooting Dogs Dead

Recalling the cruelty of Whites in Edgefield, Elder Frank recounted going hunting with the family dog. When, as dogs will do, it ran over to play with the White hunters' dogs, the Whites shot the Black family's dog dead. Whites would run Black families off desirable land. One night, he vividly recalled, White "neighbors" came to the house and shot off their guns. His father sent his mother and sisters to her brother's house, but the boys stayed. His father had an old rifle that, when shot, fired sixteen times. The White men dropped to the ground, and after a while they ran off.

Elder Frank described living as a Black man down South as "kind of devastating." Even though his father was well known among and liked by the Whites he "hauled" for throughout the county, that had not stopped his White "neighbors" from attacking the family that night. In fact, one of these neighbors had the gall to stop by to say he had heard about the shooting the previous night and wondered if his father knew what it was about. He replied, "Yes, I do know what it was about," which Elder Frank reported with a knowing laugh. "They just didn't like Black folks—that was the whole thing in a nutshell." Elder Frank went on to report that one night, a White man rode by their home on a horse and the dog barked at him. The White man shot and killed the dog, and when his father called out, "Who is that?" the dog killer's menacing response was, "Come over here, you so-and-so, and see who it is!"

Living and Working while Black in the North

Frank did not hesitate to leave for Washington, D.C., to join his sisters Thea and Molly, a move that his father encouraged and supported with fare for his train ticket. About seventeen years old when he arrived, he lived with Thea on Swann Street in the Northwest for about two years. He worked for the Pullman Company and did construction work until he relocated to Philadelphia, where four of his father's brothers had settled along with his mother and three older sisters, Holly, Thea, and Molly. He lived with one of father's brothers on Twenty-fifth in the Village until he got his own apartment. Arriving in 1942, he quickly found work at the U.S. Navy Yard. After the war, he worked in a White-owned laundry and then at the Strick Trailer Company. He fondly remembered "Ole Man Strick," the owner, who gave a party every year at a local amusement park for all his employees. He loved to dance, Frank recalled, and they said that it was while dancing in Florida that Strick expired. After leaving Strick's, he became self-employed in house remodeling.

Elder Frank agreed that Black families were safer from White violence in Philadelphia, but the North had its own kind of racism. He remembered the transportation strike in 1944, when he used to ride the trolley for just eight cents. He recalled the military being called in both to protect the Black trolley drivers and to prevent a riot "about equal rights." In the North, "most everything you got, you had to fight for," he observed. When asked about interracial interactions when he first arrived in Philly, he said that he had had no White friends; his best friend was his Uncle Ben's son. Frank noted that some Whites were "very friendly" and some were "very prejudice," in "more or less equal" proportions. "Whites just didn't want to see you have nothing." Elder Frank had no regrets over leaving the South and had no desire to return to Edgefield.

"The Word got hold to me"

Raised in Willow Springs Baptist Church like his siblings, Frank first attended Tenth Memorial Baptist Church in Philadelphia, but his wife, Elder April, was not "satisfied" with what she found. He began to visit The Church with his wife and his sister Holly, though initially he did not seek out a closer relationship with this faith community. Then, he recounted, he heard the pastor of The Church "bring out the Word of God like I had never heard it before, and the Word got hold to me." He observed that "the truth and explaining the Word" was missing from other churches.

For Elder Frank, "salvation is Jesus Christ," and you know that you are saved when you are "born again and filled with the Holy Ghost." Speaking in tongues is "a sign that the Holy Ghost is living inside." Regarding the millennium, he explained that Mother Brown's calculation had referred to the date by which Gentiles would have to embrace salvation, not the date of the millennium. He added, "As you go on in the Word, you learn that some things are different than you thought. . . . you learn as you go on, and you grow as you go on." He still "looks to the kingdom" and believes strongly that saints should not be "unequally yoked together with unbelievers," but, since God is love, saints must love people in the world as they do one another.

After coming into The Church, Elder Frank always paid tithes and served as a "brother" and then a head deacon. Now, as an elder chosen by the pastor, it is his duty to study, read, and teach the Word for the saints' guidance. Elder Frank is the chair of the elder board. He expressed appreciation for the bicameral arrangement of the elders and deacons, as it allows for more discussion on decisions than a pastor-focused organizational structure. Currently eighty-six years old, Elder Frank enjoys living independently in a community for the elderly, with the supportive attention of his children and the saints as needed.

Elder L. Ronald Wilson (1926–2002)

"How can you study the Bible if you can't read?"

Violet and Uncle Gilbert

Crisco was melting on the stove, as Elder Ronald was making lye soap during our interview. While we talked, he added the lye to the fat, let the mixture cool, and poured it into the shallow cardboard boxes he used as cooling trays. Watching this process echoed my earliest childhood memories of Elder Ronald. He died not long after our interview, so I never saw him again. This memory of him and the magic of his soap making is precious.

He was born in 1926 in Chase City, Mecklenburg County, in south-central Virginia, where his mother and maternal grandmother, the pastor and founder of The Church, were also born. Mecklenburg County is the location of the Alexander Slave Cemetery, the place of final repose for an estimated thirty enslaved Black men and women, including one Violet, whose grave received a headstone, a rarity in the antebellum South.[15] Chase City, formerly called Christianville, was incorporated in 1873. In 1880 a photograph was taken there of an African American man identified as Uncle Gilbert standing in front of an ox-driven wagon. He had been "given to Betsy Smith Brame in 1827 by her father Capt. Robert Smith" and survived slavery, continuing to live with his family in Chase City (Caknipe 2008: 7, 15, 23, 26).

Ronald was one of three sons. Both his parents and his grandparents were born after Emancipation, but his great-grandmother remembered the day the slaves were freed. His parents separated shortly after he was born, and he spent the first eleven years of his life with his "father's people." He then joined his mother in Philadelphia and lived with her for the next eleven years. In Chase City, Black men tended to be farmers and sharecroppers, though some worked as lumberjacks for sawmills. The women did domestic work for Whites and sometimes did fieldwork, both on their own farms and on White-owned farms. He attended a two-room "field school" for Black children, and in 2000 found the school building still standing but used for storage. His parents taught him that education was "very important," and his mother, Ruby, was for a while a teacher's assistant at Reynolds School in Philadelphia. On hearing that some "saved" people questioned the value of education for salvation, he disagreed and asked rhetorically, "How can you study the Bible if you can't read?"

School and Work, North and South

Elder Ronald remembered that he arrived in Philadelphia on October 23, 1937; he turned twelve the next month. Pastor Brown, his grandmother, was familiar because she used to visit the family in Virginia. His mother immediately enrolled him at J. F. Reynolds public school on Jefferson Street. Later, he was trained as an electrician at Ben Franklin High School. However, his first job was as a dishwasher at Horn and Hardart's automated cafeteria, which had opened its first automat in Philly in 1902. Ronald started working there in 1942, just twelve years after Blacks had sued in order to enter Horn and Hardart's restaurants as customers (Ballard 1984: 85). After two years there, he took a job as a skilled worker in a manufacturing company, where he remained from 1944 to 1988. After many years in this rather dangerous work, he got "hung up in the machinery" and cut badly, so he enrolled in on-the-job sales training. Selling came naturally to Elder Ronald. He liked the challenge and the travel, and he explained that he was not put off by rejection, as each rejection frees you to move on to the next potential buyer.

His interactions with Whites were almost entirely limited to work situations. Regarding job opportunities for Blacks, Elder Ronald replied that he "wouldn't say it was good and wouldn't say it was bad." Most Black men worked in unskilled manufacturing jobs; women, like his wife and his mother, also worked in factories as unskilled laborers, but his grandmother had done domestic day's work. He observed that Whites (by which he meant Gentiles) tended to hold "skilled" jobs, and "Jews owned everything," referring to businesses and factories like the one where his wife, Elder Esther, worked. When he moved into North Philly in 1946, he recalled, Jews predominated in Strawberry Mansion and other Whites lived throughout North Philly, but by 1948, when he moved to his own apartment on Twenty-first Street, North Philly was almost all Black. When he moved across Girard into West Philly, his was the only family on Pennsgrove Street. Corroborating Elder Esther, he recalled his Jewish next-door neighbors who did not "run" when the other Whites fled and later sold their home to the Wilson family.

Elder Ronald did not see much difference in interactions between Blacks and Whites in the North and in the South, as each group pretty much kept to itself. Regarding race relations in the North, he stated that "the only reason we get along now is because it's the law," so "if you need work, you can get that job." In retrospect, Elder Ronald appreciated the quality of his life in the South where he lived in a nice home with his father's people, where "we had a Victrola" record player and many homes had organs. He is one of only two elders I interviewed who considered the possibility of returning to live in the South.

Slipping, Sliding, and Salvation

In Mecklenburg County, Ronald had attended Lone Oak Baptist Church, which was still standing in 2002. In Philadelphia, he attended his grandmother's church, which was meeting at Twenty-third and Montgomery streets in 1935. It was "all I knew. . . . To me, it was just like going down to the corn field or fishing," with no special significance. He kept "slipping and sliding" "in and out" of The Church. It was his wife, Elder Esther, whom he followed into "the way of salvation" when he began to take the Word seriously. Over his lifetime, he held the positions of brother and then deacon. His duties were mainly administrative, but also involved providing transportation for saints and maintaining the grounds. He became an elder in 1980, when his duties shifted to teaching, preaching, and guiding the saints. Elder Ronald reminisced fondly about how he, Elder Jerald, and Elder Walter had their children around the same time, describing those "wonderful" times when "we all were raised up together." Elder Ronald took tithing very seriously, even tithing his Social Security check, and he continued to comply with rules of diet, dress, and Sabbath observance. Tongues were still, for him, the sign of being filled with the Holy Ghost. Without specifying a particular date, he felt that millennium was at hand. He opposed voting but spoke of education as "a must." With some regret, he observed that the younger members were not as strict as when Mother Brown was alive, and even some elders did not wear mantles all the time.

Elder Walter Nichols (1933–)

"With God, all things are possible."

"If I went out and shot somebody, I bet you'd put me on the news then!"

So Elder Walter declared as he argued his case at the door of the NBC television station. He was paying a personal visit to the television station to have his sixtieth wedding anniversary covered in a local news spot. When he was informed that his sixty years of marriage to one woman and raising a large family were not newsworthy, a Black guard overheard this rejection and told Elder Walter to wait while he "phoned someone upstairs." A White female reporter arrived, listened to his story, and filmed an interview that appeared on the television news broadcast and online relating the "good news" of this sixtieth anniversary.[16] Notwithstanding his sense of humor and contagious laughter, Elder Walter is a determined individual and natural leader.

Schooling in Edgefield

Walter Nichols was born in Edgefield in 1933, the third youngest of fifteen siblings. At the time of our interview, he was the youngest elder; his sister Rose was the eldest in his family and the oldest elder of The Church. He left Edgefield when he was a child, so his memories of his hometown are not as extensive as those of his elder siblings, although one event in Edgefield caught up with him later in life. Elder Walter recalls walking several miles to school when the White students riding on the bus threw stones and "would call us niggers and stuff." He remembers that they prepared a big pot of beans that the students had for lunch. His mother, a teacher, instilled in him the importance of "getting an education." Elder Walter declared, "I think education would enhance salvation." To support his position, he observed that while Peter was unlearned, Paul was well educated "at the feet of Gamaliel," the Jewish legal authority, and it was Paul, not Peter, whom God used to found the Christian church.

Family in Philly

Elder Walter left for Philadelphia when his sister, Beverly, collected him along with his younger brother Alvin and sister Roberta. He remembered that a soldier in uniform sat him on his lap during the ride north, although, he added jokingly, the soldier was also "looking at" his older sister. Although only a teenager herself, Beverly collected her younger siblings to join their older siblings and their mother, who was estranged from their father by this time. On arriving in Philadelphia, Walter lived with his sister Holly for a while, with paternal uncles for a couple of years, and then settled in with his older sister Thea, an elder who passed before she could be interviewed for this study.

Elder Walter described a family "system" in which the older sisters "took care of the three younger siblings" in a way that extended into his adulthood and into the next generation. As an example, Elder Thea used to give him money and buy his clothes and school supplies, and even after he married, she was always there to assist. She then "took" his daughter Celine "as her own." This niece was close to Elder Thea until her death, providing transportation and other support for her aunt. Elder Walter was close to his sister Elder Beverly, as he and his wife lived in the apartment above the Cromwells for several years in a duplex at 1812 West Huntingdon Street. I grew up in the first-floor apartment below Elder Walter and his family until we moved to Sixteenth Street near Allegheny Avenue. Later in life, Elder Walter purchased the home of Elder Jerald Cromwell's parents, who had lived across the street from the paternal uncles where Walter had lived as a child and where Beverly and Jerald Cromwell had met and "courted."

Jobs, Higher Education, and White Allies

When Walter arrived in North Philly, some Whites were still living there, but many others were moving out. He was immediately enrolled at Pratt Arnold Elementary School, and then attended Fitz Simon Junior High and Northeast High, alma mater of Elder Jerald. He was an A student in junior high, motivated in part by the fact that "girls looked up to smart guys" and would call him up for help with their homework. He missed this adulation while attending the all-boys high school. Soon, he met and married Lonetta, who was a deaconess when this study began but was recently installed as a church elder. Together, they had seven children. Remarkably, with each pregnancy, Elder Walter experienced *couvade*, in the form of sympathetic labor pains, with each delivery.

In high school, Walter worked both as a delivery boy and a "soda jerk" in the Black-owned Simpson's Pharmacy at Twenty-first and Diamond. His next job was in a metal auto-parts factory where his brother Wilbert, a deacon of The Church, worked. He also worked in a factory that made army uniforms. For a while, he worked full time in the summers for Bill Haines in south Jersey, picking blueberries and driving a farm truck not far from Egg Harbor, where his mother, Lilly Adamson Nichols, finally settled and was reunited with his father, Gordon. In 1952 Walter started working with his brother, Elder Frank Nichols, at Strick's, where he remained for the next sixteen years. After suffering a severe back injury during a car accident on his way to work, he had to retire on disability.

During this time, he took advantage of the opportunity to return to school, offered by vocational rehabilitation services. Walter completed his GED and then college. He expressed deep appreciation for the support and assistance of his wife and his college-educated daughter, Celine. This program required that applicants have a background in community service; he qualified because of his involvement in welfare rights, his elective office on the Home and School Board, and his leadership record at The Church. After completing his bachelor's degree in social work at Temple University in 1976, he worked in the District Attorney's Office in the publicity division. "I loved it," Elder Walter recalls, for he learned much about the inner workings of the legal and law enforcement systems, as well as how to "deal with people" from various backgrounds.

As Elder Walter left the South when still a child, he became aware of southern racial dynamics primarily through national news coverage of such events as the mutilation and lynching of Emmitt Till and of the violence that met civil rights workers. Of interracial and inter-ethnic interactions in the North, he recalled "friendly" interaction with some White students at Fitz Simon. At Strick's he had regular, close contact with Whites for the first time. He had little interaction with Whites or Hispanics outside of work. On the Black struggle for equality, he observed that God always puts some White people in place as our allies. The "Whites who bridge the gap" whom he cited include Eleanor Roosevelt, who supported the Tuskegee airmen, and the brothers John F. and Robert Kennedy. Since retiring, he has entertained thoughts about the benefits of living in a more rural setting, especially in the New South, but he has no regrets about having left it when he did.

The Truth

In Philadelphia, Elder Walter had visited Baptist churches as well as Mother Dabney's Garden of Prayer before he "learned about salvation" through his sister Holly. He fondly recalled Bible study on Sabbath led by Sister Ruby, daughter of the pastor-founder. At this time in his life, Walter had a sobering experience that entailed a close brush with law enforcement, during which he was given a book entitled *With God All Things Are Possible*. After carefully reading it, he promised God that he would serve Him. With the intervention and support of the family, especially the Cromwells, he turned his life around and became an active, committed saint in The Church.

When he started "going to The Church" seriously, the only male members were Brothers Jerald Cromwell and James Stables, so he was incorporated into the duties of The Church right away. As a lay "brother," he had extensive management and maintenance responsibilities. Later, he served as a deacon for thirty-seven years and acted as the deacon board's secretary. Now he is an elder and secretary of the elders. He became an elder when Elder Jerald Cromwell phoned him and told him that God had put it in his heart to invite him to join the elders. All the elders had reached a consensus to accept him, welcoming his experience as secretary, his youthful energy, and his tendency to be meticulous in record-keeping and complete any task he undertook.

Although a crisis may have contributed to Elder Walter's coming into The Church, what has kept him in it, he says, is "the truth" that comes with studying the scripture. When speaking of his beliefs as a saint, he speaks of salvation as a "way of life" left for us by Jesus Christ. He explained that "You know you are saved by this life you live, which is possible because you have been born again, filled with the Holy Ghost, and speak in tongues, the sign of God's presence." He still looks to the millennium, but he believes that, "like Jesus," we should love people outside The Church, and he votes as a responsible American citizen. Regarding church organization, Elder Walter appreciates the advantages of having a pastor to centralize decision-making processes, particularly if that individual can exercise a reasonable degree of objectivity and not favor one family over another, for The Church is a family of families.

Echoes of Edgefield

Elder Walter left Edgefield as a child, but Edgefield followed him into his adulthood. During his first cruise with his wife in the 1980s, he met a woman who, on learning that he was a native of Edgefield, explained that Davis Timmerman had been her father. She gave Elder Walter the detective magazine she was reading, which included a piece relating the Logue-Timmerman feud and the infamous events later chronicled in *The Guns of Meeting Street* (Dorn 2006). The feud between the Logues and Timmermans culminated in a shoot-out between the Logues and law officers in 1942 and, the next year, in the executions of Wallace Logue, Clarence Bagwell, and Sue Logue, the first woman to be electrocuted in South Carolina (O'Shea 1999: 320).

Elder Rose Nichols Horten (1912–)
"Mother Brown did know the Word!"

Essie Mae and Strom

Elder Rose, the oldest living elder at the writing of this book, reached her ninety-seventh year in 2009. Born in Edgefield County, the oldest of fifteen children in the Nichols family, Rose recalled Essie Mae, the Black daughter of Strom Thurmond, South Carolina's virulent pro-segregation governor and U.S. senator. Essie Mae Washington-Williams waited until her father's death to reveal their kinship publicly, although she had been aware of it since she was sixteen. In 2005, Essie Mae Washington-Williams published *Dear Senator: A Memoir of the Daughter of Strom Thurmond*. What stood out about Washington-Williams's public presentation of this previously private history was the grace with which she addressed what was obviously still a painful matter. Throughout her talk at the Quail Ridge Book Store in Raleigh, North Carolina, she spoke of her father as a "good man" who was always kind and generous toward her. With almost childlike wonder, she said that she never understood why, before the end of his very long life, he never claimed her as his daughter. As Elder Rose pointed out in her recollections of life in Edgefield, such behavior was commonplace and Essie Mae's story was commonly known.

The story of Essie Mae and Strom was interwoven among the many family recollections that I heard grown-folk recount during seemingly endless summer afternoons of picking blueberries in southern Jersey. I cannot remember when I did not know about Strom Thurmond's Black daughter. This information was not confined to Edgefield natives; it was discussed at the lunch table among my African American classmates at Philadelphia High School for Girls, who seemed to know as much about the affair as I did. Strom Thurmond had sexual relations with Essie's mother, Carrie Butler, a Black woman who had been working in the Thurmond household and was sixteen years old when she bore their daughter in 1925. Yet, Strom Thurmond vehemently opposed integration and filibustered against the 1957 Civil Rights Act for over twenty-four hours, longer than any individual senator had ever done in congressional history. A Black uncle of Thurmond's and two of his cousins had made the news in 1948, the same year Thurmond was the presidential nominee of the segregationist States Rights Democratic Party (Yoes 2003: 5).

Farming, Sharecropping, Surviving

Elder Rose recalled life on a farm where only two things had to be purchased: rice and sugar. The family ground their own meat to make sausage, grew their own peanuts, and raised their own chickens, turkeys, guinea fowl, geese, goats, cows, and hogs. They picked fruit from the trees and made cane syrup, which they enjoyed with biscuits. Her mother "kept a garden" with greens, tomatoes, peas, okra, and other vegetables.

Rose's mother, Lilly Adamson Nichols, instilled an appreciation for education in all her children, but Rose was only able to attend until she was about twelve years old and when they were not working in the fields. She and her siblings picked cotton so efficiently that, by the time their father had delivered a bale of cotton and returned, the children had picked another. Her father "hauled" cotton for White farmers and cut and sold ties for the railroad. Elder Rose observed that she had never seen a White woman in the fields; White men hired Black women so that their White wives "would not have to get out there and hoe." Elder Rose married at eighteen and sharecropped with her husband until they migrated north.

When asked about interactions with Whites in Edgefield, Elder Rose said things were fine as long as you said "yes ma'am and no ma'am and stayed in your place. . . . they didn't bother you if you didn't bother them." She remembers the night her father defended their home with a shotgun when Whites tried to run them off the land. She vividly recalls her fourteen-year-old cousin being tied up to a tree and beaten until he confessed to a rape he had not committed in order to escape being murdered.

"So we took off"

When asked why she left the South, Elder Rose replied that she and her husband "got tired of working like dogs from sunup to sundown . . . so we took off." Her husband left first and settled in Washington, D.C., before sending for her. She recalls the Depression and the work opportunities created by President Roosevelt's New Deal, especially the Works Progress Administration (WPA, 1939–43) and the Civil Conservation Corps (CCC, 1933–42). Her brother Jonathan worked and lived at a CCC camp during the week, returning on the weekends with money that helped the family survive those difficult times.

Not long after the bombing of Pearl Harbor, Rose moved to Philadelphia, where her father's other brothers had already settled. She lived with her sister Holly in an apartment at Twenty-fifth and Diamond, where they had White neighbors. She did piecework in a factory up to six hours per day, but she was never hired on a full-time basis. Elder Rose recalled regretfully that she could have had a well-paying job at the shipyard, but it required a test and she had not had enough education in Edgefield to pass it. She worked at the Campbell's Soup factory where her sister Holly and sister-in-law April had worked, but had to stop after two years when she developed a persistent cough. Thereafter she did day's work, often in Jewish homes; Elder Rose complained that Jewish women could "work you to death" around the high holidays. Comparing life down South with life up North, she said that in the South they "worked hard for no money" to speak of and in the North they worked just as hard but made enough money "to save a little." On being asked if she would return South to live, she unhesitatingly replied in the negative, saying that there was "nothing there anymore." Like other elders, she recalled that in the North there was little social interaction with non-Blacks unless it was job-related. She remembered when Blacks "tore up Ridge Avenue" because White transit employees "didn't want the Black men to drive the trolleys," but President Roosevelt had sent in soldiers to protect Black drivers and keep the peace.

Finding the Truth

Like the rest of her family, Rose grew up attending Willow Springs Baptist Church. When she first arrived in Philadelphia, she attended Jones Tabernacle AME Church, established in 1877, which had been moved from its earlier site to 2021 West Diamond Street near Holly's apartment.[17] Following her sister Holly to services at The Church, she discovered something that other churches lacked: they did not teach you to call on the name of Jesus for the gift of the Holy Ghost, and "Mother Brown did know the Word."

Elder Rose said that before she "found the truth," she was "full of hate" because of "what people had done to me," but Jesus "moved it out" and she learned what it meant to love your neighbor as yourself. "Jesus kept me in The Church," she asserted, for although she had the greatest respect for the pastor-founder, Elder Rose recalled that Mother Brown "could be so hard on you sometimes." Still, the pastor preached the truth and Elder Rose wanted the truth, so she became an active member, "more so upstairs than downstairs," coordinating activities in the upstairs kitchen rather than in the sanctuary. She and her sister Elder Thea worked closely and effectively in catering matters. Elder Rose used to get up at 5 a.m. to prepare unimaginably light and rich biscuits from scratch for General Assembly breakfasts, which also included her fried chicken, cheese grits, and gravy. She was also responsible for the tongue sandwiches that the youth craved. As a church elder, she preaches, teaches, and provides spiritual guidance to the saints. Along with her grandchildren and great-grandchildren, she lives on her mother's property in Egg Harbor, New Jersey. She is provided with transportation to and from The Church on Sabbath. Regarding interaction with nonmembers and "people in the world," her position is that saints should "show no partiality" to anyone. Still, saints should not be "unequally yoked together with unbelievers" or "caught up in the world." She approves of fellowshipping with other commandment-keeping Christians. Elder Rose prefers spiritual leadership by a group of elders to having power centralized in a pastor. She is a voting citizen, and in the 2008 presidential election she cast her ballot for "that ole smart Obama," thanking God that she "lived to see this day."

Conclusion

Although the oral histories of ten elders preclude broad sociological generalizations, they put flesh on the bare bones of social history. Looking back in 1909 at the profound economic disruption and social dislocation wrought by the Civil War that made Reconstruction a task of immense proportions, W.E.B. Du Bois wrote that "Property in slaves to the extent of perhaps two thousand million dollars had suddenly disappeared. One thousand five hundred more millions representing the Confederate war debt had largely disappeared.... 250,000 men had been killed and many more maimed.... Add to all this the presence of four million freedmen and the situation is further complicated" (Du Bois 1910: 781). In an 1865 report to the president, Secretary of the Interior Carl Schurz described the utter vulnerability of freedmen and freedwomen amid a postwar reign of terror. Federal troops helped to protect the egalitarian institutions and policies that emerged during the brief and incomplete Reconstruction of the South. With the withdrawal of these troops in 1877, what Benjamin Brawley called "the Vale of Tears" began (Brawley 2001: 297–335).

Living while Black after Whites' "Redemption" of the South

Founding saints heard a little about slavery and Emancipation from their parents and grandparents, who passed on stories they had heard from older generations. Their own narratives relate the lived experience of what Whites called "redemption," when Whites throughout the South took back "their beloved homeland from the clutches of Union victory and the political empowerment of former slaves and their descendents" (Giggie 2008: xvi–xvii). Some elders were born less than fifty years afterward, into a world in which White supremacy had been reestablished across political, social, and economic institutions. Black lives were still expendable, as the murder of Will Jones on church property attests, and any sign of resistance to the racial hierarchy was met by force. Protocols of linguistic and behavioral deference buttressed unequal power relations, and even being *perceived* as violating them could be disastrous, as the flight of J. Moses shows. Elder Esther's narrative is witness to the "trickery" by which the land allotted to her newly freed family was taken back by Whites. Economic exploitation in the form of sharecropping and domestic labor is reported throughout these narratives. Elder Hannah was reduced to tears when watching footage of destitute children in the Third World because it "brought back so much" about conditions when she was "coming up."

The South sketched in these narratives is a society in which Black parents could not protect their children from being beaten into a false confession and incarcerated at the age of fourteen, as cousin James learned. Black children learned from parents like Gordon Nichols to "wear the mask" and not to resist White oppression so as to avoid being killed. Narratives from both South Carolina and Virginia speak of White children throwing stones at Black children, who already knew that they must not retaliate. Black children saw that their racial identity relegated them to walking to a one-room schoolhouse and writing on their laps, compared to White children who rode the bus to a school with several furnished rooms designed for various functions.

Up North

During the Great Migration, many Blacks moved North in stages. Some relocated to southern cities first: Elder Esther left Moncks Corner for Charleston, South Carolina, and Elder Holly went to Augusta, Georgia, after fleeing Johnston, South Carolina. Some children followed their parents to the North: Elders Ronald and Esther followed their mothers. Sometimes parents followed their children: Lilly Nichols joined her children in Philadelphia after separating from her husband. Others had assistance from friends: Elder Hannah's friend convinced her to leave the South for the big city and offered her a place to stay until she found work and housing. These networks of family and friends were crucial to getting established, creating family in a strange place and sharing financial and informational resources. Living together reduced housing costs and reinforced kinship ties, and helped newcomers adapt to new social settings and cultural rules.

The migrants' lived experience of Philadelphia was hardly utopian. The early death of Elder Jerald's sister from tuberculosis brings home the health disparities between Blacks and Whites. The founding saints' recollections personalize the impact of constitutional law and legislation, including the effects of the 1954 desegregation decision and the 1964 Civil Rights Act on their families' access to public education and housing. While all the elders who left the South as adults expressed no desire to return there to live, their narratives of finding "home" in the North suggest that this process had been protracted, difficult, and incomplete.

They had left behind confrontations with the Klan only to encounter the avoidance strategy of White flight. In Philadelphia, the saints were systematically excluded from "good" neighborhoods with well-funded schools, reasonably priced stores, and healthy, safe environments. When they managed to move into better areas, Whites were already fleeing the "changing" neighborhood. The day my family moved into a new house at 1812 West Sixteenth Street, not far from Temple University's School of Dentistry, the White family next door was moving out, and the little girl talked with me just long enough to ask why I had not bothered to wash my face that morning.[18] Our family moved to the Germantown area after many Sundays spent scouting out neighborhoods, never certain if we would be "let in" or how long the neighborhood would last before White flight leached away the schools, stores, tax base, and property values. Growing up meant living through an extended urban migration that mirrored the Great Migration, a protracted quest for home that yielded only temporary and tentative resting places.

Commitment to Education

All the narratives contain strong affirmations of the value of education. Elders were shocked by and critical of the notion that education might conflict with "being saved." In the South, publicly funded schools for Blacks were always inadequate and sometimes entirely absent, so Black independent churches provided primary and, especially, secondary schooling: Elder Hannah's Baptist church schools and Elder Beverly's Baptist-founded and church-sustained Bettis Academy filled the educational gap created by *Plessy v. Ferguson*. Sometimes better-off relatives, like Elder April's distant kin, contributed financially in order to support the education of talented Black youth.

This tradition of valuing and supporting education was reinforced by the teachings of The Church, which interwove notions of salvation, "chosenness," and academic excellence. As working parents of school-age children, several elders carpooled to Logan School in the 1950s, then a "demonstration" school comparable to magnet schools today, until the children were old enough to take public transportation to the White section of the city where it was located. Although domestic work was low-paying, it provided female saints with flexible schedules that allowed them to spend time with their children after school. Some adults also pursued higher education: Elders Jerald, April, and Walter earned college degrees after their children had reached young adulthood; Deacon Alvin Nichols, Elder Walter's younger brother, earned his college degree and became a financial aid officer at Community College of Philadelphia. Elder Ace Gaye, who was installed after the interviews for this book had been conducted, completed his degree in construction engineering from Drexel University; his wife, Erin, a deaconess and evangelist, went back to school and earned her master's degree in social work. Like many educated African Americans, the saints have tended to work in professions that served the community.

Whites and Blacks, North and South

These narratives support the notion that, in both the South and the North, Blacks depended on Whites for jobs and Whites relied on Blacks for labor. The texture of these relationships differed significantly between the agricultural South and the industrial North. Elders' narratives suggest a pattern of relationships between southern Blacks and Whites in which Blacks sharecropped on White-owned land, worked as farm laborers, and toiled as domestic servants. These relationships were grounded in a long history of chattel slavery that entailed publicly acknowledged, as well as unrecognized, biological kinship. Black and White family and local community histories were interwoven, as exemplified by the Logue-Timmerman feud. Their recollections of southern race relations are rife with intimacy, violence, congeniality, conflict, and contradiction. In contrast, their recollections of race relations in the North are flat and cold—literally so in the case of Elder Holly's "snowman." Racial violence in the North tended to be subtle and structural in nature. Racialized tracking in public schools steered Blacks away from preparing for college and into manual occupations. White flight and legalized police brutality made Black neighborhoods inferior and dangerous. Having a few African Americans in positions of authority did not always help. As Elder Jerald's narrative attests, the danger that lay beyond the Black "pockets" of the city came not only from the various White ethnic gangs but also from the Philadelphia Police Department (PPD), which was known for arresting and brutalizing Blacks they found "in the wrong place at the wrong time." So common were such events that Mother Brown warned parents that if they failed to keep their children in line with corporal punishment, then "the police would." This warning was brought home by reports from neighborhood families whose sons had returned badly beaten by the PPD, or had not returned at all. A saint once spoke in church of a local boy who had been taken to the police station; when his mother was called to collect the corpse, his fingernails appeared waterlogged, as if he had been tortured. She never learned what caused her child's death.

The saints' narratives distinguish Jews, who were also considered White, from White Christians, whom they called Gentiles. Elder Beverly spoke highly of her Jewish employer, who took an interest in her, adjusted her work schedule to accommodate her family's needs, and fought for her after the war when the union wanted a male to take her job. Elder Esther identified with Jews when she asserted, "We were all hated—them for being Jewish and us for being Black." The teachings of The Church value the Jewish people as God's first "chosen people" and as Jesus's cultural ancestor. The saints also follow selected Levitical laws. (For more details, see Crumbley 2000.) How much this sense of religious connectedness colored the elders' recollections is not clear, but entirely negative characterizations of Jews are absent from these recollections. Narrators did not withhold criticism of Jewish people when they felt they deserved it, but these tended to be criticisms of individuals and not of Jews as a group.

Sex, Gender, Race, and Power

Growing up, I used to hear older women in the community say that the only free people in America were White men and Black women. In time, I came to understand that they were relating a larger story about White men's access to Black women's bodies, first as slave masters and later as alpha males in American sexual hierarchies. The interplay of sex, gender, and race is explicit in the incarceration of fourteen-year-old James and in the unidentified but visible White ancestry of the African American boy his Black schoolmates nicknamed "Whitefolks." The elders lived in times when secret sexual relationships between Black women and White men were not only common but regarded as normal. The lynching of Black men was justified by the often entirely unfounded rumor that they had raped a White woman. The reigning assumptions were that no White woman would have sex with a Black man unless she was forced and that Black women had sex with White men willingly, wantonly, and without moral restraint.

Lilly Adamson Nichols, daughter of the half-White Duke Adamson, spoke of her White grandfather as "scandalous," having sired children "all over the county." Her Black grandmother's sister also bore children by her White grandfather's brother. The Black and White families lived on the same property with full knowledge of one another. When I asked why she had become a White man's mistress, I was told, "So she wouldn't have to work so hard." This explanation made more sense after I learned how hard life could be for Black people in those days. A Black woman being "kept" by a powerful White man could expect her children to be well fed and clothed year round, unaffected by the seasonal fluctuations and chronic debt that plagued Black sharecropping families. She was less likely to be in danger from other Whites in the community, and her half-White children might fare better in life; Duke Adamson's White father regularly took him into town and eventually deeded him land. On the other hand, a Black woman who rejected a White man outright could be courting danger not only for herself but for her husband, family, and community. Seen in this light, having a sexual relationship with an economically, politically, and socially powerful White male could be considered a survival strategy for Black women.

According to these narratives, Black women negotiated male-dominated institutional structures in both sacred and secular worlds. Elder Beverly would have been unable to learn to be a cutter, a skilled trade that was usually exclusively male, had it not been for the wartime labor shortage, and she would have been forced out of this position earlier had her employer not been willing to stand up to the local cutters union on her behalf. Elder Hannah pointed out that in those days "women weren't allowed too much" in the Baptist church, so that Pastor Dudley "didn't have a free hand" in mentoring her. However, Pastor Dudley recognized her spiritual gifts and introduced her to Mother Brown. Mother Brown not only mentored Elder Hannah as a preacher but also supported her as a single mother. While The Church may not have been able to provide a women's "hospice," as Bishop Robinson's Mount Sinai did, the female saints were there for each other. Like scholar-cleric Robert Franklin's grandmother (Franklin 1995: 263), my mother often "admonished" and "encouraged" the young women who came to our home to "visit" with her. Sometimes they cooked and ate together and sometimes the women stayed overnight, especially if "their nerves were bad" or when they had experienced an emotional "break," which was much worse.

The narratives recount relationships between Black and White women in the North and the South. In the South they ranged from the gracious "Miss Cornelia" to self-serving White women who presumed that Black girls who had gone as far as the public school system allowed would work for their daughters, who had graduated and married. Stories about interactions in Philadelphia range from White women selecting day workers from Black women "lined up" on North Philly street corners to Elder Esther's female Jewish neighbor who "stayed" and became a close friend when the other Whites abandoned Penngrove Street. The strongest connection between Black and White women is economic; most of the female elders who had performed domestic work for White women in the South continued to do so in the North.

Self-Criticism

The elders pulled no punches. They related the stark reality of everyday White racism and domination that constrained their lives both North and South of the Mason-Dixon Line. They also recounted Black people's inhumanity and injustice to one another in the form of color prejudice, internalized racism, and economic exploitation. Elder Esther's husband's brother did not like Black women as dark-skinned as she was. Elder April's father felt compelled to undermine the colorism of his day by informing his children that two of their teachers, one very dark- and the other very light-skinned, were equally endowed intellectually and yet were paid the same salary. In a critical voice, Elder April made a point of informing me that the landowner who took three-fourths of the harvest, while her father retained only one-fourth, was a dark-skinned Black man. Elder Beverly pointed out that the deacons who called for Magistrate Logue to discipline Will Jones knew full well that the Logues, who blamed Jones for the acquittal of their brother's murderer, Cliff Owdom, were likely to kill him; nevertheless, to curry the favor of this powerful White family, these deacons forfeited an opportunity to exercise self-determination in the one institution Blacks controlled, the Black church. With deep regret, Elder Jerald recalled his African American school counselor who, acting as a surrogate White gatekeeper by weeding out a potential Black competitor, had tried to convince Jerald that he was not college material.

Spiritual Sojourn

The journeys that these narratives recount are more than geographical; the elders also relate spiritual journeys from established independent churches into a Sanctified church they helped to create and sustain. All of the elders grew up in older, independent Black churches, but explored other options after arriving in Philadelphia. Several said that they were "looking for something," and others had experienced a divine call to serve God. The Church offered them "the truth of salvation" guided by Mother Brown, "who knew the Bible."

These lives unfolded during the period Brawley called "the Vale of Tears," which extended from the late-nineteenth century until World War II. In the South, the elders witnessed a demoralizing denial of human and civil rights on a daily basis. Their collective response to this situation was well expressed by a freedwoman in Texas who, when repeatedly confronted by the Klan, "just built a wall of the Lord 'round me, so they couldn't get at me" (quoted in Brawley 2001: 293; Wilson 2005: ix). Finally they responded by "voting with their feet" and leaving for the North. After their migration, the saints "built a wall of Jesus" around themselves in The Church.

Finally, why is the life history of the pastor-founder not included in this chapter? Mother Brown died many years before she could be interviewed. Much of the information about her is drawn from secondary sources rather than of her own recounting, making it quite different from the elders' narratives. Moreover, her story is intimately tied to the institutional history and organizational processes of The Church. For this reason, chapter five, which analyzes The Church's organization, opens with her biographical sketch.

4

BECOMING SAINTS

WHAT DOES IT MEAN to become a saint—ritually, symbolically, and culturally? For first-generation saints, becoming a saint entailed much more than just going to church. Furthermore, becoming a saint in this particular Sanctified faith community entails compliance with selected Levitical laws, a practice that is absent from many, if not most, Sanctified churches. Thus, this chapter starts by immersing the reader within the ritual experience of Sabbath worship. It then explores four elements of "being saved": "keeping the commandments" (law); "being in but not of the world" (holiness); "rightly dividing the word of truth" (scripture); and "being filled with the Holy Ghost" (spirit). The chapter concludes with a diasporic reflection on cultural and historical sources of these beliefs and practices.

Going to Church

"Will a man rob God?" Mother Brown often posed this rhetorical question as tardy saints tried in vain to slip into the church after the sun had set and Sabbath had begun. Although this passage from Malachi 3:8 explicitly refers to robbing God of "tithes and offerings," Mother Brown taught that being late for Sabbath was robbing God of time. Besides, to arrive late was to "break" the Sabbath, the fourth of the Ten Commandments, and to break one commandment is to be "guilty of all" (James 2:10–11).

There were two other Sabbath services the saints might choose to attend. However, during the late 1950s and early 1960s, when founding saints who had entered as young couples in the 1940s were raising their children in The Church, most saints attended all three services. Founding saints chose their jobs accordingly and, if necessary, made special arrangements with employers so that they could arrive at church just before sunset on Friday evening, attend Sabbath morning service at 9 a.m., and return for the Sabbath afternoon service at 3 p.m.

The set order of the service was familiar to the saints, although it varied depending on how "high" the spirit was and with the changing time of sunset through the seasons. When the pastor established eye contact with Elder Laura Smythe, then a "sister," she reached for her tambourine and "pitched" the key, which the pianist would pick up, and the congregation sang "Down at the Cross."[1]

> Down at the cross where my Savior died,
> Down where for cleansing from sin I cried,
> There to my heart was the blood applied;
> Glory to His Name!
>
> (Refrain)
> Glory to His Name, glory to His Name:
> There to my heart was the blood applied;
> Glory to His Name!

The rest of the saints joined in with their tambourines or clapping, while a head deacon playing the drums set the pace. Meanwhile, the ushers, dressed in white like the other female saints but wearing white gloves, removed chairs from the central aisle and placed them in the back of the room, making space for the shout should the spirit be high during the devotional service. I always aspired to join the ushers and eventually, as a teenager, was allowed to do so. After about two hours, when the devotional service ended, the chairs were replaced so that the saints could sit, although saints might shout at any time the spirit fell on them. The whole service lasted, on average, three hours. As Robert Franklin observed, "Because worship is sacred, one never rushes it" (Franklin 1989: 19).

When the spirit died down, Mother Brown would stand, joined by the saints. Now Elder Frank Nichols, who along with Elder Ronald Wilson sat at a table positioned directly in front of the altar behind which the pastor sat, intoned, "And God spake all these words, saying" (Exodus 20:1), signaling the congregational recitation of the Ten Commandments that hung on the front wall of the sanctuary next to the Lord's Prayer. At the end of the commandments, Elder James Stables intoned, "Jesus said," and the saints repeated a passage from Matthew 22:37–40 printed just below the Ten Commandments: "Thou shalt love the Lord thy God with all thy heart, and with all thy soul, and with all thy mind. Thou shalt love thy neighbor as thyself. On these two commandments hang all the law and the prophets." The saints then repeated the Lord's Prayer. At this point Elder Frank, with his hands raised, led the congregation in prayer. The saints responded to his supplications by singing or humming "Amen," "Jesus," and "Yes, Lord," adding their own personal prayers as well.

After Elder Frank finished his prayer, the table where he and Elder Ronald sat was set aside so that anyone needing prayer could come forward and kneel at the altar. Three head saints, usually Elders Holly Stables, Laura Smythe, and Beverly Cromwell, and sometimes Elder April, joined the pastor in "laying on of hands." A head deacon, usually Jerald Cromwell, accompanied the pastor as she proceeded down the line of kneeling saints. The olive oil he carried was contained in a small, flat glass bottle wrapped in a white handkerchief. The saints went up to the altar with health complaints ranging from ringworm to cancer; personal matters could include a stormy marriage or an upcoming test at school. Every year, just prior to the opening of school, all school-age children "went up for prayer" and were anointed with oil.

After the Ten Commandments and prayer service were over, the saints sang "Sweet Sabbath Home":

> Sweet Sabbath school more dear to me
> Than fairest palace dome
> My heart e'er turns with joy to thee
> My own dear Sabbath Home.
>
> (Chorus)
> Sabbath Home! Sweet Home!
> Blessed Home! Sweet Home!
> My heart e'er turns with joy to thee
> My own dear Sabbath Home.

Next, if the Holy Ghost had "spoken" during the devotional service, the interpreter of tongues, who at that time was my mother, would stand and say, "The Holy Ghost spoke from . . ." and read those passages that had been revealed to her as the saints spoke in tongues. The pastor expounded on these verses by relating them to other verses in the Old and New Testaments, with the saints following in their Bibles reading each passage aloud in unison. If the Holy Ghost had not spoken, the pastor might "bring a message" that explored a passage of scripture, relating it to other passages from both the Old and New Testaments. Mother Brown, while an effective preacher, was first and foremost a teacher who instructed the saints in the "Word of Truth."

On Sabbath afternoons, especially during the long summer days when the sun did not set until after 8 p.m., the service might be "turned over to the children." Children attended all three Sabbath services along with their parents, but on Sabbath afternoons they became the focus of activity and would read and respond to scriptures. They also went up to the front of the sanctuary and performed music on instruments that included piano, drums, accordion, Hawaiian steel guitar, and xylophone. Similarly, on the fifth Sunday of each month and during General Assembly, when our loosely affiliated sister churches in Brooklyn met with us, children performed to warm applause, encouragement, and praise. Some of the youth have gone on to compose church music and lyrics that not only express spiritual longing for salvation but also document the history of The Church, the centrality of the pastor, and the valuing of the founding saints' sacrifice.

Sabbath afternoon was also when testimony service took place, although any saint could testify at any time if they were so moved. The saints, including the youth, would rise and open with "Giving honor to God, his Son Jesus, the pastor, deacons, and saints" and then proceed to thank God for the blessings in their life. Testimonies often requested that other saints pray for the person, for example, that God would be with the saint during an upcoming doctor's visit or intervene with a supervisor at work who did not want to give the saint the Sabbath off. Saints ended their testimony with "Pray for me that I'll grow stronger in the Lord."

At the end of Sabbath evening service, the pastor announced, "Service is dismissed until nine o'clock tomorrow morning," and on Sabbath morning she said, "Service is dismissed until three o'clock this afternoon." Sabbath afternoon service ended when the sun set, which could be as early as 5 p.m. in the winter and as late as 8 p.m. in the summertime. Sabbath was over when the pastor rose and intoned, "The nineteenth Psalm and the fourteenth verse," and the saints rose and recited, "Let the words of my mouth and the meditation of my heart be acceptable in thy sight, O Lord, my strength and my redeemer. Amen."

The worship services profoundly engaged body, mind, emotions, time, resources, and the energies of the saints.

Law: Keeping the Commandments

Faith without works is dead.

James 2:20

Mother Brown's church was not the only Sanctified storefront church that the founding saints encountered on settling in Philadelphia. What distinguished it from many is that it was a "commandment-keeping church." Mother Brown taught the saints about the manifestation of indwelling spirit and Jesus's redemption, but she also taught the saints the "law," for "What doth it profit, my brethren, though a man say he hath faith, and have not works. Can faith save him? . . . But wilt thou know, O vain man, that faith without works is dead" (James 2:14, 20).

For founding and first-generation saints, the law had several dimensions, with sources in the Jewish Torah, the Christian Old Testament, and the New Testament gospels as well as paraenetic books of the New Testament containing advice and admonition written by the apostles to the early church. From the Old Testament, the saints repeated the Decalogue verbatim from the King James Version of Exodus 20:1:

> And God spake all these words, saying, I am the LORD thy God, which have brought thee out of the land of Egypt, out of the house of bondage.
>
> 1. Thou shalt have no other gods before me.
> 2. Thou shalt not make unto thee any graven image, or any likeness of any thing that is in heaven above, or that is in the earth beneath, or that is in the water under the earth: thou shalt not bow down thyself to them, nor serve them: for I the LORD thy God am a jealous God, visiting the iniquity of the fathers upon the children unto the third and fourth generation of them that hate me; and showing mercy unto thousands of them that love me, and keep my commandments.
> 3. Thou shalt not take the name of the LORD thy God in vain: for the LORD will not hold him guiltless that taketh his name in vain.
> 4. Remember the Sabbath day, to keep it holy. Six days shalt thou labor, and do all thy work: but the seventh day is the Sabbath of the LORD thy God: in it thou shalt not do any work, thou, nor thy son, nor thy daughter, thy manservant, nor thy maidservant, nor thy cattle, nor thy stranger that is within thy gates: for in six days the LORD made heaven and earth, the sea, and all that in them is, and rested the seventh day: wherefore the LORD blessed the Sabbath day, and hallowed it.
> 5. Honor thy father and thy mother that thy days may be long upon the land which the LORD thy God giveth thee.
> 6. Thou shalt not kill.
> 7. Thou shalt not commit adultery.
> 8. Thou shalt not steal.
> 9. Thou shalt not bear false witness against thy neighbor.

10. Thou shalt not covet thy neighbor's house, thou shalt not covet thy neighbor's wife, nor his manservant, nor his maidservant, nor his ox, nor his ass, nor any thing that is thy neighbor's.

The saints repeated these divinely given commandments verbatim and understood them literally, so that in addition to venerating the one true God and avoiding murder, adultery, covetousness, dishonoring their parents, stealing, and lying, they did not take photographs or have "images" in their homes. They kept Sabbath from sunset Friday to sunset Saturday, when secular activities such as watching television, listening to the radio, cooking, and washing dishes were avoided, in compliance with Isaiah 58:13. Significantly, special blessings accompanied Sabbath keeping, for as the Bible put it, "If thou turn thy foot from the Sabbath, not doing thy pleasure on my holy day; and call the Sabbath a delight, the holy of the Lord, honorable . . . I will cause thee to ride upon the high places of the earth, and feed thee with the heritage of Jacob, thy father, for the mouth of the Lord hath spoken it" (Isaiah 58:13).

Torah and Gospels Conflated

In addition to these fundamental commandments, law included selected Levitical rules and regulations from the Old Testament. While founding saints did not "keep kosher," they rigorously avoided pork and other "unclean" foods indicated in Leviticus 11 and Deuteronomy 14. First-generation saints did not eat shellfish (clams, shrimp, lobster, or other mollusks and crustaceans) because they lacked scales and fins. Saints were especially particular about the popular and accessible all-American hot dog. They usually purchased kosher hot dogs to cook at home, except for the hot dogs sold at the Jewish-owned Cherry's Kosher Restaurant in Strawberry Mansion. Certain saints, including Mother Brown, sometimes shopped at the Jewish market on Ninth Street.

The Church adopted another feature of Levitical instruction: after a saint gave birth to a child, she did not come to church for thirty-three days for a son and sixty-six days for a daughter. Indicating the selective nature of its observation of Levitical laws, however, menstruating women were not deemed "unclean" and prohibited from the sanctuary, as in some African Instituted Churches which selectively wed traditional African menstrual seclusion with the laws of Hebrew scripture (Crumbley 2006).

Law also included the injunctions and teachings of Jesus. The church's conflation of the Jewish Torah and Christian gospels is exemplified by the celebration of the Lord's Supper, which the first-generation saints referred to as both Passover and Communion. This ritual was celebrated only once a year, on the fourteenth day of the month of Abib, the exact date being determined in consultation with a Hebrew calendar (Exodus 34:18; Leviticus 23:5).

The saints were constantly reminded that the New Testament made it perfectly clear that Jesus was Jewish. Furthermore, he had not come to destroy the law or the prophets, but to fulfill them (Matthew 5:17). Jesus kept Sabbath, and his "last supper" was also his ancestors' last supper in Egypt. During the protracted communal fasting and praying that occurred for the month preceding Passover/Communion, Bible study tended to focus on the books of Exodus, Leviticus, and Numbers, and prophetic scriptures related to the Messiah and the death and resurrection of Jesus Christ.

As the admonishing and exhorting apostolic letters also contributed to the first generation's notion of law, their injunctions regarding women's dress were taken quite seriously. Women covered their heads at all times, did not cut their hair, dressed "in modest apparel," and comported themselves "as becometh holiness" (1 Corinthians 11:6; Titus 2:3; 1 Timothy 2:9). However, Mother Brown taught and preached despite the assertions of 1 Timothy 2:10–12: "Let the woman learn in silence with all subjection. But I suffer not a woman to teach, nor to usurp authority over the man, but to be in silence."

Law was understood to have both Old and New Testament sources and authority, and keeping all the commandments, especially the Sabbath, established a special covenantal relationship with God. This covenant guaranteed not only an intimate relationship between God and the saints of The Church but also blessings of well-being, wealth, and success, for as the saints and their children were frequently reminded: "And the LORD shall make thee the head, and not the tail; and thou shalt be above only, and thou shalt not be beneath; if that thou hearken unto the commandments of the LORD thy God, which I command thee this day, to observe and to do them" (Deuteronomy 28:13).

White Jews, Black Saints, and Chosenness

Unlike Bishop Cherry, who founded the Church of the Living God Pillar and Ground of Truth, and William S. Crowdy, who led the Church of God and Saints of Christ of God, also in Philadelphia, Mother Brown did not hold that her congregation represented the "true Jews." For her and the founding saints, the issue was not Jewishness but keeping the law, for by keeping the law the saints participated in the same promises and covenant that had existed between God and ancient Israel.

The relationship between Jewish law and Christian salvation, which Mother

Brown and the founding saints struggled with as they carved out their soteriology—that is, their understanding of salvation—was not a trivial matter. This issue has been debated since the apostles Peter and Paul disagreed over whether or not to circumcise non-Jewish converts to the newly emerging Christian faith (Galatians 2) and has informed institutional schism and theological debate throughout the history of Christianity (O'Neil 1975: 12–17, 53–58, 176–77; Jervis 1991: 11). Mother Brown approached the matter by grounding her argument in scripture. Citing germane passages, primarily from Romans 11, Mother Brown taught that through spiritual adoption "salvation is come unto the Gentiles": "And if some of the branches be broken off, and thou, being a wild olive tree, were grafted in among them, and with them partakers of the root and fatness of the olive tree, boast not against the branches. . . . blindness in part is happened to Israel, until the fullness of the Gentiles be come in" (Romans 11:17–19, 25).

The saints' identification with Jews was reinforced by the shared centrality of Old Testament law, especially keeping Sabbath and eating clean food, as well as the recognition that Jesus was a Jew. This connection tended to undermine anti-Semitism and led the saints to distinguish Jews from "other White people" by associating them with God's first chosen people from whom a higher standard was expected.

While I have explored the nuances of first-generation saints' interactions with and perceptions of Jews elsewhere (Crumbley 2000), it is important to note here that the saints criticized Jewish employers as freely as they commended them. When Elder Beverly's Aunt Julia, who also came from South Carolina, lived briefly with her niece, she helped a young man who reported how "hard" these Jewish employers "worked him" and how little they paid. They had him make a special soup for their Sabbath, but gave him only a cup of thin broth for his lunch. Elder Rose Nichols Horten shook her head when recalling what Jewish women "put [her] through" to prepare for the high holidays. The issue was not the hard work, for they were accustomed to heavy physical labor. Their complaint was that they were not compensated for the additional tasks, and so they chose not to work in those homes again.

Two of the elders' narratives contain critiques of Jewish women who distanced themselves from the economic plight of the Black women they employed. Elder Hannah's poignant experience of being "lined up like horses" contrasts dramatically with Allen Meyers's rather distanced observation about Jewish women's "need to have a domestic clean the house" at a salary of "25 cents per hour in the late 1940's" (Meyers 2002: 50). Elder Beverly commented that "they took care of themselves, and didn't care what it did to us," when a Jewish employer reported that she and her daughter were moving to a newly built, all-White neighborhood.

In contrast, the narratives of Elders Esther and Ronald tell of a Jewish next-door neighbor who refused to join the White flight from their neighborhood. The Kaufmanns, who employed Elder Jerald's father, wrote to him when he was overseas during the war. Meyers documents Hanna Silvers's fight for justice in Strawberry Mansion after it had become a Black neighborhood (Meyers 2002: 55). Despite acknowledging Jewish uses and abuses of White privilege to the detriment of Black people, the saints generally viewed Jews as God's people, among whom both good and bad were found. Jewish classmates in school were held up as models, not only to be emulated but also excelled (Crumbley 2007: 7, 18).

Law, Works, and Grace

For first-generation saints, academic excellence was normative: being the "head and not the tail" applied to the classroom as well as the workplace. On report cards, As were expected, Bs were acceptable, and Cs were tantamount to failure. The biblically grounded link between law and excellence was reinforced regularly by social-historical conditions and saints' shared values. As a child of the church, I grew up hearing that "an education is one thing no man can take away from you." This refrain, combined with the stories of how hard it was to get an education down South, made academic excellence seem the least a young person could do. The 1954 ruling in *Brown v. Board of Education* that desegregated public schools occurred around the time that the founding saints were raising children. This generation had access to educational opportunities that their parents had been denied, as well as the opportunity to compete on more equal terms in the job market (Crumbley 2008b: 77–78; Crumbley 2000: 14–16).

My parents, as well as my aunts and uncles, arranged their lives so that their children could attend Logan Demonstration School, an experimental elementary school located in an all-White and heavily Jewish neighborhood in the North Broad Street area of Philadelphia (Meyers 2002). We were among the first Black children to integrate the school and were greatly outnumbered by White students. I recall having to sing both "Dixie" and "Old Black Joe" from a school songbook, and a boy called Luke insisted that my blood was black like my skin! Yet, influenced as I was by the teachings and values of The Church, it never occurred to me that White students were anything more than fellow students; I never assumed that they would be my superiors. A sizeable number of the other students were Jewish, as they were at

Masterman Junior High School and the Philadelphia High School for Girls, which I attended later. My interactions with Jewish students at Logan might best be described as healthy competition bordering on sibling rivalry. I had no close Jewish friends until I was a student at Temple University, where I got to know two Jewish women who invited me to their homes. One was a redheaded woman of Russian Jewish background who lived in the Northeast; the other, Toni, was a witty and articulate woman whose parents owned a store in Chester.

There was no school bus service to Logan School; Philadelphia had not bussed students even before desegregation. While many of my White classmates lived within walking distance of the school, our parents had to transport us to and from school until we could manage the subway or the slower Broad Street "C" bus. Because not all saints owned cars and those who did had only one car for the two working parents, they set up carpools that included children from about five different households. Coordinating schedules must have been difficult for these working mothers and fathers, and sometimes the car was exceptionally crowded, but no one was ever left behind.

In the end, "keeping the commandments," especially Sabbath, was a source of salvation and "all the good things in life" for first-generation saints, who were at ease with being "separate and peculiar." They saw themselves as a light not only to a sinful world but also to so-called Christians who treated Sunday as the Sabbath. Unlike some Sanctified and Pentecostal churches that have been associated with anti-intellectualism, The Church viewed educational excellence as a sign that one was a commandment-keeper. Keeping the law enhanced the self-image of founding saints and their children, countering the dominant society's racialized images of Black people by fostering an invaluable combination of a covenant-grounded sense of self-worth with a competitive formal education.

This discussion of law is incomplete without reflecting on law and love. When I have tried to describe the place of law in the life of The Church to non-commandment-keepers, at some point they raise the issue of legalism, or salvation by works. Accusations of exchanged, bartered, and earned salvation are leveled, and they query, "What about grace?" Additionally, they charge that The Church has dehistoricized itself by standing outside the traditions of the early church. What has been almost impossible to communicate to my fellow Christians is that, within this belief system, grace goes hand in hand with an experience of law as duty steeped in love. In this light, divine law is a gift that gives structure, meaning, and order to life, and because law affects all of daily life, it is a constant reminder of the intimate connection we have with the divine. Being human, we constantly break the law; but, as the Old Testament relates time and again, God always forgives, restores, and saves. Herein lies grace, which for Christians culminates in Jesus. Moreover, we model our lives on Jesus, who was Jewish. Out of love and reverence for him, the saints keep the law of his ancestors, as he did. Regarding the charge that The Church situates itself outside traditions of the early church, that depends on which early church is claimed. The saints see themselves standing in the early church tradition, not Christianity after it was co-opted and reformulated by the Roman Empire but the faith when it was still a revitalization movement within Judaism and the first Christians kept Sabbath. Why be like Constantine when you can be like Jesus?

Holiness: "In but Not of" the World

Having therefore these promises, dearly beloved, let us cleanse ourselves from all filthiness of the flesh and spirit, perfecting holiness in the fear of God.

2 Corinthians 7:1

The founding saints saw themselves as a "strange and peculiar people," not only because they kept God's commandments (Deuteronomy 26:18) but also because Jesus died so "that he might redeem us from all iniquity, and purify unto himself a peculiar people, zealous of good works," who had been called "out of darkness into his marvelous light" (Titus 2:14; 1 Peter 2:9). To walk in this light was to live a life of holiness.

Holiness, here, refers to a way of life best described by Mother Brown's injunction that we "wear the world like a loose garment." Saints should live in the world but simultaneously distance themselves from it and from the people in it, being in, but not of, the world (John 17:11, 16). Founding saints knew that they had been "called to come out from among them . . . be ye separate . . . and touch not the unclean thing" (2 Corinthians 6:7).

Holiness and Danger

For first-generation saints, wearing the world like a loose garment meant that the world was less a place within which you lived and more like a thin sheath of removable apparel, barely worth noticing. The ability to slough it off in an instant was crucial, for founding saints had embraced Mother Brown's profoundly millenarian teachings. The millennium, a thousand-year reign of Jesus Christ in which the saints would rule with him until God established his Kingdom, was understood to be imminent. Employing Old Testament prophecies, a date in the late 1960s was calculated for "the end," both as the absolute "end of time" and more loosely as "the time of the end." Either way, Christ's return was understood to be so imminent that some saints would not see death (1 Corinthians 15:51–52).

Growing up in this milieu of millennial anticipation, I imagined that the Parousia—the second coming of Christ—would be marked by a bright light and a loud explosion, but then I may have been conflating the apocalypse with the new danger I was being prepared for at school. Regular air raid drills were held at Logan to teach us how to protect ourselves during an atomic bomb attack. Like Bert the Turtle in the Civil Defense Administration pamphlets sent to public schools in the 1950s, we were taught to "duck and cover" to protect ourselves—as if that would actually protect us from the kind of incineration the United States had inflicted on Hiroshima and Nagasaki.[2]

Fear laced those times. While this 1951 civil defense drill reminded us that "we must all get ready now, so we know how to save ourselves," Matthew 25:13 exhorted us to "Watch therefore, for ye know neither the day nor the hour wherein the Son of man cometh." News reports reminded us of how dangerous the present could be for youth like fourteen-year-old Emmett Till, a Chicago native lynched and mutilated in Money, Mississippi, in 1955, reportedly for whistling at a White woman. Indeed, my mother spoke of being on pins and needles when my brother Stephen was visiting with our Uncle Jim in Edgefield, South Carolina, for fear that her Philadelphia-raised son might unknowingly digress from southern racial etiquette and be murdered. Emmett Till's brutal murder, along with the public assassinations of Medgar Evers (1963), Malcolm X (1965), and Martin Luther King Jr. (1968), brought home the ease with which Black lives could be ended in America, especially when Blacks showed elements of the spontaneity, assertiveness, self-determination, and strategic organizational skill so valued in their White counterparts. The assassinations of President John F. Kennedy (1963) and his brother, former Attorney General Robert F. Kennedy (1968), overlay these times with such a sense of dangerous unraveling that the millennium offered a welcome reprieve—at least for those who were "ready."

Prohibitions, Comportment, and Exceptions

For founding and first-generation saints, the boundaries between The Church and the world were explicit. Mother Brown taught that to be saved required strict separation from the world, which meant not being "unequally yoked together with unbelievers" (2 Corinthians 6:14). Unbelievers, or "worldly" people, might include relatives as well as acquaintances. As Elder April observed, the resulting "dividing line" caused familial rifts that the saints accepted as an unavoidable aspect of "taking a stand." Numbered among "unbelievers" were members of other churches, including the Sabbath-keeping and Sanctified storefront churches that proliferated in North Philadelphia. Like many children of the saints, I grew up virtually unaware of the larger religious life of the city, although occasionally Mother Brown referred to Bishop Johnson, Daddy Grace, and Father Divine, usually pointing out their digressions from the truth. Only when, as a divinity school student, I came across Arthur Huff Fauset's *Black Gods of the Metropolis* did it become clear that The Church was embedded within a vast and variegated Black religious landscape in post–World War II Philadelphia. The Church had emerged against a background of Black Seventh Day Adventists and Black Jews who "kept Sabbath" and "ate clean." Other women, such as Mother Dabney, Bishop Ida Robinson, and Bishop Tate, had pioneered and led Holiness-Pentecostal congregations in Philadelphia. To the children growing up in The Church, however, these other churches were as foreign as the rest of the world.

Holiness entailed avoiding not only unbelievers but also worldly places and activities. Founding saints did not attend clubs, bars, or social gatherings with nonmembers. An exception was made for business-related events, such as annual picnics at a local amusement park for the families of postal workers and of Strick's employees. Founding saints, expecting the imminent end of the world in a millennial apocalypse, did not become involved in political organizations or even vote. Parents did attend PTA meetings at their children's schools, however. Church youth did not go to movie theaters and did not join the Girl or Boy Scouts. They participated in sleepovers only with other children of The Church, not with schoolmates. They did not attend sports events, including the University of Pennsylvania–sponsored track and field "Penn Relays," or "Negro Olympics" (Wiggins and Miller 2003: 247). Dancing was prohibited, so they did not attend parties or go to the shows and dances held at the renowned Uptown Theater at Broad Street and Susquehanna Avenue, where Martha Reeves and the Vandellas, Otis Redding, the Temptations, B. B. King, Ray Charles, James Brown, Jackie Wilson, Patti LaBelle and the Blue Bells, Diana Ross and the Supremes, and the Jackson Five, among other R & B stars, regularly performed.[3]

The Church sponsored numerous activities for children, including an annual picnic held at the Philadelphia Zoo sponsored by the Elders Cromwell, with Elder Beverly's signature fried chicken and homemade potato salad gracing the picnic menu. During a weeklong series of events during the summer called the Dedication, children were taken on educational outings to such places as the Benjamin Franklin Institute of Technology, the Philadelphia Museum of Art, the outdoor Rodin Museum, and the Museum of Natural Sciences. We were also taken to the city's Fairmount Park, including Smith Memorial Playground and Playhouse with its gigantic wooden slide.

Boundaries between The Church and the world were permeable at points of intersection that were work-related or educational. Although, like all the saints' children, I was forbidden to attend movies, as a teenager I attended Philadelphia Orchestra performances as well as live theatre. While I could not hang out with schoolmates after school because they were worldly, I spent hours roaming and completing my homework in the seemingly endless corridors of exhibits in the Philadelphia Museum of Art.

Saints were supposed to behave "as becometh holiness" (Titus 2:3), expressed in general comportment and dress codes. Women covered their heads; little girls wore wide ribbons. Sisters wore long or three-quarter-length sleeves. Wearing a bathing suit was regarded as a form of "nakedness." Women also avoided apparel that was similar to men's attire, including pants and shorts, in keeping with the text "The woman shall not wear that which pertaineth unto a man, neither shall a man put on a woman's garment: for all that do so are abomination unto the LORD thy God" (Deuteronomy 22:5). Constraints on males were not as extensive, and the male saints did not appear so obviously different from their counterparts in the world. They wore long pants and shirts, avoiding shorts. During Sabbath, women and girls wore white dresses and mantles that hung down their backs, while males wore dark suits, white shirts, and bow ties. Proper comportment meant that slang was meticulously avoided. Youth did not even use the common expression "OK," or "okey-dokey."

Scripture: Rightly Dividing the Word of Truth

Study to shew thyself approved unto God, a workman that needeth not to be ashamed, rightly dividing the word of truth.

2 Timothy 2:15

Biblical Revelation, Cumulative Revelation

Each of the four elements of being saved—law, holiness, scripture, and spirit—is introduced with a passage of scripture that corroborates and validates it, because for the founding and first-generation saints all aspects of salvation are grounded in scripture. The centrality of law is articulated in James 2:20, which asserts that faith without works is dead. The rigor of holiness is affirmed by the exhortation in 2 Corinthians 7:1 that saints should perfect holiness in their lives. The saints are directed to study and carefully parse out scripture's meaning as a demonstration that they are, indeed, God's workers (2 Timothy 2:15). Even the Holy Ghost, which under no circumstances is to be "quenched" (1 Thessalonians 5:19), is constrained by the Bible, for it is through scripture that the Holy Ghost speaks.

For the founding saints, the "Word of Truth" alluded to in 2 Timothy 2:15 is not limited to the New Testament. First-generation saints valued both the Old and New Testaments, which were studied with equal care, committed to memory, and understood to corroborate each other. Jesus, a Jew, kept the Old Testament laws and was the subject and voice of the gospels, as well as inspiration for the paraenetic letters of the apostles. The Bible is the source of divine revelation, that is, God's will and the way for salvation. Interpreting scripture, however, is a complex task: its meaning is not merely a matter "of any private interpretation" (2 Peter 1:20). Despite their literal approach to the Bible, founding saints saw scripture as a set of texts into which each saint and The Church as a whole must delve deeply for understanding. Mother Brown taught that it behooves every saint "to work out your own salvation with fear and trembling" (Philippians 2:12).

This orientation promoted an understanding of the Bible as a source of ongoing, "cumulative" revelation rather than fixed or "perfect" revelation. This openness helps to explain the ease with which the saints accepted the passing of the date calculated for "the end." As Elder Frank pointed out, "You learn as you go on, and you grow as you go on." Although Mother Brown taught this perspective to the saints, it competed with the notion of her as God's "anointed." While this disparity was a source of tension, it helped enable The Church to survive the death of the founder. As central as her personality was to the organizational cohesion of the founding generation, God, speaking through the "Word of Truth," is always the final arbiter.

Bible Study

Mother Brown rarely "preached" a sermon while standing at the podium, but rather "taught" what the Holy Ghost spoke by directing the saints to germane verses in the Old and New Testaments, which the saints located in their Bibles and then read aloud together.

At Tuesday Bible study services, the saints worked their way through the

Bible from Genesis to Revelation. Each saint stood and read a verse of the Bible section designated for that night. Mother Brown led Bible study, but each saint was allowed to present what "to their mind" the scripture was saying. Children participated when it was their turn to stand and read, their mothers or neighbors helping with unfamiliar words. For children too young to read but old enough to be conscious of the process, mothers would read the verse phrase by phrase and the child would repeat after her, interjecting more words as their literacy skills improved. The Bible was often one of the first books that a child of The Church learned to read. All were encouraged to participate in Bible study and state what the text "said" to them, and children could join in the conversation as soon as they were able.

The assertion, "The Bible says," ended debate, because biblical authority is the ultimate authority. At the same time, scripture was the subject of spiritual and intellectual reflection, which produced not so much a creed as an ongoing revelation of how one is to behave in the world. James Bielo, in his research on the Lutheran Church–Missouri Synod, found that the significance of Bible study lay not so much in its intellectual byproduct as in the process of studying a holy text and affirming a shared faith (Bielo 2008: 1, 2, 5, 7, 18–19). Similarly, for founding saints, Bible study entailed the affirmation of a shared faith grounded in Holy Scripture. In addition, for founding saints and their children, Bible study fostered literacy, mental discipline, and skill for the public presentation of self, which had been denied to many founding saints by an underfunded and unequal education in the segregated public school systems of their southern hometowns. Bible study also engaged their children in the exercise of intellectual discipline as groundwork for academic excellence.

As adults, the saints' jobs offered few opportunities for stimulating intellectual exchange, as racial discrimination meant that Black men and women worked longer hours at lower wages to meet the economic needs of their families. They had little time for intellectual endeavors, such as enrolling in continuing education. During Bible study, however, the saints were encouraged not only to study scripture but also to share their ideas publicly and freely. Their children grew up in an environment that provided divinely sanctioned preparation for the presentation of self in the larger society. When speaking their memorized "pieces," youth were taught how to project their voices, articulate clearly, and comport themselves with dignity. In the process, they learned that what they had to say mattered (Crumbley 2008b: 76–83). Additionally, youth were regularly reminded to choose the divine gift of wisdom and directed to this biblical passage: "And God said to Solomon,

Because this was in thine heart, and thou hast not asked riches, wealth, or honour, nor the life of thine enemies, neither yet hast asked long life; but hast asked wisdom and knowledge for thyself, that thou mayest judge my people, over whom I have made thee king: Wisdom and knowledge is granted unto thee; and I will give thee riches, and wealth, and honour, such as none of the kings have had that have been before thee, neither shall there any after thee have the like" (2 Chronicles 1:10–12).

Adult saints not only studied scripture in church and at home, but also memorized and recited long biblical passages for special services devoted to this performance, such as the annual Dedication. At every quarterly General Assembly, the young people repeated the "pieces" that Mother Brown had them commit to memory. For children, these might be poems, which the pastor personally selected and assigned. As youth matured, they were expected to memorize progressively longer passages of scripture. The very young began by memorizing the shortest verse in the Bible, John 11:35: "Jesus wept." Sometimes the little ones also wept as they repeated these two words after their mothers in front of the congregation. Soon, however, they developed confidence and a personal style encouraged by high praise and enthusiastic applause from the congregation.

Biblical Primacy and Doctrinal Fusion

"Tell them that we believe in the Bible." This is what my mother told me to tell the girls at school when they pressed me to explain why I dressed differently, avoided eating pork, and attended church on Saturdays. But the Bible says many things, necessarily making creeds selective. What The Church emphasized had much to do with what Mother Brown had brought to it from her religious journey. Much of our church discipline drew from the *Doctrinal Points of the Church of God (7th Day Apostolic) Re-organized 1933*, into which "the original 40 points of doctrine are herein incorporated, having been established in the year 1933, and were accepted by the ministerial council assembled at Salem, West Virginia, March 5, 1950, and reaffirmed by the Apostolic Council, July 7, 1951" (Church of God 1951). The "points" articulate biblically buttressed beliefs and practices, including: keeping the Ten Commandments, especially Sabbath; eating clean food; separation from worldly people and places; and Old Testament prophecies related to the millennium. Nevertheless, Mother Brown took seriously the document's opening statement that "these articles of faith are not to be construed a closed creed, as the Church of God stands ready at all times to consider further light of the Bible (2 Timothy 2:15; 1 John 1:7)." The Church never addressed point 23, a pacifist position on "carnal warfare," and the saints spoke in tongues despite point 6, "That we stand opposed to the gibberish called 'speaking in tongues.'"

Mother Brown spoke of herself as "Baptist bred and Baptist born," but during her peregrinations in the North she was exposed to various Holiness, Pentecostal, and Sabbatarian traditions including the Seventh Day Adventists. In Orange, New Jersey, she was introduced to the "Sabbath Truth" in the Church of God Seventh Day. From the time she arrived in Philadelphia in 1914 until 1937, she ministered in association with this faith community, which was led by Brother Gayle, breaking with him over matters of moral comportment and doctrinal interpretation.

Mother Brown distanced The Church from other Sabbath-keeping churches in Philadelphia during the 1940s and 1950s by focusing on how they differed from The Church and digressed from scripture. For example, Mother Brown, like the Seventh Day Adventists, took seriously Levitical dietary codes, the Decalogue, and the Sabbath. However, she asserted that just as they physically placed the book of their prophet Ellen G. White atop the Bible in their sanctuary, so they placed her prophecies above biblical teachings. Bishop Cherry's Church of the Living God Pillar and Ground of Truth "kept the commandments," observed Sabbath, and prohibited smoking, dancing, drinking alcohol, and taking photographs. However, she explained, unlike The Church, its members did not speak in tongues or "shout." Furthermore, Cherry's followers claimed that they were the true Jews and Jesus was Black, which she saw as a gross deviation from scripture. In contrast, Mother Brown taught that the saints were heirs to the promise made to the Jews not because of a genetic connection to Abraham but by the spiritual in-grafting of the Gentiles through redemption (Romans 11:17–24). This spiritual adoption through Jesus Christ required neither describing ourselves as Jewish nor deprecating White Jews.

Similarly, without articulating the notion of "trinity," Mother Brown took issue with the "Jesus-only" teaching of Bishop Johnson, leader of the Church of the Lord Jesus Christ of the Apostolic Faith. He had amassed a large following at his nearby church on Twenty-second and Montgomery with his internationally broadcast sermons (Hopper 2008: 40). Mother Brown interpreted his "Jesus-only" doctrine as equating Jesus with God, which she argued diverged from Jesus's own words when he spoke of himself as the "Son of God." This stance may well have been her response to the Apostolic "oneness" movement within Pentecostalism, which affirmed that the Father, Son, and Holy Spirit are only "titles" of God, not distinct persons (Daniels

2003: 167). Mother Brown was also keenly aware of other Sanctified churches in North Philly at the time. For example, Mother Dabney's COGIC Garden of Prayer was located just around the corner from where the saints met above the horse stable.

The selective use of the *Doctrinal Points*, the compliance with selected Levitical law, and the spirituality of Sanctified religion all inform the beliefs and practices of The Church in a way that echoes Barbara Savage's observation about "the adventuresome range of religious ideas and practices" that populated the diverse religious landscapes of Great Migration Philadelphia (Savage 2002: x, xvi).

Unbiblical Celebrations and Gendered Scripture

If a common Christian practice was not mentioned in the Bible, it was invalidated and avoided by founding saints. For example, children were taught the pagan origins of Christmas and Easter. Santa Claus was represented as the first lie that parents told their children, and Christmas trees were a pagan celebration anticipating spring with evergreens. Like their schoolmates, children of The Church received holiday gifts, often musical instruments played during worship service, but the occasion was referred to as "Chanukah."

Similarly, there was no biblical basis for Sunday worship. The custom was understood to be a pagan Roman tradition of sun worship entirely distinct from, and even in opposition to, Sabbath-keeping, which was commanded by God and observed by Jesus. In the same vein, the practice of taking communion often or regularly was un-biblical, as Jesus's last supper was part of the Passover observance that occurs once a year. So the saints took communion only once a year, preceding it with at least a month of frequent tarries (periods of extensive prayer, fasting, and Bible study), carefully determining the date with a Jewish lunar calendar, and using the terms "Passover" and "communion" interchangeably for this ritual observance.

As in most literal biblical traditions, biblical authority in The Church is employed selectively. Nowhere is this selectivity more obvious than in matters of gender. While other faiths argue against female ordination by quoting Timothy 2:11–15 and Ephesians 5:22, in The Church these passages, though not entirely dismissed, were consistently offset by the passage in Galatians 3:28 that "in Christ there is neither male nor female" and by the fact that the Bible includes narratives about Judge Deborah in the Old Testament and the beloved "Elect Lady" of the New Testament.

Spirit: Filled with the Holy Ghost

Quench not the Spirit.

1 Thessalonians 5:19

While the Bible legitimates the four elements of salvation, Spirit infuses them all. To "behave as becometh holiness" and to keep the commandments entails more than mere self-discipline; it requires "receiving" the baptism of the Holy Ghost, being "born again," and living a new life. This sentiment is communicated in a song favored by Brother Jonathan Nichols, which was composed by blind street evangelist Reverend Gary Davis, another participant in the Great Migration:

> Things I used to do I don't do no more (3x)
> been a great change since I been born
> Things I used to say I don't say no more (3x)
> been a great change since I been born
> Lies I used to tell I don't tell no more (3x)
> been a great change since I been born
> People I used to would hate I don't hate no more (3x)
> Great change since I been born
> Roads I used to would walk I don't walk no more (3x)
> been a great change since I been born.[4]

In addition to keeping the saints in the law and the "way of holiness," the Holy Ghost actively guides the saints through scripture, as Jesus promised his followers: "It is expedient for you that I go away: for if I go not away, the Comforter will not come unto you; but if I depart, I will send him unto you.... Howbeit when he, the Spirit of truth, is come, he will guide you into all truth: for he shall not speak of himself; but whatsoever he shall hear, that shall he speak: and he will shew you things to come" (John 16:7, 13).

For founding saints, the Holy Ghost "speaks" in unknown tongues. In turn, a Holy Ghost–filled interpreter of tongues reads from the scripture that the Holy Ghost speaks to "edify" the church (1 Corinthians 14:5). The mystical experience of being filled with the Holy Ghost and the intellectual activity of studying scripture went hand in hand for first-generation saints. They believed that speaking in tongues is a "sign" of true followers of Jesus (Mark 16:17). First-generation saints were also convinced that the Holy Ghost reveals "things to come" through Old Testament prophecies; they studied those prophecies regarding the millennium with special care.

The saints regard the Holy Ghost as a source of healing power, as Jesus asserted: "The Spirit of the Lord is upon me, because he hath anointed me to preach the gospel to the poor; he hath sent me to heal the brokenhearted, to preach deliverance to the captives, and recovering of sight to the blind, to set at liberty them that are bruised" (Luke 4:18). For first-generation saints, healing pertained not just to the body but also to the mind, as well as to situations in their lives. When doctors could not arrive at a diagnosis, or treatment was too costly or nonexistent, Mother Brown, who always could "get a prayer through," laid hands on the sick. She and the head saints also laid hands on those plagued by deep mental distress, protracted unemployment, or an impending deadline to repay a loan.

Pressing Through, Shouting, and Tarrying

The Holy Ghost is active in the bodies as well as the lives of the saints. It is manifest when saints "press through" or "shout," carried away by holy dance. The sacred dance of shouting is biblically legitimated as a delight to God, for King David shamelessly "danced before the Lord with all his might" to the point of nakedness (2 Samuel 6:14–23). A single saint might start to shout, but when the Spirit is high more saints joined in a communal shout, with the saints playing the piano or the drums sometimes leaving their instruments to join in.

"Pressing through" entails praying with one's whole self—body, mind, and spirit—until the repeated name of Jesus "becomes tongues." Pressing through entails much more than this simple-sounding technique suggests, however. Like any mystical experience, being filled with the Holy Ghost's power defies articulation. An especially powerful account comes from James Baldwin, who was raised up in a storefront church and, after "getting saved" at the age of fourteen, preached throughout Harlem, where his parents had arrived during the Great Migration (Baldwin 1948: 29, 42). "While John watched, the Power struck someone, a man or woman; they cried out, a long wordless crying, and arms outstretched like wings, they began the Shout. Someone moved a chair a little to give them room ... then another cry, another dancer; then the tambourines began again, and the voices rose again, and the music swept on again, like fire, or flood, or judgment. Then the church seemed to swell with the Power it held and like a planet rocking in space, the temple rocked with the Power of God" (Baldwin 1953: 15). Pressing through is not likely to happen the first time the prospective saint attempts it. It may well be preceded by tarrying—protracted praying and fasting—during which the prospective saint engages in intense Bible study.

Once "received," the Holy Ghost must be maintained. First-generation saints regularly tarried both as individuals and communally. At any time, a saint may go on a fast, during which they intensified their Bible reading with a view to "growing stronger in the Lord." Mother Brown might "call a tarry" when she felt led to do so for the spiritual well-being of The Church. A month of communal "tarries" preceded the Passover/Communion. Held over the weekend, these tarries entailed fasting, with adults taking only water, though bouillon and saltines were allowed if needed. Mother Brown regularly made a large pot of soup which, along with soup provided by parents, sustained children during the fast. During tarries, saints stayed overnight at the church, making pallets for sleeping on the floor in places that roughly corresponded to where they usually sat during services.

Holy Ghost infilling is profoundly democratic. This divine knowing does not require protracted or permanent retreat from mundane reality, vows of celibacy, or long training to master technique. Nor does it represent an anti-authoritarian protest against organized religion and fundamentalism, as some scholars have suggested (Soelle 2006: 34, 61–67). Being filled with the Holy Ghost occurs *within* the structures of this Bible-based church. By tarrying, a saint may not only worship but "experience" the Holy.

This experience of the spirit was so important that, during worship, the shout was never arbitrarily cut short, in accordance with the biblical injunction "Quench not the Spirit." A saint might break out in tongues during a sermon or start shouting during a moving musical performance if the spirit struck him or her. In this light, music was not performed *for* an audience but *with* a spirit-filled congregation whose members enter the musical moment with clapping, singing, and swaying. What in other churches might represent a transgression of liturgical boundaries here represents junctures where the spirit breaks through liturgical form (Dodson and Gilkes 1995).

The blurring of boundaries between audience and performance, pulpit and pews, has been noted in other Black Sanctified congregations. Melvin Williams describes the African American Zion Holiness (COGIC) congregation as "a church where they are the performers rather than the audience" (Williams 1974: 11). Among Jamaican Pentecostals, John Hopkins noted, music was "fundamental" to religious expression and comprised half the service; it involved singing "with the choir scarcely differentiated from the rest of the people" and was accompanied by handclapping and tambourines (Hopkins 1978: 23, 26, 29–30, 32).

Shouting was accommodated temporally, spatially, and through designated personnel. Temporally, the shout lasted as long as the spirit was high.

Spatially, at the start of a service, ushers removed chairs from the inner aisle to create space for saints to shout freely and safely. Specific saints were designated to "hold" shouting saints so they would not hurt themselves or others, while the shouting saints were in altered states with eyes closed. If the spirit were especially high, an usher also might start shouting and have to be held. Even after the chairs had been returned to their original position, the Holy Ghost could fall and a saint might shout between the rows of chairs, which were pushed aside to make room.

Privileging Spirit and Pressing Through

The accommodation of the shout in The Church demonstrates the degree to which founding and first-generation saints privileged spirit. Robert Franklin identifies the shout as an important feature of "southern, rural, Black religion" that includes "ecstatic utterance, weeping, speaking in tongues, spontaneous singing, dancing, running and other forms of behaviors associated with revivalist piety and with some African traditional religions" (Franklin 1989: 18). While the ring shout of the Gullah is well known, Guy and Candie Carawan observed shouting without the ring among the Gullah of Johns Island, transforming the entire sacred space into shouting space (Carawan with Carawan 1995). Nor is the shout limited to the Gullah or explicitly Sanctified churches. Timothy Nelson observed the pastor of a Holy Ghost–filled AME church in Charleston, South Carolina, encourage his congregation members to shout and speak in tongues, defending these practices by alluding to Methodist origins of American Holiness (Nelson 2005: 43).

In Jamaican Pentecostalism, John Hopkins observed, "possession by the Holy Ghost occurred at high points of preaching" (Hopkins 1978: 27). Spirit-privileging churches do not draw only people of African descent, as I have explored elsewhere (Crumbley 2008c: 76). Hopkins has argued that Black Jamaican Pentecostal churches differed from the White American churches from which they derived institutionally in the way they "bring on" the Holy Ghost. White American Pentecostals bring on the Spirit through "concentration and prayer," while Black Jamaican Pentecostals do so through communal worship, during which music becomes a "*means* to the experience" (emphasis added). Furthermore, Hopkins suggests that, for worshippers of African descent, the "ultimate end" of the service is "possession by the Holy Spirit" (Hopkins 1978: 25, 28, 34). Building on Hopkins, I suggest that there are spirit-privileging elements in both European American and African religious traditions. I also suggest that the European American tradition selectively reinforces and legitimates the African tradition in the religious practices of the Black Jamaican Pentecostals Hopkins studied and in the Sanctified church that is the subject of this book. I am arguing, then, that European American revivalism, which made personal knowledge of embodied spirit central to the Christian experience, reinforced such spirit-privileging elements in West African spiritualities as spirit possession. In light of this shared affirmation of overarching spiritual power, is it so surprising that during the nineteenth-century emergence of Holiness and Pentecostalism (and again during the twenty-first-century Memphis Miracle) "saved" Blacks and Whites transcended American conventions of racial separation to worship together?

The particulars of an individual pressing through in The Church entail that person repeating the name of Jesus until they begin speaking in tongues. With the help of "head saints," the supplicant is rolled on the floor, rocked, and moved freely to the rhythm of the piano and drums in the background. After saints press through and "receive the Holy Ghost," they rise from the floor and engage in the shout. "Dancing in the spirit" is found throughout the Atlantic African Diaspora and has been associated with possession by divinity, whether by the Holy Ghost or the Yoruba *orixa* divinities. This possession experience represents what Rachel Harding calls a transforming and "privileged form of communication with the spirit," during which dancing bodies of devotees both "echo and beckon" divinity (Harding 2006: 16).

It is worth noting that in The Church females are central to the pressing-through process, bringing to mind Harding's observation that, in the African-derived Candomblé religion of Afro-Brazilians in Bahia, women "are the main resource of devotional labor" (Harding 2006: 13). Additionally, the physical effort that is part of pressing through is reminiscent of "struggling" in the Church of the Lord, an Aladura church that selectively weds Yoruba and Christian traditions, including Holiness and Pentecostalism introduced by missionaries and their literature.[5] "Struggling" can entail rolling, prostrating oneself, running, and other forms of physical exertion. Similarly, the evoking of the spirit in The Church through the repetition of the name of Jesus resonates with my observations in Christ Apostolic Church, another Aladura church that I studied during my fieldwork on African Instituted Churches in Nigeria. In Christ Apostolic worship, it was not unusual for the congregation to repeatedly shout en masse during prayer, "Sokale!" calling the Holy Ghost to "Come down!" Such engagement of the body in the pursuit of spiritual heights not only points to interesting parallels, but also identifies an agenda for future comparative research in the global study of Black religious expressions.

The Sanctified Female Body

Hopkins points out an intriguing contradiction: the physical body is central to worship in churches whose teachings associate the body with carnality and sin (Hopkins 1978: 25–26). For insight into this question, he turns to the cultural history of enslaved Africans, arguing that because "recognizable manifestations of African religion were suppressed, specific African beliefs and practices survived only in incoherent fragments in Jamaica." These include such practices as spirit possession, drumming, and "magical techniques" as well as "attitudes and approaches" toward religion, which continue "to operate in Jamaica as they had in Africa" (Hopkins 1978: 24). This view finds persuasive echoes in other spirit-privileging churches formed by people of African descent.

Diane Austin-Broos elucidates the nuances of cultural change that Hopkins implies by insightfully exploring cultural and historical dimensions of "eudemonia," or profound joyfulness, of Jamaican Pentecostal worship. Austin-Broos argues that Pentecostalism unites "psyche with soma" and conjoins biblically grounded moral discipline with the joyous celebration of physical and social well-being (Smith 1997: xviii; Austin-Broos 1997: 6–7, 13). For Austin-Broos, the capacity of Jamaican Pentecostals to accommodate such seeming opposites can be traced to non-dualistic West African legacies in which good and evil are "ambivalent companions."

In line with Hopkins, Austin-Broos argues that the enslaved bodies of West African descendents, despite the constraints of slavery, became foremost culture-carriers of West African cosmologies. Pentecostalism's physically expressive worship forms reinforced the positive sense of the human body as a vehicle of divinity found in West African spirit possession and religious dance forms. Simultaneously, Pentecostalism's world-rejecting, moralistic, and ascetic features lend social propriety and credibility to church members, who tend to be from the poorer, less educated, darker-skinned social strata of Jamaican society. Austin-Broos skillfully elucidated the process by which the West African cosmological "trick" infuses Pentecostalism with an element of African spirituality that "sanctifies" both the sinful body and forbidden secular dance within the context of worship. She observed that Pentecostal worship becomes an arena of both eudemonia and Pentecostal piety. Within this non-dualistic cosmology, not only are bodies and minds healed, but so are social inequalities (Austin-Broos 1997: 34–35, 38, 116, 156, 195–204, 233–34).

Similarly, in his study of the Zion COGIC congregation, Melvin Williams noted the "ambivalence" of the very physical manifestation of the spirit within a constellation of rituals and symbols that surround the body with negativity and sin. He turned to psychology to explore what he described as an "obsessive" concern over "sexual potency of the body" and preoccupation with covering the female body, which is represented as a source of temptation (Williams 1974: 124–33). Hopkins and Austin-Broos employ psychosexual explanations for the paradoxes surrounding the body in spirit-privileging churches. For example, Hopkins refers to spirit possession as "sexual surrender to Jesus" (Hopkins 1978: 26), and Austin-Broos observes that female members "have a strong sense that in-filling involves entry of the Spirit through the vagina—a process not described as such but sometimes signaled by tapping the abdomen. The Spirit fills the cavity of the belly, now cleansed of unsanctified semen, and moves up to the heart in order to revive the soul" (Austin-Broos 1997: 146). Such psychosexual explanations for infilling by the Holy Ghost recall the description of a storefront church service during which a woman "suddenly . . . reached a climax and fell to the floor" (Eddy 1958–59: 73).

Human sexuality, which I personally view as a delight and a gift, is a thread interwoven throughout our humanity, which to varying degrees and in myriad ways permeates all that we do. Still, I am uncomfortable with psychological explanations that would reduce the infilling of the Holy Ghost to sexuality. Not only do such explanations overly simplify the complexity of this religious experience, but they contribute to the ambivalently charged sexualizing of the Black body in Western intellectual traditions (Rigby 1996: 9–10; Pandian 1985: 70–84). I am, nevertheless, very much at ease with Austin-Broos's notion of "eudemonia" to explore the sheer joy that accompanies the religious experience of Holy Ghost infilling. Drawing on the works of Roger Caillois (Caillois 1961), I would add to her conceptualization of eudemonia the dimension of "holy paideia"—that is, moving the body in space in spontaneous, pleasurable ways that celebrate the ecstasy of divine connection.

Dealing with the body in the study of religion is "more than a notion." As Rebecca Norris has remarked, this line of scholarly inquiry is complicated by dualistic and dichotomous conceptualizations of the body in western culture (Norris 2001: 112; also see Norris 2005, 2009). In a similar vein, Timothy Landry, drawing on Ann Stoler's work among the Songhai, reminds us that all of us, including scholars, are products of socially constructed sensorial landscapes. Sensorial landscapes vary cross-culturally and privilege certain senses over others, and in the West, we tend to favor the sense of sight.

Thus, the anthropological fieldworker becomes an "observer" who "watches" those she studies, privileging what can be seen to the virtual exclusion of that which might be experienced as bodily feeling. As Landry explains, we leave a lot out of the ethnographic portraits we write, publish, and teach to our students. These omissions include how the body of the researcher informs the ethnographic process. Alternatively, Landry embraced "the total ethnosensorium" of spirit possession and came to know sacred space in Haitian Vodun as circumscribed not only by the sanctuary but also by the body of the practitioner (Landry 2008).

Not all anthropologists are prepared or inclined to follow Landry's exhortation to do "anthropology through our bodies"; nor must they be, for outsider positioning has produced respectful and moving ethnographic insights. Still, like Landry, I would like to see the conventional visually oriented ethnosensorium expanded to take more seriously the embodied experiences reported by practitioners. I would also like to see more ethnographers exploring how their own socially constructed sensorial landscapes inform their interpretation of the body in religious experiences such as the shout in Sanctified religious experience.

Spiritual Gifts and Personal Power

Though democratic in its accessibility to anyone willing to press through, the Holy Ghost is not manifested in the same way, or to the same degree, in every saint. As 1 Corinthians 12: 1–11 explains, spiritual gifts are universally available but take diverse forms: "Now concerning spiritual gifts, brethren, I would not have you ignorant. . . . Now there are diversities of gifts, but the same Spirit. And there are differences of administrations, but the same Lord. And there are diversities of operations, but it is the same God which worketh all in all. But the manifestation of the Spirit is given to every man to profit withal. For to one is given by the Spirit the word of wisdom; to another the word of knowledge by the same Spirit; to another faith by the same Spirit; to another the gifts of healing by the same Spirit; to another the working of miracles; to another prophecy; to another discerning of spirits; to another diverse kinds of tongues; to another the interpretation of tongues: But all these worketh that one and the selfsame Spirit, dividing to every man severally as he will." Among founding saints, no one was deemed better than another because of their spiritual gifts, for individual spiritual gifts were for the edification of The Church as a whole. Still, being "anointed" accorded the pastor divine protection: "Touch not my anointed" (1 Chronicles 16:22). However, in time, even anointment ceased acting as a buffer against human criticism.

Saints recognize the distinctive gifts of the spirit in one another. Elder Esther was described as having the gift of tongues, while Elder Beverley and Deaconess Helga have the gift of interpretation. Some founding saints have the gift of dreams: while asleep, they "see" what is to come. Others have the gift of visions: they "see" while awake. For example, when a young woman was missing from home and could not be found, one of the head saints was consulted, and she told the parents the intersection where she had "seen" her. They went to the location and found her standing there.

Diasporic Reflection

The Church is Judeo-Christian, but the saints' reworking of Christianity has occurred within an African Diasporic cultural crucible. What does this larger context imply for studying The Church in particular, and the Black Church in America in general? I address these questions by looking at how saints have conceptualized spiritual power, considering the shout diasporically, imagining independent church movements transatlantically, and by addressing Afrophobia.

Working Roots

Although the founding saints believed in the Devil as the personification of evil, some recognized a more diffuse evil. While this evil could be overpowered by the Holy Ghost, it was believed that certain adepts could manipulate this power skillfully and effectively. "Working roots" was rarely discussed by the saints, and not all first-generation saints believed in its power to the same degree. As Yvonne Chireau points out, these extra-Christian folk traditions exist on the cultural fringe of Black lives and are whispered about when acknowledged at all (Chireau 2003: 27, 47, 140–41). Root workers manipulate a variety of natural substances, called "roots," to produce outcomes that range from the relatively innocuous, such as making a lover loyal, to the dangerously malign, such as "fixing" someone so that they go mad or die. The root worker is paid by the person for whose benefit the operation is performed.

Roots are generally believed to "turn" on whoever uses them. When I was a college undergraduate, a friend confided that she had fallen in love with a married man and consulted a woman who worked roots. My friend confessed that she later regretted doing this because the roots had turned on her. After the wife of the married man she loved lost the child she was carrying, my friend began to have accidents, which she explained as a consequence of what she had "done" to him and his family. Similarly, my great-aunt, a churchgoing woman, was known for "putting something" in her husband's food because she constantly worried about him having affairs with other women. As a widow in her eighties, she became extremely fearful. Once, she refused to come out of the house because doing so required her to step over what looked like dust but she feared was powder that someone who wanted to "fix" her had put on the steps, because stepping over roots activates them.

The power of roots can be successfully combated through practical action and by the power of the Holy Ghost. For example, as a youth, one of the elders saw her father take a lock of his wife's hair and bury it under a flight of stairs. She noticed that her mother "stayed sick all the time" and doctors could not find a cause. She and her siblings responded by bringing their mother with them when they migrated to the North. There she recovered and lived to be 101 years old. The move to Philadelphia changed two crucial things: it "put water between" her, the roots, and the root worker, which dampened the spell; and when she became a saint in The Church, the power of the Holy Ghost further protected her.

These beliefs about root-working resemble witchcraft beliefs found among the Aladura in Nigeria who, though Christian, believe that some people use power for evil ends, but that the power of the Holy Ghost can protect them from harm. Belief in witchcraft goes hand in hand with faith in the power of God to triumph over it. Among the Aladura, this view was publicly stated and the problem was ritually addressed within the church. Among the saints, this cosmos was acknowledged to the degree that it was deemed subordinate to the Christian power and divinity. In this light, Yvonne Chireau's observation may be applied not only to Black American but to African contexts, when she suggests that the spiritual lives of Blacks have historically spilled beyond institutional churches into coexisting but marginalized religious spaces that permeate everyday life (Chireau 2003, 1995).

Shouting Diasporically

Were you to ask the saints why they shout, they would likely refer to King David who "danced" before his God, grounding this practice of praise in biblical scripture. But where is the specific biblical reference to "shouting" that corresponds with what the saints do when they dance in the spirit? And how is it that this particular set of bodily motions has been passed down from the time of the enslavement? Shouting has roots in West African spirituality, but how likely are the saints to claim these African origins? As Sterling Stuckey notes, shouting is integral to systems of rituals and symbols found among peoples from the western coast of Africa, including the Fon, Temne,

Mende (Mandinka), and Bakongo. Furthermore, the shout can occur with and without the ring formation. Stuckey argues that, because members of different ethnic groups recognized the ring shout among each other, this religious ritual transcended cultural and linguistic differences to unify enslaved Africans. It continued to be reinforced by newly imported Africans and was passed on to American-born people of African descent from one generation to the next (Stuckey 1987: 11, 22–25, 40, 58–59, 83, 89–91, 97, 364n53).

Even in 1790 Philadelphia, when only 2 percent of Pennsylvanians were African-born, African-derived traditions were selectively preserved, as urban Blacks interacted with Africans from rural areas and with those continuing to arrive from Africa and the Caribbean.[6] Philadelphia annalist John Fanning Watson recalled in 1850 that Blacks danced "lightheartedly" and for long stretches of time at the Washington Square burial ground. According to Stuckey, Watson missed not only the devotional significance of the dancing but the connection between the locus of the dancing—a burial ground where Black ancestors had been interred since the early 1700s—and the West and Central African ring shout's association with funerals and other rites of passage (Stuckey 1987: 22–23, 75; Nash 2006: 40–41).

While conducting fieldwork among the Aladura, I witnessed an event that struck a shout-related trans-Atlantic chord. On the last night before the annual Mount Taborah pilgrimage celebration in the Church of the Lord–Aladura, the Ghanaian delegation that was leading the evening service began to run in a counterclockwise circle as they sang (Crumbley 2008a: 75). During four years of fieldwork, I had not seen a ring formation among Yoruba Aladura, though they regularly "danced" in the pews during worship. I also had seen Aladura members, like saints in The Church, touched or "shaken" by the spirit and speak in unknown tongues. Church of the Lord–Aladura "spiritual exercises" engage the body to achieve spiritual heights in ways that resonate with how saints in The Church "press through." Drawing on Faye Harrison's notion of bifocality, I am suggesting here that the engagement of the physical body in the Sanctified Church and Aladura Christianity is an outcome of African spirituality being selectively reinforced by European American revivalism, which was encountered by both enslaved Blacks in America and colonized Nigerians.

Both Sides of the Atlantic: Independent Church Movements

In addition to these ritual and symbolic parallels, institutional parallels exist between the rise of independent church movements (ICMs) on both sides of the Atlantic. As I have explored elsewhere (Crumbley 2010), ICMs have occurred in at least two waves. Aladura churches were not the first ICMs among the Yoruba of Nigeria, just as Sanctified churches were not the first ICMs among Black people in America. In Nigeria "African Churches," such as the United Native African Church (UNAC) and African Church Bethel (ACB), emerged in 1891 and 1901, respectively (Sanneh 1990: 176–77). Much like the AME, AME Zion, and Black Baptists in the United States, this first wave of ICMs represented more of an institutional than a cultural break with European missionary churches (Sanneh 1990: 180).

As the first wave of ICMs on both sides of the Atlantic became more established, they began to distance themselves from what they called "atavistic" African syncretism and "corn-field ditty"–singing Negroes (Adeyemi 1979: 17, 20; Ola 1978; Omoyajowo 1982: 223; Washington 1984: 58). In contrast, second-wave ICMs represent a cultural departure from the worship practices, doctrines, and organizational models of mission and mainstream Christianity. Thus, the legitimating effect of Protestant revivalism on selected African religious elements resulted in more than calling old African gods by new names (Hurston 1981: 106; Dodson and Gilkes 1995: 537, 528). Rather, the centrality of spirit in both African religious traditions and European American revivalism culminated in a second wave of ICMs in ways that have enriched Christianity and expanded contexts in which the Black Church in America can be interpreted.

Beyond Afrophobia in Studying Religious Expressions

This diasporic reflection concludes with a call for students of religion to take a global, interdisciplinary, and cross-cultural look at what peoples of Africa and African descent do when they encounter various forms of Protestant Christianity. Research on the intersection of African religious practices with Catholicism has produced a rich and extensive literature on Santeria, Candomblé, and Vodun, identifying ways in which the constellation of Catholic saints corresponds to and sustains African expressions of pluralized divinity. But no body of literature systematically and comparatively explores what happens when Protestantism intersects with the religious traditions of African and African Diaspora people. Such a line of inquiry requires a de-territorialization and re-territorialization of African and African Diaspora studies to ensure that local Black cultural expressions are conceptualized in terms of transnational dialogues (Harrison 2008: 106; Matory 2005: 3; Gordon and Anderson 1999: 282–90). In the study of the Black Church in America, we should be willing to think of things-African and things-African-American in the same intellectual breath, as well as be open to expanding the interpretation of the Black Church from a marginalized religious minority within America to a reformulation of Christianity occurring within diasporic cultural flows.

To move in these methodological and interpretive directions means coming to terms with what Dianne Stewart calls "Afrophobia." Drawing on the work of Englebert Mveng and Elias Farajaje-Jones, Stewart argues that Africans and people of African descent have suffered from the demoralizing conflation of civilization with Christianity, which has rendered any other religious tradition—particularly African religious practices—not just culturally inferior but evil (Stewart 2005: 5, 43, 70, 255n68). Afrophobia has led to selective cultural forgetting among people of African descent, and this gap in awareness has prompted theologians and everyday practitioners to legitimate spiritual practices that have African origins by finding biblical texts that lend them Christian support. Transcending Afrophobia entails not simply dismantling internalized racist notions of African peoples as culturally and religiously impoverished, but also coming to terms with Christianity's exclusive claims on divine revelation.

5

FAMILY

THE CHURCH IS "FAMILY." The notion of family that undergirds this chapter draws on African American usages of the term to refer to relationships of mutual obligation, responsibility, compassion, duty, and loyalty between persons who may, or may not, be connected through conventional ties of descent and marriage. The Church is "family," then, not only because so many of the saints are actual "blood relations" or marriage partners but also because the saints relate to each other in terms of who brought whom to "the truth." In many African American churches, members call one another "brother" and "sister," but in The Church, many saints are siblings. The Church also grew by saints bringing friends and neighbors into the fold. Growth has occurred through recruitment both of conventional kin who belong to extended families and of spiritual kin, who are absorbed through "spiritual adoption." At its founding, the head of The-Church-as-family was Mother Brown, whose role combined the kin-based position of parent with divinely legitimated authority as God's mouthpiece. The role of spiritual parent has persisted in the male and female elders, who take their stand at the head of this church family today.

This chapter focuses on emergence of the beliefs, practices, and organizational processes of The Church and on how they changed over time. It falls into three major sections. I begin with the life and vision of its pastor-founder. As the major church figures were women, this section also addresses gender as an organizing element in this emerging institution. The next section analyzes the organizing theme of family, tracing how connections based on conventional kinship and spiritual adoption inform recruitment and, in turn, are informed by boundaries between the Church and the world. The last section focuses on continuities and change in The Church after the founder's demise in 1984 and until the present.

A Voice, a Vision, a Church

The voice came when she was down on her knees in a rented room above a horse stable. It was not the first time Mother Brown had heard this voice. She had been listening to, and for, it ever since her "call" as a young woman in Mecklenburg, Virginia, where she was born in 1879. The leaders of her Baptist church responded to her report of being called with the words, "God never called a woman to preach." Nevertheless, on arriving in Philadelphia in 1914, she started preaching on the city's "highways and byways" and held services in saints' homes. She also preached in some of the "big churches" where they wanted "to put her up" because of her gifts of preaching and "getting a prayer through" for the sick and suffering. She said that she did not stay with these more established churches because she "got tired of their fornication and lies." She criticized clever, self-serving male ministers who seduced women by posing such rhetorical questions as "How can two clean sheets dirty each other?" Mother Brown was determined that her church would be "a clean church," free of "fornication."

She was in a little upper room that she had rented above a horse stable, praying fervently for divine direction, when the voice came. "You will never be saved doing what the world is doing," the voice said. She replied, "Lord, what must I do?" The voice said, "Follow me and my Word." She looked up and saw wild goats on hilltops, and then they ran down the slopes to sit at her feet. At this point, she knew that God would "send me a church" and she would lead the saints into the kingdom by teaching them the Word as long as she lived.

Mother Brown was nearly sixty when she had this vision and was approaching one hundred years of age when she related these events to me in the late 1970s for a paper that I was writing for a class at divinity school, before I had studied ethnographic interviewing methods. That interview, combined with the saints' recollections, obituaries, and other printed matter, constitute the basis of this biography.

Mecklenburg Call, Philadelphia Ministry

Mother Brown was born in Mecklenburg County, Virginia, near the North Carolina border, in 1879, just sixteen years after the Emancipation Proclamation was signed. According to the 1860 census, 6,778 Whites, 898 "free colored," and 12,420 slaves resided in the county. Mecklenburg was a center of the Great Awakening, and the first recorded Black Baptist congregation in America was convened there on the plantation of William Byrd in 1758.[1]

No information about Mother Brown's childhood experiences, family background, or marital life was available. However, documents show that Mother Brown married at the age of twenty-one and, on leaving Virginia, she first traveled to East Orange, New Jersey. There she "was introduced to the Sabbath Truth" and began her interaction with the Church of God Seventh Day. She relocated to Philadelphia in 1914, the year World War I began in Europe. In Philadelphia, she reconnected with this Sabbath-keeping faith community through one "Brother Gayle."

Separated from her husband, she supported her two small children by doing domestic day's work, often in Jewish homes. Despite the responsibilities and pressures of single motherhood, she remained true to her call and "preached in hospitals, nursing homes, and in the streets, teaching the Sabbath Truth" in association with the Church of God Seventh Day from 1914 to 1937. Between 1937 and 1938, Mother Brown rented a place to hold worship services at Twenty-third and Montgomery streets. When the rental space became unavailable, she held services in her home. Then, in 1939, Mother Brown rented a room situated above a horse stable. (As late as the 1950s, horse-drawn wagons traversed North Philadelphia, hauling ice for the "ice boxes" that kept food cold and vending some of the sweetest watermelons Georgia ever produced—far superior to those sold at the local A&P grocery store.)

By 1954, the saints had outgrown the upper room and moved into a corner building on Berks Street. The saints raised funds through "rallies" to renovate it into a sanctuary with a basement and second floor for meals and other social gatherings. Mother Brown had the final word on these renovations, as she did in all matters; however, she seriously considered what the deacons had to say. Although the saints were growing in number, they only left Berks Street in 1960 because the city decided to build a public clinic at that location. Two properties were purchased near Susquehanna Avenue and converted into one church building. Again, the pastor had the final say, but she was well advised by her deacons.

It is difficult to specify the size of the congregation in the past because The Church did not keep membership statistics. The Church's literal interpretation of the Bible helps explain this refusal to count members. According to Scripture (2 Samuel 24; 1 Chronicles 21), King David angered God by "numbering" eligible males for military service to determine his fighting power, rather than trusting God to use however many there were to win the battle. The elders whom I consulted in the 1990s enabled me to estimate the congregation's membership over time. The Church began with a handful of people "at the horse stable." There were from forty to fifty members, including adults and children, by the time they moved to Berks Street in 1954. The congregation continued to grow steadily for the next decade, despite the death of the founder in 1984. In 1990 there were approximately one hundred members: forty-five lay members, twenty-eight elders and deacons, and twenty-eight children. Over the last two decades, that number is said to have stabilized.

Affiliations, Finances, and Business Matters

The Church is not part of any established Protestant denomination. The pastor considered these to be "carnal-minded" digressions from the purity of the early church founded by the apostles after the ascension of Christ. The Church was not ecumenically engaged with local Philadelphia churches, with the exception of informal interactions with two other commandment-keeping churches. One of these was a predominantly White Sabbath-keeping holiness church led by a White married couple, the Pihiras, who occasionally visited, shared meals, and occupied the pulpit, although they visited The Church more than The Church visited with them. A Black couple, the Martins, who pastored a church in New Jersey, visited with greater frequency, and even today pulpits and choirs are shared between The Church and this church, now led by the Martins' daughter.

The only sustained institutional affiliation during the history of The Church was with a female-headed ministry on Pitkin Avenue in Brooklyn, New York, pastored by Elder James with the assistance of two other women ministers, Elders Williams and Captoria. Initially, the weekend-long "General Assembly" services of these churches alternated between Philadelphia and Brooklyn, where Elder Esther had her life-changing experience. By the 1960s, however, the Philadelphia church had grown considerably larger than the Brooklyn church, and quarterly General Assemblies began to be held primarily in Philadelphia. At these gatherings a business meeting was held, and each church contributed a tithe of its tithe and made donations to pianists, secretaries, and overseers of the respective churches. During General Assembly, Elders James and Williams sat on either side of the pastor on the raised platform at the front of the sanctuary, and they both preached a sermon. The gathering was accompanied by specially prepared communal meals. A children's program on Sunday highlighted their musical performance and biblical memory skills.

Financial matters of The Church were handled by the deacons. Mother Brown had the final say, but took their advice seriously. Regular income was generated by the religious paying of tithes and "freewill offerings." First-generation saints regarded paying tithes as a biblically grounded requirement and, as elders' narratives attest, they continue to tithe even their Social Security checks. Mother Brown regularly cited the prophet Malachi: "Will a man rob God?" and reminded the saints that paying tithes is accompanied by blessing: "Bring ye all the tithes into the storehouse, that there may be meat in mine house, and prove me now herewith, saith the LORD of hosts, if I will not open you the windows of heaven, and pour you out a blessing, that there shall not be room enough to receive it" (Malachi 3:7–9).

The accumulation of tithes and freewill offerings comprised "the treasury," which was used to pay church bills and loans. When The Church was young and growing, tithes and offerings were not always enough to meet these financial demands. So the pastor would "call a rally," during which each family contributed a lump sum determined by the pastor in consultation with the deacons. Parents purchased the folding chairs for each member of their family as well. With time and the accumulation of contributions, the treasury became a source of interest-free loans that members were to pay back by a designated date. For financial and legal matters, particularly regarding property, the church lawyer, Mr. Buchman, was consulted; he also served as lawyer to individual saints.

Authority, Deference, and Gendered Roles

Mother Brown was a charismatic woman, commanding in comportment and skilled in managing people and power. Her knowledge of the Bible was commendable: not only had she memorized most of it, but she could skillfully refer to specific passages to support or develop a line of thought. She was the voice of God to people who were looking for "something more" than the Baptist or AME churches offered. She offered a divinely sanctioned way of life grounded in the Bible, keeping the law, and being filled with the Holy Ghost. The millennial element of her teaching trivialized aspects of institutional process, such as developing a church mission statement, constitution, or bylaws. These fell under the category of "man's laws" and "carnality," and rare attempts to press for transparency and explicit organizational process were perceived as questioning her authority and losing sight of the weightier matter of "getting ready for the kingdom." When a decision had to be made, it tended to be unilateral. For example, when two of the deacons began to miss deacon board meetings and services, the pastor had them step down. As Elder Walter, a former deacon, explained, the deacon board did not contest Mother Brown's decision because it seemed a reasonable response to these men's conduct.

Criticism directed at the pastor herself was met with the scriptural caveat "Touch not mine anointed, and do my prophets no harm" (1 Chronicles

16:22). The saints who were convinced of their pastor's calling and who aspired to "make the kingdom" retreated. The deference shown Mother Brown included her being the first person the saints greeted with a "holy kiss" prior to "shaking hands" with the other saints before service began. For this, the pastor was usually seated on the same level as the saints. Once service began, however, she moved to her seat on the platform, where large chairs with high backs were arranged side by side with hers in the middle. Normally no one else sat in these special seats, unless they were guest preachers.

Mother Brown wielded ultimate authority in both political and ceremonial arenas of power. Yet she was wise enough to know her limits and, like any effective leader, surrounded herself with people who had a variety of skills. Elder Walter said that "she listened to us" and the deacons could change her mind when they convinced her that their ideas and approaches were well informed. Key women, who tended to be central figures within their family groups, were the bearers of spiritual gifts that supported the pastor and the saints of The Church. These "head saints" interpreted tongues, taught, preached, had visions, and helped the aspiring saints "press through." These were the saints to whom new aspiring saints could bring questions about the Word and the personal struggles that accompanied "taking a stand" for truth. Thus, male deacons functioned on the level of management and saw to matters involving the physical plant, while the "head saints" were sources of spiritual guidance and power central to the life of The Church (Crumbley 2007).

Empowered Lives, Degendered Bodies

The notion of Black women occupying positions of authority and being associated with spiritual purity is in sharp contrast to the dominant society's images of Black women during the Great Migration era. As discussed in "City Tales," Black southern women who came to northern cities threatened notions of domesticity and gendered propriety held by both the White establishment and aspiring middle-class Blacks. As Cheryl Townsend Gilkes suggests, the Black Sanctified Church provided an alternative to the "ideological attacks," abuse, and exploitation that Black women suffered in the dominant society by "providing the moral support for their role within their families and their communities." In the Sanctified Church, older Black women whom younger Whites addressed as "girl" or "auntie," or familiarly by their first name, were accorded "titles of respect," such as deaconess, elder, evangelist, pastor, or even bishop (Gilkes 1986: 29).

Anthea Butler has noted that, at a time when racist images of dangerous Black female bodies flourished in American popular culture, Sanctified churches accorded Black women merit and status (Butler 2007: 64–70, 100). Just as Jamaican Pentecostalism "sanctifies" the sinful bodies of lower-class women associated with illegitimacy and fornication into "transcendent brides" (Austin-Broos 1997: 195, 196–98), so the recently arrived and minimally educated Black female domestic and factory workers who flocked to these churches were treated with a respect and authority that was legitimated by the Holy Ghost power that dwelt within them (Butler 2007: 75). For example, Elder Beverly's family circumstances, coupled with systemic discrimination, meant that this high school valedictorian became a domestic worker rather than the teacher that she aspired to be. In contrast, in The Church she "worked with the young people" teaching them scripture, and as "interpreter of tongues" she revealed the scriptures that the saints studied each Sabbath. She lays hands on the sick, presses-through new members and, as an elder, shares responsibility for the spiritual guidance of The Church.

Still, elements of concern and discomfort with the Black woman's body linger in the Sanctified Church tradition for reasons that are ritual, social, and political. Melvin Williams describes an "obsession" with covering women's bodies in the Sanctified COGIC congregation that he studied. In The Church, male saints also covered their bodies; however, whether at church or in the world, men's dress codes did not distinguish them from their male counterparts outside the church. When female saints covered their heads, wore dresses down to their calves, and avoided makeup and jewelry, they stood out from their neighbors, coworkers, and employers. The dress code for Sabbath was even more distinguishing: women wore white dresses and mantles that hung to the middle of their backs.

The significance of dressing "as becometh holiness" has been fruitfully explored by historian Anthea Butler, who argues that the interpretation of this Biblical phrase entails ritual codes that "degender" and "cleanse" the Black female body in preparation for the Holy Ghost infilling. She suggests that "dressing as becomes holiness" also effects a strategic approximation to middle-class respectability that makes Black women "more palatable to whites" (Butler 2007: 79–81). To this I would add that covering and avoiding makeup have valuable implications and consequences for sexual politics, an insight provided by my respected colleague N. Y. Nathiri, executive director of the Association to Preserve the Eatonville Community. Nathiri has been the general manager of the annual Zora Neale Hurston Festival since 1990, when she started the festival, and is a trailblazer in cultural heritage tourism as a strategy for sustaining community development (Nathiri 1991).[2] During a discussion about her successful fundraising efforts in both the private and public sectors, Nathiri referred to the full hijab that she wears as her "business suit," which sets a professional tone for interaction with the predominantly male business representatives with whom she negotiates matters of money and power. In this light, degendered and desexualized dress codes can be viewed as protective ritual action that introduces an element of control in sexual politics so that women are less likely to be sexually approached and abused.

Perhaps the most degendered and desexualized of all the saints was Mother Brown. Her clothing, regardless of where she was, was visibly modest, and her head coverings were complete. She was the antithesis of the Black male Pentecostal pastor who, John Hopkins writes, has a sexual presence and is a "father-lover figure" to whom supplicants "surrender" as they do to Jesus (Hopkins 1978: 26). In contrast, Mother Brown was an asexual Madonna figure.

Recruitment and Boundaries

Kith, Kin, and Holy Office

"Daniel is my child in the Lord." This is how Elder Walter described his relationship with a saint who is now one of the four ordained deacons. Daniel is not biologically related to Elder Walter, but the elder was instrumental in his becoming an active member of The Church and an ordained church officer. Deacon Daniel is married to Helga, the niece of Elder Walter's wife, Lonetta, who brought Deaconess Helga into The Church. Elder Walter and Elder Lonetta's four daughters, Celine, Denisha, Brandy, and Eudora, are church musicians and have served on the usher board; now some of their grandchildren are ushers and musicians. These relationships exemplify the ways people are "brought into" The Church: they are recruited along kinship lines, through marriage, and by spiritual adoption.

As the case of Deacon Daniel illustrates, being in The Church is not a matter of sitting on the sidelines and being entertained. Saints participate in the activities that maintain the church as a religious organization when they take on the duties and responsibilities of musicians, ushers, deacons, deaconesses, evangelists, and elders. The offices of elder, deacon, deaconess, and evangelist are "ordained" offices; musicians and ushers are offices for which congregants volunteer. Church offices are age-related, though no fixed rules specify how old a person has to be to occupy them. Elders have tended to be in their seventies or older, and youth often begin their church duties as musicians and ushers. The informal way young people step forward is illustrated by a youth named Jabari, the great-grandson of Elder Walter and

Elder Lonetta. During a Sabbath worship service, when his great-uncle Elder Frank was performing a selection on his harmonica, the four-year-old Jabari walked up to the front of the church, took out *his* harmonica, and joined his uncle in "My Faith Looks Up to Thee." Now a teenager, Jabari is one of The Church's drummers.

A saint might rise from usher to deacon/deaconess, then to evangelist, and finally to elder, but this trajectory is neither inevitable nor set in stone. Offices are not mutually exclusive; a saint might hold more than one office at a time, or step down from one and rise to another. A saint can be removed from a post. One of the two deacons who were retired from this office when they became less active in deacon board matters has remained an active member of the congregation and is a key musician. Offices are gendered, but not in the same ways they were in mainstream churches: musicians and ushers may be of either sex; only men are deacons; and evangelists and elders may be of either sex.

Figure 1 combines genealogy with organizational process as it indicates who brought whom into The Church and how these ties are reflected in the distribution of church offices among the families that comprise The Church. Unlike a family tree, this diagram does not line up the generations horizontally but rather fans out in networks of interconnection. The diagram differentiates clearly between kinship through biology and marriage and kinship through spiritual adoption since saints brought in their siblings, spouses, children, and relatives but also mentored and guided others to whom they were not related. The multifarious connections that have developed over time within this faith community require simplification in order to be presented intelligibly.

It is important to note that the diagram in Figure 1 focuses on offices rather than the laity. It focuses on current holders of "ordained" offices—elder, deacon, deaconess, and evangelist—and includes "service" offices, such as musicians and ushers. It indicates the current or highest of several offices that a saint may hold simultaneously. Additionally, it does not include those loyal participants who hold no office but are the glue that holds this religious community together.[3] Examining the diagram reveals certain patterns. First, the majority of the male and female elders are members of the Nichols family. Secondly, the all-male deacon board consists of one biological member each from the Tompkins, Brown-Wilson, and Winston families and one in-law of a biological member of the Nichols family. The laity is comprised mainly of "young people," which in The Church refers to young adults in their twenties through their forties. Currently, the Nicholses are not the majority among the young people, which reflects the fact that many

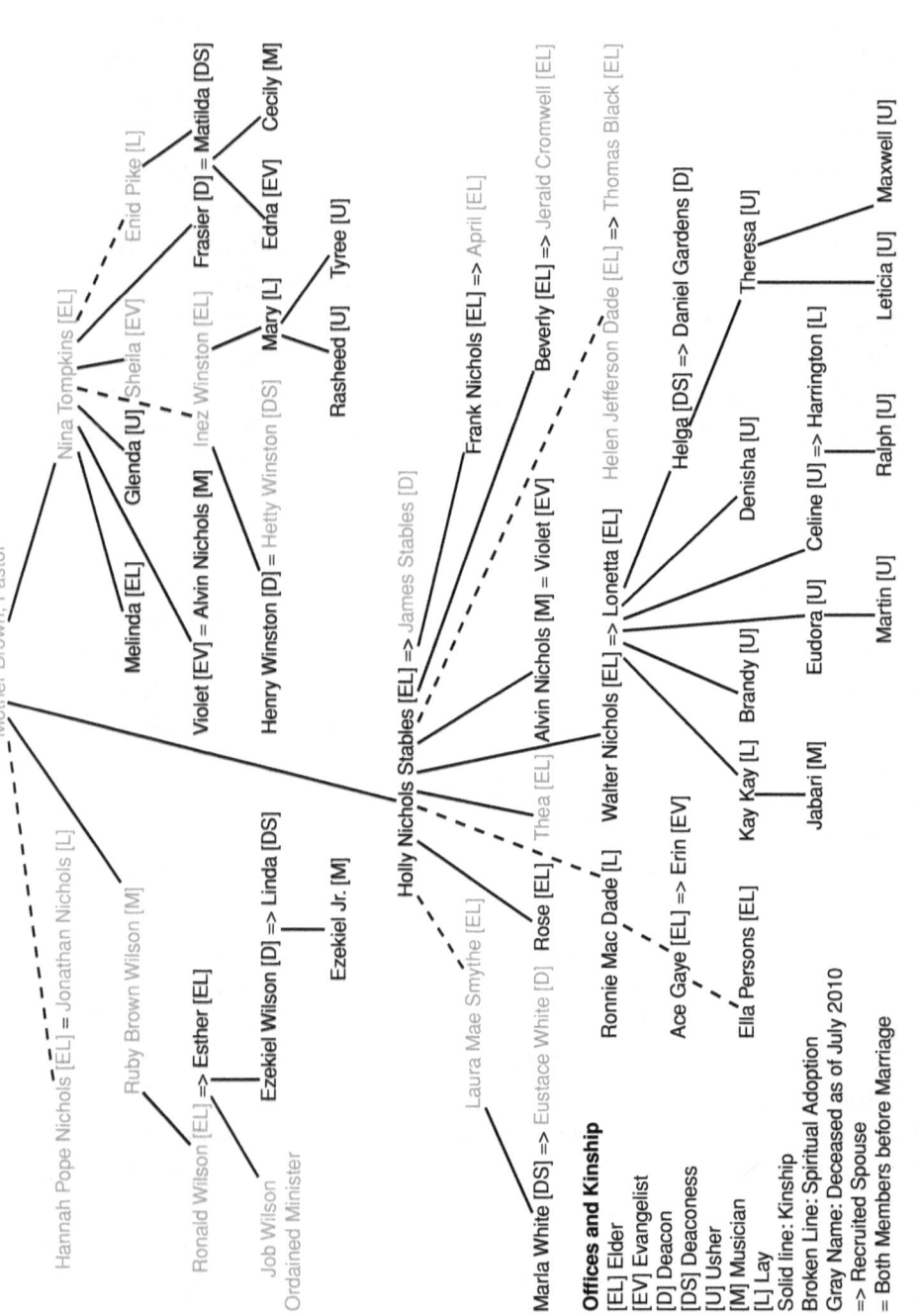

Figure 1. Genealogical and organizational structure of The Church.

of the children of the Nichols founding members left the church on becoming adults. Thus, while Nichols family members have a plurality on the elder board, and while Nicholses were the majority of the laity in the twentieth century, in the twenty-first century they are not the majority among the deacon board or among the "young people." This informs changing interfamily dynamics and policy formation.

The saints prefer not to talk about "joining" The Church; instead, they speak of "coming into" or being "brought into" it. People "join" social clubs and "sign up" for organizations, they explain, but being part of The Church requires more than formal membership. A saint must be born again, keep the commandments, and live a Holy Ghost–filled life. Recruitment to The Church has not been effected through large-scale evangelical programs but rather through one-on-one introductions to "the truth," often in the context of family, household, and neighborhood.

In the founding generation of The Church, the Nichols family was the largest in number and predominated among the congregation's first deacons and deaconesses, who were married to each other. Lilly Adamson Nichols was the Nichols matriarch. However, in terms of recruitment, the apical figure (that is, the figure at the apex of one of the three family clusters on the diagram) was Holly Stables, Lilly's third-oldest daughter, who brought so many of her siblings into The Church. Elder Holly's husband, James Stables, was one of the first deacons. Eight of her fifteen siblings have been active members to varying degrees; her brothers Willy and Jonathan are not indicated in the diagram because they did not hold church offices before their demise. The Nichols siblings produced twenty children, but with the exception of Elder Walter, most of the founding Nichols children are no longer active members. Still, they maintain their ties to varying degrees: attending church services when they are in town, making donations, and sustaining close relationships with family who are church leaders. Keeping these ties is rather easier than breaking them, for to speak to family is to speak to the saints of The Church.

Elder Walter and Elder Lonetta's oldest daughter, Celine, brought her husband, Harrington, into The Church. She, her son Ralph, her sisters Denisha, Brandy, and Eudora, and Eudora's son Martin have all been ushers. Elder Walter's wife, Lonetta, was recently installed as an elder; previously she had been an usher, deaconess, and evangelist, stepping down from one office as she took on another. Many years ago, Elder Lonetta brought her niece, Helga, into The Church, and Helga brought in her husband. As all new saints are, they were referred to as "brother" and "sister"; now they hold the offices of deaconess and deacon. Their daughter, Theresa, is an active member and an usher, as are Theresa's daughter Leticia and her son Maxwell, who also plays the drums.

Deaconess Helga is vice president of the usher board and serves as the "interpreter of tongues." The role of interpreter is crucial to the spiritual life of The Church. Drawing on scripture, The Church considers speaking in tongues fruitless unless there is an interpreter to whom the Holy Ghost reveals the tongues as biblical passages, which are then read and studied for the edification of the saints (1 Corinthians 14: 5, 12, 23, 27, 28). Deaconess Helga was called to this spiritual service after the death of Elder April, who, in turn, had taken over from Elder Beverly when she and Elder Jerald relocated to Virginia. Her husband, Deacon Daniel, is one of the four church deacons.

When Ace Gaye entered The Church as a "brother," he had no kinship tie to the Nichols family, yet he speaks of Elder Holly as "my mother." He was introduced to The Church through a friend, Ronnie McDade, who had become part of The Church through Elder Holly when Ronnie was a "roomer" in her household. Ace Gaye married, brought his wife Erin into The Church, and briefly lived with Mother Brown. Elder Holly is his mother-in-the-Lord. He was also very close to Elder Beverly, as he was to her husband before Elder Jerald's demise. Elder Ace rose from a "brother" to the office of deacon and was also an evangelist. Recently, he was installed as an elder and celebrated his seventieth birthday. Both of the Gayes have returned to college to complete degree programs; their daughter graduated from the Philadelphia High School for Girls, and they also paid tuition for their son to attend a prestigious private school attended by members of established Philadelphia families. Deaconess Erin is an evangelist, as well as serving on the usher board. She and her husband brought Ella Persons into The Church. Sister Persons rose to the office of evangelist and was recently installed as an elder. Another case of spiritual adoption is that of Elder Helen, who was Elder Holly's next-door neighbor. Elder Dade brought her mother, Luanne Jefferson, into The Church, as well as her younger sister Mae, who is no longer active but had been a church usher. After Elder Helen's first husband died, she brought her second husband, Thomas Black, into The Church; he too rose to the level of elder. Elder Helen was unable to be interviewed for this study before she died; her husband has since relocated.

The Smythe family's apical head was founding member Laura Smythe, who rose to the position of elder before her death (which occurred before this research project began). Elder Laura and Elder Holly had been neighbors when they lived on Diamond Street. Elder Laura's husband was the brother of Mother Brown's daughter-in-law, so Mother Brown and Elder Laura were related through marriage. Elder Laura served faithfully and effectively as church treasurer until Elder Jerald took over the position, which she reportedly welcomed because of the competing duties that being an employed mother entailed. Elder Laura had one daughter, and Elder Laura's husband, though not a sustained active saint, visited The Church from time to time until his demise. Elder Laura also brought her sister's daughter, Marla, into the church. In turn, Marla introduced her husband, Eustace, to the faith. He and she became deacon and deaconess. Deaconess Marla was actively engaged in The Church until she relocated permanently to Delaware. A natural archivist, she lovingly collected biographies of founding saints, which have been invaluable for reconstructing the lives of those who passed on before this research project began. Deacon Eustace was a natural teacher and worked closely with the youth before he passed on. Deacon Eustace started and then led "The Band," composed of church youth who played musical instruments, including drum, piano, maraca and other shakers, xylophone, Hawaiian steel guitar, accordion, and autoharp. In some cases, children began playing toy instruments received as gifts during Chanukah and then worked up to the adult instrument.

Elder Nina Tompkins came into The Church through Mother Brown. They lived in the same neighborhood, and Mother Brown was a source of ready support to Elder Nina as she raised her nine children. Elder Nina's husband was not drawn into The Church, but several of her children and grandchildren became leaders. Her son Frasier is one of the four current deacons, and his wife, Matilda, is a deaconess as well as an usher. Their daughter Edna is an usher and an evangelist as well, and Edna's daughter Cecily is a musician who plays the drums and a handheld percussion instrument called a *shakere*. Elder Nina's daughter Melinda was installed as an elder after serving as an evangelist. Elder Nina's daughter Glenda is a church usher, and Glenda's son Derek, along with his wife and child, who live in New Jersey, attend The Church as well. Additionally, Elder Nina's daughter Violet is a deaconess and president of the usher board. Violet married Brother Alvin Nichols, the youngest brother of Elder Holly. He has served The Church as a musician since he came into the congregation. As a young adult, he composed the words and music to "Elect Lady" and "The Little Upper Room on Vanpelt Street," which celebrated the pastor and the founding history of The Church. He also accompanied and led a choir of his peers. It should be noted that Elder Nina brought Sister Pike into the church. Sister Pike brought in Matilda, who became an usher and on marrying Deacon Frasier became a deaconess.

For many years, Elder Nina lived in the same building with Inez Winston, who along with members of her immediate and extended family—as many as fourteen of them—came into The Church and became active to varying degrees. Like Elder Tompkins, she passed on before she could be interviewed for this study. Her son, Henry Winston, is one of the four deacons and is a musician in his own right, composing the words and music to "Don't Doubt God," "The New Jerusalem," and "They Bore the Burden," which refer to the founding saints by name. Deacon Henry married a young woman named Hetty who was already an active member of the church. Hetty was an usher, and when Henry became a deacon, she became a deaconess and served in this capacity until she passed on too early. Their daughter, who came later in life and as quite a surprise, has graduated from college. Elder Inez's daughter Mary is an active and loyal saint. Sister Mary brought two adopted sons, Rashid and Tyree, into The Church, and they recently became young ushers.

Mother Brown, the pastor-founder, though married, lived separately from her husband. She was a single mother of two children. Her son, Enoch, whose wife's brother married Elder Laura, did not become part of The Church. Her daughter, Ruby Brown Wilson, became an evangelist in her own right and was church pianist, a position that Elder Holly took over when Ruby passed. Ruby separated from her husband and lived with her mother, the pastor, until Ruby died at the age of forty-three. She bore two sons: Hosea, who did not become part of The Church, and Ronald, who did. Ronald became a church deacon and later rose to the elder board, as did his wife Elder Esther. Ronald Jr. had been a musician, playing steel guitar, before he died. His brother Job was ordained as a "minister" before he was thirty by the pastor just before her death. He "went out" to start his own church. Sadly, he too has passed on. Elder Esther and Ronald's youngest son, Ezekiel, is one of the four church deacons. As minister of music, Deacon Ezekiel played the piano and led the adult choir in the gospel album entitled *Touch Me Lord* in 2002.[4] The song that begins and ends this recording is his arrangement of "Down at the Cross," which has always been sung to start worship service in The Church. The second performance of "Down at the Cross" at the end of the recording is sung in Spanish by the vocal group Coro Gospel de Madrid, which had been introduced to the deacons' rendition of the song through an evangelical missionary colleague of Deacon Ezekiel. The Spanish choir so loved his arrangement that they asked to record it, which he graciously allowed. Deacon Ezekiel has since released another gospel album which, like the first, includes both standard gospel tunes and his original compositions. Deaconess Linda is married to Deacon Ezekiel and they have two children. Ezekiel Jr., who is a church musician and plays the drums, is completing high school; his older sister Krystal is a graduate of the Philadelphia High School for Girls.

The life of The Church, in large part, is generated by the interaction within and between these kin-based and spiritual family complexes. The relationships are finely nuanced, and analyzing their social-psychological dynamics would require a separate book.[5] As Melvin Williams notes in his ethnography of the Zion church community, "primary group intimacy . . . also fills this community with anxieties, stress, fears, jealousies, and competition that are expressed in member to member relationships" (Williams 1974: 13, 28). Despite such tensions, the saints are "there for each other" in ways that range from helping with burial costs to making themselves available during the everyday challenges of life. The saints wed deep love for one another with critical assessment of each other's particular strengths and defects of character. They attend others' celebrations, which in some cases involve renting halls and inviting nonmembers. In 2010, these events included the celebration of Deacon Ezekiel and Deaconess Linda's silver wedding anniversary, Elder Ace's seventieth birthday, and Elder Walter and Elder Lonetta's sixtieth wedding anniversary. Bridging age and offices, younger saints are paired with an "adopted" elder who mentors them and to whom they offer respect and pampering, both in and outside church contexts. The explicit formal division of labor between deacons and elders that emerged after the death of the founder is humanized and complicated by close personal relationships between spiritual mothers, fathers, brothers, and sisters.

Regarding the nexus of institutional organization, family relationships, and gender, it is notable that the apical figures of founding family complexes—Brown, Nichols, Smythe, Tompkins, and Winston—are female: Mother Brown, Elder Holly Nichols Stables, Elder Laura Smythe, Elder Nina Tompkins, and Elder Inez Winston. All had married, although some may have lived separately from their spouses. Nevertheless, the centrality of women in The Church does not discount the institutional significance of males. As deacons, men were depended upon to handle money matters and the physical plant. Male and female elders have the same duty of providing spiritual guidance for the congregation through teaching, preaching, admonishing, and praying.

Wall of the Lord

The Church under Mother Brown was modeled on the family. That matters because of what Elder April described as a "dividing line" between the saints and the world. For first-generation saints, "taking a stand" and being in The

Church entailed distancing themselves from their family of origin. The motivation to recruit family, then, came not only from wanting to see them "make" the kingdom, since Judgment Day was imminent, but also because it kept family ties intact. The notion of the "dividing line" brings to mind the strategy of the former slave in Texas who dealt with the threat of the Klan by building a "wall of the Lord 'round me, so they couldn't get me." Under the leadership of Mother Brown, "a wall of the Lord" was built around the saints to protect them from a world that they experienced as spiritually contaminating, physically dangerous, and racially excluding. Within the "wall of the Lord" built around this commandment-keeping church, parents could rest in the knowledge that their children would be blessed (Proverbs 8:32; Psalms 147:13) and that God would spare them the iniquities experienced by their forebears.

The sins and distractions of the world represented obstacles to saints getting ready for the kingdom. For this reason, worldly places and people, including unsaved family members, had to be avoided. Their new inner-city environment was alien. While it was a less likely site for racist violence than their southern hometowns, its social structures and processes marginalized them from free and fair participation in White-controlled social, political, and economic institutions. The world of inner-city Philadelphia where the founding saints settled was, as it is now with the exception of a few gentrified areas, a world where the working poor and the impoverished live in neighborhoods lacking the political might and resources to secure the amenities of a stable, salubrious, family-oriented environment.

In the part of North Philly where I grew up, there were very few tree-lined streets and no nearby recreation centers. There was a bar across the street on the corner, and the only stores were White-owned mom-and-pop stores whose owners did not live in the neighborhood and whose prices were unfairly high. North Philly was not as devastated by drugs and violence as it is today, but an alternative economy based on activities such as "running numbers" and the presence of numerous poolrooms and bars contributed an element of danger to life in the ghetto. The Church was disconnected from that world. By spending most of their free time at church and avoiding "worldly" activities, the saints were unlikely to be "at the wrong place at the wrong time," making them less likely to get caught between warring gangs or to be arrested and brutalized by the police.

Although North Philly would await us, unchanged, when church services ended, during worship the world paled into nonexistence. The "wall of the Lord" that the founding saints, led by Mother Brown, built around themselves can be understood as a tradeoff between spiritual security and secular safety on the one hand and, on the other, the loss of an immortal soul and possibly loss of limb or life. Competition between intimates is to be expected in a face-to-face community like The Church. Still, founding saints found in one another equals and peers who shared familiar ways of being Black that they brought from the rural South. In The Church, the first generation of saints did not have to negotiate the racialized hostility and White-dominated hierarchy that they encountered daily in the larger society. At church, time and space were equitable, unracialized, self-determined, and sacralized.

Power and Gender Shifts

Everything changes, including The Church. When The Church was just starting, Mother Brown's charisma maintained its families in orbit around her powerful persona. Her leadership style usually entailed unilateral decision-making rather than proposing an idea for discussion or consensus-building. She ruled with an iron first that was not necessarily cloaked in a velvet glove. Mother Brown was especially determined to have a "clean church" free of "fornication." She was vehement about "openly rebuking" any saints caught engaging in premarital sex. For anyone taking umbrage, her position was simple: "There's the door the carpenter cut."

In time, the absolutism of her leadership was questioned. One elder recalled that when she came into The Church, she had been warned by a relative who was not in The Church that one day the saints would "grow up" and begin to question the pastor. That day came. For example, the pastor wanted to add to the three Sabbath services a Sunday Bible school for children followed by an adult class on Sunday evenings. Several parents decided not to have their children attend, feeling strongly that the children needed some free time when they were not in church or at school. The parents communicated among themselves on the phone and virtually all decided to keep their children home. Consequently, the children's Bible school meetings ceased to be held.

Mother Brown agreed strongly with the sentiment of Proverbs 27:5, that "open rebuke is better than secret love." When the first teenager in the history of The Church became pregnant, she was required to stand before the congregation and apologize for her misconduct. Even after doing so, she continued to be the object of "open rebuke" from the pulpit. One day a deacon from the Nichols family walked out of the church and returned with a large stone that he placed on the table before the altar, and then silently walked back to his seat. This act, which was clearly directed at the pastor, was understood by all present as an allusion to Jesus directing the "scribes and Pharisees" intent on stoning an adulteress: "He that is without sin among you, let him first cast a stone at her" (John 8:7).

Critical leveling of the pastor was indirectly lodged through the singing of this gospel song:

> Oh, you can't hide—no need of trying.
> You can't get by, 'cause you don't know how.
> God's got your number and he knows where you live.
> Death's got a warrant for you.

This verse is varied by addressing it to different constituencies, so that "Oh" is replaced by "children," "mothers," "fathers," "Church," and "preacher." By including "preacher," the pastor-founder was placed on the same level as all the other saints, who are unable to hide from God or death.

The singing of "You Can't Hide," the silently enacted parable of the first stone, and the refusal of parents to bring their children to another service, while poignant expressions of opinion, did not entail open verbal confrontations with Mother Brown. Although some saints were "growing up" and becoming critical of what they saw as her abuse of power, they did not question the fundamental truth of her teachings. They continued to hold the greatest respect for Mother Brown's teachings of the way to salvation through keeping the commandments, being filled with the Holy Ghost, and living a life of holiness grounded in the Bible. Moreover, while the caveat "touch not my anointed and do my prophets no harm" no longer made her immune to critique as a human being, it was a powerful reminder of the legitimacy of her authority as a religious leader.

In the late 1970s, I had a fortunate conversation with Deaconess Marla White about the changes I was noticing in The Church. She observed that "No one is in a corner anymore. No one is bound. There is no more living for man." The deaconess proceeded to explain that earlier in the history of The Church, Mother Brown had to be firm with the saints to instruct them in the way of salvation, but she had taught the saints the Bible and instructed them to "search the scriptures" for themselves and to "work out our *own* soul's salvation with fear and trembling." Deaconess Marla added that she had recently faced her mortality during surgery for a life-threatening condition, at which point she came to the realization that if she died, she would have to "die for myself." Subsequently, she decided, it was time for her to "live for myself."

With increasing frequency, saints began to take exception to the pastor's seeming preference of one family over another. Pitted against each other, the families too often worked at cross-purposes, missing golden opportunities to develop more democratic, transparent, and accountable leadership strategies among themselves. Some of the children of founding saints left The Church in part because they felt themselves caught in the crossfire between warring factions and families, leading to experiences that left them wounded and led them to question the validity of church teachings that contending parties claimed to espouse.

Reorganization

Mother Brown was an indomitable charismatic personality. She was also very clever and deeply committed to the future of the church she led. Aware of strained relationships between herself and the saints, the conflict between families, and her advancing age, she did something that is rare among charismatic leaders. Most are too caught up with visions of transcendent realities to attend to mundane matters of institution-building. Before her death, Mother Brown installed a biblically grounded organizational structure that decentralized decision-making, replacing the pastorate with a bicameral committee that included women in leadership roles. That structure has survived her death into the twenty-first century. This new governance did not arise from a vacuum; its source is found in the New Testament: "And in those days, when the number of the disciples was multiplied, there arose a murmuring of the Grecians against the Hebrew, because their widows were neglected in the daily ministration. Then *the twelve* called the multitude of the discipline unto them, and said, It is not reason that we should leave the work of God, and serve tables. Wherefore, brethren, look ye out among you seven men of honest report, full of the Holy Ghost and wisdom, which we may appoint over *this business*. But we will *give ourselves continually to prayer and to the ministry of the word*" (Acts 6:1–4, emphasis added). It is significant that, despite the tendency to interpret the Bible literally, the new arrangement includes women among the elders, although in the Bible the "twelve" were all males. The deacons, who had management-related responsibilities before Mother Brown's death, continue to perform the same duties, and the office remains male-gendered.

The criteria for becoming an elder or a deacon are guided by Paul's instructions to Titus to "order the things that are wanting, and ordain elders . . . as I had appointed thee": "If any be blameless, the husband of one wife, having faithful children not accused of riot or unruly. For a bishop must be blameless, as the steward of God; not self willed, not soon angry, not given to wine, no striker, not given to filthy lucre; But a lover of hospitality, a lover of good men, sober, just, holy, temperate; Holding fast the faithful word as he hath been taught that he may be able by sound doctrine both to exhort and to convince the gainsayers" (Titus 1:6–9). The selection process for elders currently employed in The Church entails a careful examination of a saint's family life, personal comportment, and spiritual life. Two criteria seem to be foundational: the person has to "have age" and "know the Word." When, playing devil's advocate, I suggested that there is a difference between "knowing" the Word and "living" it, Elder Beverly responded, "Not in *this* church." The newly installed elders live the Word, and as they all were previously evangelists, they have demonstrated the ability to teach and preach the Word for the edification of the saints.

The point that elders have made in their interpretive discussion of the passage from Acts is that the deacons do the work that would distract the church leaders from the "real work" of The Church, which is the spiritual instruction and guidance of the saints. Mother Brown identified the first set of elders around 1978, when she was in her nineties. By 1980, Mother Brown had appointed a second wave of additional elders. Elders were male and female saints, often founding deacons and deaconesses, and received formal credentials from the municipality recognizing their church-conferred status. Several have died, and younger saints who were serving as deacons, deaconesses, and evangelists have risen to the office of elder. New evangelists continue to be identified; youth take on ushering duties and enter the ranks of musicians.

The governance arrangement that Mother Brown put in place has survived her death for thirty years. Not having power centralized in a pastor has entailed some dramatic changes in organizational processes. The saints have had to learn how to make policy through the new structures, which are designed in a way that fosters governance by consensus. After Mother Brown died, what Elder April described as "one dominating force" was replaced by shared leadership among the elders. They have brought diverse perspectives to bear on church teachings and introduced different styles of spiritual guidance to the congregation.

Democratization and diversity can be both a blessing and a curse. As Elder Walter pointed out, the elders are still developing a transparent consensus-building process among themselves that balances their varied viewpoints with a commitment to being a unified source of spiritual wisdom on which The Church can depend for decision-making. They must learn to hear one another's perspectives and offer support as well as constructive criticism in regularly scheduled meetings. Elder Walter suggested, for example, that elders generate an agenda of priority matters that they can keep before themselves and present to the deacon board during biannual meetings. The deacon board and the elders also meet ad hoc to address issues as they arise, but Elder Walter pointed out the importance of meeting regularly to avoid a crisis management approach that leaves little time and energy for envisioning the future.

What of women's power since the demise of the female pastor and the office itself, which had centralized power in a female leader? As I have explored in greater depth elsewhere (Crumbley 2007), when Mother Brown was pastor, she was the only woman in The Church who exercised the "political" power of administration and policy formation; the other female saints exercised "ceremonial" power as interpreters, seers, healers, and teachers. The new arrangement she put in place made it possible for more women to participate in policymaking than when power was centralized in the pastorate. As elders have pointed out, the elders do the "real work" of The Church, and both men and women share this power. Still, women are prohibited from serving as deacons, which excludes women from setting financial policy. It should be noted, however, that when serious financial matters arise beyond paying bills and the like, the deacons bring the issues before the elders. Although the elders have not done so to date, they can stop a measure from going forward if, after fervent prayer and searching the scripture, they determine that the proposal is not in line with "truth" or for the edification of The Church. More importantly, the formal boundaries that distinguish the duties and powers of the deacon board from those of the elder board are regularly breached by personal interactions and close relationships, both those based on kinship and marriage and those based on spiritual adoption. This humanizing boundary-breaching process helps to undermine potential institutional tension and competition between the two boards, and it fosters the sharing of information and collaborative efforts.

Continuity and Change in Beliefs, Practices, and Family Dynamics

While the new governance strategy brought organizational changes, those shifts have been experienced within a context grounded in the same ritual and symbolic elements on which The Church was founded: keeping the commandments, knowing the Bible, being filled with the Holy Ghost, and living a life of holiness. These fundamentals are being reinterpreted with an eye to the future as well as the past. The Church now has bylaws in place, and people appreciate the more efficient running of church affairs. Ritual use of space also has changed. The platform still seats The Church's spiritual leaders, but it is now shared by all of the elders, with the presiding elder for that Sabbath seated in the center chair where Mother Brown used to sit. When the presiding elder is introduced and rises to the podium, the saints all stand.

Codes of dress during worship continue to emphasize modesty. The elders still wear white dresses, but some wear modest caps or hats rather than mantles. Some lay female saints also wear colored, though modest, garments to church; none wears pants. A female saint must still dress modestly and cover her head, according to scripture, but how she complies is left up to individual discretion. Sabbath continues to be the most central communal ritual in the life of The Church. Sabbath evening service still begins at sunset Friday night, and Sabbath morning services are still held. Recently, however, there has been a dramatic change regarding afternoon service; how it occurred provides a window on current church governance.

In July 2010, the elder board came to a momentous decision after protracted, careful, and prayerful deliberation over an issue that had been of concern for some time: whether to hold Sabbath afternoon services which, in the summer, could be protracted, even when service began at 6 p.m., as had become the practice after Mother Brown's death. The elders came to a consensus that Sabbath afternoon services should no longer be held, and were rather surprised that this announcement met strong and emotional opposition, mainly "came from the young people," men and women in their forties and younger. There were two major objections: that ending Sabbath afternoon services would be "tearing down what the pastor had built up," and that the young people would lack the instruction and discipline they need to grow in their faith as commandment-keepers. On the first point, the elders' spokesperson asserted that while Mother Brown may have established the practices, there is no biblical requirement for a Sabbath afternoon service, making the practice "man-made," not divinely ordered. Besides, the elders' spokesperson added, rather self-reflectively, her generation of parents had made their children "sit in church all day"—when Sabbath afternoon service began at 3 p.m.—but in the end "they left anyway." The elder also pointed out that during afternoon services the young people often gather to socialize on the second floor of the building, only returning to service when it is about to end.

During the discussion that followed, the deacons maintained a certain distance, in keeping with the division of labor that makes decisions such as this the preserve of the elders. In response to the young people's concern, elders suggested youth-oriented modifications to Friday evening and Saturday morning services and said that they would take the matter under consideration. This did not appease the young people, who seemed to see Sabbath afternoon services as their space for leadership and expression. Still, the elders' decision would have remained if two of the elders had not changed their position and agreed with the young people. One of these, a member of the Tompkins family, had recently been installed; the other, an older elder, is a member of the Brown-Wilson family.

The two elders made it clear that they would be in the church Sabbath afternoons and welcomed anyone else to join them. They are joined by the young people who insist on the importance and value of this service, which includes religious education as well as forums for discussion. The four deacons also attend, one of whom provides instructional leadership; however, it is not clear whether the other deacons are present because they too feel the need for this service or because deacons have to return to the church anyway to handle the tithes and offerings after the sun has set—or both. The majority of the elders do not attend this service; nevertheless, they have not insisted that the church building be closed Saturday afternoons. As one consultant explained, the problem is not with *what* but the *way* it was done: the matter should have been taken back to the elders for reconsideration before any action was taken. It is difficult not to notice inter-familial and intergenerational dynamics of this issue, and for those concerned with institutional sustainability, the question is this: How willing are the saints to put the future of their faith community before family affiliation and personal revelation?

Intentionality, forethought, and planning are playing an increasingly important role in the life of The Church. Printed programs are prepared for each Sabbath service, demonstrating greater attention to time management and indicating the time by which the shout is expected to be over. Relatedly, removal of chairs to make room for the shout no longer occurs. Still, the spirit is not "quenched" even though it may mean "running over." For example, the printed program for June 22, 2002, states that Sabbath morning service begins at 10 a.m. with the presiding deacon opening the service. The opening selection, "Down at the Cross (Glory to His Name)," is followed by the reading of the Ten Commandments and morning prayer led by the presiding elder, followed by the morning song selection. The designated elder then leads the "Prayer of Requests," followed by a musical selection and two congregational songs. The plan is for the shouting to end by 11 a.m., when a designated brother reads a passage and the presiding elder preaches "Holy Ghost Scripture" ("Hear what the spirit saith to the Church"). This is followed by a choir selection and testimonies by visitors, elders, and the congregation. A deaconess reads the announcements, and at 1 p.m. service is dismissed until 6 p.m. Youth Bible study is now held separately on the second floor of the church. The program lists other services and programs, including Sabbath evening service and Tuesday evening Bible study, noting the name of the presiding elder.

Among upcoming activities listed on the programs are events involving other churches. Church-related enclosures range from a lined sheet for taking "Notes from the Sermons" to secular materials, such as information related to health conditions that are disproportionately prevalent among African Americans. Other printed materials include programs for other Church events such as the General Assembly, for special musical events such as the twenty-sixth anniversary of the Sunbeams choir and voluntary society, and instructive materials, such as "The Seventy Weeks Prophecy: A Predication of the Coming of Jesus, of His Mission, His Anointing and His Death" prepared by Deacon White. In the past, the Gospel Pearls Song Book and the Doctrinal Points were the only printed matter regularly consulted beyond the Bible. Now, in addition to the program and its enclosures, secular information and material found on the Internet finds its way into the hands of the saints. The "wall of the Lord" that the founding saints built around themselves is much more permeable as information from the world is readily, though selectively, accessed and disseminated.

General Assembly was the only formalized relationship The Church had with other religious institutions, but all three of the women who headed the Brooklyn church have passed on. The informal relationship with the Martins has intensified through their daughter, who realized her parents' dream of creating a retreat and vacation center in southern New Jersey. She heads the church there, and her members and the saints of The Church regularly exchange choir performances and have shared social gatherings. In the same vein, Elder April initiated the "annual fellowship day" at The Church, to which the New Jersey church has been invited, along with other nonmembers. Since Elder April's passing, Deacon Ezekiel has continued such outreach endeavors, especially the exchange of choirs. It is interesting that a founding saint, Elder April, would take such an active role in creating linkages between The Church and other churches when outreach was not practiced or encouraged under the pastor.

Saints still pay tithes faithfully. Rallies are no longer called, and The Church appears to be financially solvent. Indeed, there has been some talk of purchasing a new building outside of North Philadelphia, although the matter is still under consideration in light of the fact that North Philly, because of its proximity to Center City, is likely to be gentrified. Gentrification would make the property extremely valuable in the not-too-distant future and transform the presently neglected neighborhood into a more attractive, safe, and livable part of town. Interest-free loans are no longer available from the church treasury, a policy put in place by the deacons that some older saints see as a great and regrettable loss. However, there is a voluntary fund to which saints may choose to contribute and from which they are free to borrow if and when they need to do so.

Entirely new is the Education Fund started by Sister Brandy, one of Elder Walter and Elder Lonetta's daughters. Bravely, she introduced a fundraising talk at church by reminding The Church that she had broken a crack habit because of the power of the Holy Ghost and the support of The Church. She told the saints that other young people of The Church needed its support, and contributing to the Education Fund was a wonderfully concrete way to do this. Education Fund members are a very committed group of saints who contribute monthly dues, although one-time gifts are encouraged and fundraising events are held as well. The fund is self-governing, rather than under the control of the deacons. Members meet at least once every other month after Sabbath service, and membership is open to all. The only criterion for scholarship eligibility is that the student be accepted into an institution of higher education and submit a copy of the letter of acceptance. The Education Fund cannot give as much as its members would like, so they are considering new fundraising strategies. Still, its monetary gift helps to defray the cost of books and fees.

Education continues to be highly valued among the saints, and over time the educational achievements of the saints and their children have risen. In 2002, all high school graduates were attending some institution of higher learning, whether a four-year college, technical school, or community college. In spring 2008, The Church celebrated two high school graduates. Krystal, the daughter of Deaconess Linda and Deacon Ezekiel, graduated from the prestigious Philadelphia High School for Girls. Penny, who had been absorbed into the Wilson family, graduated from the Widener Memorial School for the physically challenged and medically fragile. Penny had been a student of Sister Sally Wilson Leary, Elder Ronald and Elder Esther's youngest daughter, a passionately engaged special-education teacher who also introduced "signed" praise to The Church's youth choir. When chatting with adult saints while I was finishing this book in 2010, those who are my peers almost always begin the report of their children's and grandchildren's progress by listing the degrees, diplomas, or qualifications their offspring are completing at institutions of higher learning.

The enculturation of youth has shifted significantly. Under the founding generation, young people were expected to comply with all church rules along with the adults. Now the elders tend to emphasize the importance of youth reaching a point of maturity before they are expected to embrace church beliefs and practices wholeheartedly. Until that time, the goal is to gradually, but consistently, ground them in biblically based doctrine and to reinforce their efforts to develop "a spiritual mind" that will stand them in good stead not only in the kingdom to come but also as adults in the larger society. The Church also provides secular activities for younger members that include picnics with the Sabbath-keeping church in Jersey, and celebrations of members' anniversaries and birthdays. In addition, the tradition of the annual "church picnic" has been continued, although at different locations. In 2010 it was held at Clementon Park, an amusement park where The Church reserved its own area of the grounds and arranged for both barbecued chicken and "good quality" all-beef hot dogs to be catered. Two buses transported the saints between Philadelphia and New Jersey, though elders were transported by car for their comfort and convenience.

In the end, The Church, as an experiment in organic institution-building, has succeeded in doing two things that new religious movements founded on charismatic authority often fail to do. It has survived the death of its founder, which has much to do with Mother Brown's biblically grounded organizational creativity. Just as remarkably, despite the male-centered biblical model, it has incorporated women into the spiritual leadership of the church. When I expressed my concern to Elder Walter that excluding women from the deacon board effectively excluded them from decision-making, he reminded me that cumulative revelation can intersect with institutional change. He observed that "in these last days," according to Daniel 12:4, "knowledge would be on the increase" and the Holy Ghost is able to reveal the need to make this change to the saints if this is what God "has in store" for them.

What lies ahead in the institutional future of The Church? The authority of the pastorate has been replaced by a consensus-based leadership of elders. The Church is retaining youth and incorporating them into church offices. Openings in the "wall of the Lord" have made the "dividing line" between The Church and the world less severe, as is evidenced in relaxed dress codes, ecumenical outreach, and a general air of being at more ease in the wider society. The challenge to the saints during this time in its institutional history is the challenge to all new religious movements throughout human history and across the globe—balancing a critical appreciation for the new and upcoming with those elements of the past that are tried and true.

6

RESPONSE

IN KEEPING WITH AFRICAN AMERICAN traditions of worship, this book was written as a response to several calls. The founding saints' narratives, which form the heart of this work, are a direct response to Cheryl Townsend Gilkes's call to replace "flat images" of African Americans with three-dimensional representations of their "nuanced humanity," giving voice to those silenced by oppressive social processes and thereby "writing the culture and its members into existence" (Gilkes 2002: 176). The project also answers Melvin Williams's call for "anthropological ethnography" that reveals "the beauty and the good that reside in the adaptive life styles of poor black people" which have too often been ignored or misrepresented (Williams 1974: 3). The chapters on social organization, "Family," and on rituals and symbols, "Becoming Saints," are responses to Anthea Butler's call for scholars of African American religious history to assess the organization, beliefs, and practices of Black churches beyond the main independent denominations (Butler 2007: 6). Ira Harrison has called for more anthropological case studies of storefront churches because they provide invaluable insights into a classical concern in anthropology of religion: how legitimate authority is established and reproduced when informal groups routinize charisma and become enduring formal institutions (Harrison 1966: 164).

At the same time, I have been inspired by Faye Harrison's call to rethink, revision, and rework anthropology by defying disciplinary practices that have relegated ethnography about and by African Americans to "veiled" and peripheral intellectual spaces (Harrison 2008: 15–19, 69). Like her, I experience myself as an anthropologist whose sociocultural location as an African American woman not only marks my positioning in the academy and larger society but also influences how I approach anthropological research. This study responds to the call for intellectual honesty about how the researcher's vantage point informs ethnography. I have resisted the temptation to "disappear" the ethnographic self for the sake of social-scientific distance and objectivity (Harrison 2008: 2–3, 67; Spickard 2002: 249–51; Harrison and Harrison 1999: 1–3; Okely and Callaway 1992: 5; Clifford 1986).

This study responds to the call for new perspectives in the study of the Black religious experience in America by situating The Church in relation to the Black Church in general and the Sanctified tradition in particular. To examine how African Americans have reformulated Protestant Christianity, I have drawn on the work of scholars who have de-territorialized and re-territorialized African and African Diaspora studies beyond the boundaries of the nation-state by exploring diasporic flows and transnational dialogues across the Atlantic (Harrison 2008; Yelvington 2001; Matory 2005: 3, 268–69; Alpers and Roberts 2003; Gordon and Anderson 1999; Gilroy 1993). Thus, The Church has been treated as a case study in the historical sociology of independent church movements (ICMs) in Africa and its Diaspora, making it possible to compare the first wave of ICMs among Blacks in North America to the rise of independent African churches among the Yoruba of Nigeria. Moreover, the selective legitimating of African-derived slave religion in Sanctified churches can be considered in tandem with the institutionalization of selected features of Yoruba spirituality in Aladura Christianity.

This book has nuanced the notion of Diaspora by addressing it through the prism of founding saints' lives in both the South and the North. Their personal stories foster a subtler understanding of the Diaspora in terms of micro-migration, or migration within migration, fostered by unrelenting dislocations. My point here is that the Diaspora of people of African descent in America did not end with the involuntary and deadly Middle Passage. Black people's history in the South included constant movement: the experience of being sold from one plantation to another, often far away from kin; searching for freedom and family through the Civil War and Emancipation; and changing from one White-owned plantation to another to try to eke out a living by sharecropping. In the urban North the journeying continued, as the search for home was hindered by factors such as job discrimination, health discrepancies, educational inequity, and White flight. With the collaboration of realtors, White citizens, and politicians, these factors created and reproduced segregated neighborhoods of Black people with lower incomes and less political capital, which are so important to making a community's voice heard and ensuring that its needs are met. The Great Migration, then, entailed mass flight from a familiar land of oppression to an unknown one within the same nation-state.

Rethinking Routinization: Gender, Age, and Pragmatic Visionaries

The Church made the transition from a religious movement led by a female charismatic personality to a formal organization in which power is decentralized, decision-making is consensus-based, and women and men share decision-making power. Before Mother Brown died at age 105, she put in place a biblically based organizational structure that replaced leadership centralized in a pastor with a more inclusive form of governance. The all-male deacon board continues to handle church business while elders, who can be male or female, make decisions regarding the spiritual life of the church. The distinction is not rigid; deacons also bring major administrative issues before the elders. Although they have not yet used it, elders have the power to veto proposals that, after fasting and prayer, they determine to be contrary to scripture. The potential for conflict between the board of elders and the board of deacons is mitigated by intimate relationships of kinship and spiritual adoption, which undermine structural tensions.

During her lifetime, Mother Brown was the only woman with the authority to establish formal church policy. The new arrangement reconfigures women's roles so that several women exercise decision-making power as elders. Figure 1 highlights the fact that women have been central to the growth of The Church as they recruited kin and absorbed spiritual relations into extended family complexes. Males remain crucial to the life of the congregation, beyond their administrative roles as deacons. Men can be ordained as evangelists and as elders, who in the words of one saint conduct the "real work" of leading the saints. In addition to skills, gifts, and gender, another organizing principle in The Church is age; elders in particular must not only "know scripture" and live "the Word" but also "have age."

That The Church has survived for twenty-five years since the death of the founder; that its membership is stable; that its offices are refilled; and that the bicameral body of elders and deacons has established functional decision-making strategies suggest new insights into the routinization of charisma. Not all charismatic leaders are so caught up in visions of the transcendent that they ignore the nuts and bolts of creating an enduring institution. Significantly, bureaucratic forethought and creative organizing require neither formal education nor the resources of class, gender, or racial privilege. Mother Brown was a working-poor Black single mother faced with the challenge of negotiating the transition from southern rural life to northern urban living during the first phase of the Great Migration. Motivated by divine inspiration, energized by indomitable determination, equipped with deep insight into human nature, and possessed of that rarest of human capacities, good common sense, she ensured that The Church would outlast her as a Holy-Ghost–filled, commandment-keeping church.

New Perspectives on the Sanctified Tradition

The ethnographic material presented in this book has contested stereotyped representations of storefront Sanctified churches as static, anti-intellectual, escapist, and world-rejecting religious arenas in which Black people release stress and compensate for their low socioeconomic status in the dominant society. The Church continues to address the challenges facing any living institution in regard to balancing change with respect for tradition. Although Mother Brown forbade voting as carnal and worldly activity, the saints in The Church today are more active citizens; some are professional social workers, and others have been very involved in welfare rights and public school issues. The Church has begun to engage in tentative ecumenism with other commandment-keeping churches by exchanging pulpits and choirs and attending one another's social events. Dress codes are less stringent and less gendered, and the youth tend to be "heard" and considered rather than made to comply unquestioningly. Still, the faith remains millennial, and commandment-keeping, lived holiness, biblical primacy, and Holy-Ghost–infilling remain at the core of the faith.

In sharp contrast to the anti-intellectualism often attributed to the Pentecostal and Holiness tradition, formal education has been valued by the saints since The Church was established; indeed, the narratives of founding saints suggest that they brought this aspiration with them as they moved north. Mother Brown promoted formal education and set high standards of achievement for the youth, which were reinforced by their parents and other saints. As commandment-keepers, children were, and still are, expected to perform well in school and reach the highest levels of academic excellence, as attested by the Education Fund and by the normative matriculation of high school graduates in institutions of higher learning.

I suspect that a systematic study of attitudes toward education among Black Holiness and Pentecostal churches may well show that The Church is not alone in valuing formal education. For example, Ida Robinson started schools, and the Church of God in Christ founded Bible colleges. Any anti-intellectualism that did exist is likely to have been doctrine-specific, rather than a general deprecation of formal education. Radical anti-intellectualism is a luxury that Black people in America cannot afford, for as the saints instruct the youth of The Church, "education is one thing that they can't take away from you."

The interpretation of storefront Sanctified churches in terms of "compensation," according to A. G. Miller, not only fails to take seriously the believers' faith claims but suggests that they are too weak or inept to deal with their circumstances in "constructive" ways. An alternative explanation, suggests Miller, is to view these faith communities as institutional vehicles that "shape and direct change" in believers' religious and social lives by tapping into divinely inspired power (Miller 1996). In this vein, this book delineates the organizational processes and institutional development of The Church as a creatively adaptive expression of self-determination in which the history, culture, humanity, and well-being of Black souls is not an afterthought. While the founding saints may have been viewed by outsiders as "deprived," their narratives portray the saints as people who, despite the denigrating labels applied to them, and in defiance of the structural violence of American hierarchies, knew themselves to be both profoundly human and "saints of the Most High God."

A Sanctified Hermeneutics of Suspicion

Sanctified religion has been characterized as uncritical. I contend, instead, that there are aspects of Holiness-Pentecostalism that situate the faith "over and against" majority culture by assessing the status quo as intrinsically suspect. Saints do not strive to conform to dominant norms or aspire to keep up with the Joneses. No matter how much money or power people in the world might have, "if they aren't saved, they're going to hell." The saints' interpretation of the parable that compares the wealthy seeking admission to heaven to a camel trying to pass through the eye of the needle makes material accumulation questionable, except as a sign of God's blessing. Divinely sanctioned idealism, asceticism, and suspicion of the status quo can foster an effective critique of institutionalized inequity as sin. As youths who repeated scripture and said prayers while being carpooled to Logan School, we were instilled with belief in the equality of all people before God, which countered the racist words and actions of White students and teachers alike.

Although it is little known, some spiritual leaders of Sanctified churches have engaged in political witness. For example, both Bishop Ida Robinson of Mount Zion Church and COGIC founder Bishop Charles Harrison Mason expressed their pacifist commitments during World War I. The *Official*

Manual with the Doctrines and Discipline of COGIC explicitly opposes the death penalty. Mount Sinai's newsletter, *The Latter Day Messenger*, criticized economic discrimination and lynching. During the Civil Rights Movement, Addie Wyatt and Fannie Lou Hamer, who organized communities around issues of voting and economic equity, had been leaders within Holiness churches. More recently, Harvard-educated Reverend Eugene Rivers formed the Pan African Charismatic Evangelical Congress (PACEC), a coalition of grassroots organizations committed to protesting and dismantling oppressive social structures (Alexander 2008: 128–34; Daniels 2003: 164–82; Best 1998: 158–61, 168). The House of the Lord Pentecostal, which began as a storefront church, has consistently wed social justice, sustainable community development, and biblically grounded spiritual zeal to address issues such as the anti-apartheid struggle in the 1970s, well before other Black churches were taking the matter to heart.[1] Indeed, Oberlin College professor A. G. Miller, who began a branch of this church in Ohio, was inspired to "reclaim" his Sanctified roots when in the House of the Lord he encountered saints who "did not see a contradiction between spirituality and social involvement" (Grossman and Lipton-Lubet 2009).

It is also worthy of note that James Baldwin grew up in a Sanctified church and, after being saved as a teenager, preached at several Harlem churches (Baldwin 1948: 29, 42). Never looking to the majority for self-validation when he "took a stand" against a sinful world may well have prepared Baldwin to take an unrelenting literary stand against the sin of social inequities rooted in racism, classism, and heterosexism. I contend that the protest and activism of the House of the Lord and PACEC; the Civil Rights activism of Wyatt and Hamer; the critical publications of pacifist Bishops Robinson and Mason; and the indomitable critical voice of James Baldwin have roots in a spirit-grounded "hermeneutics of suspicion" that questions surface meanings to reveal truths concealed by those with the power to represent realities in ways that serve their own interests.

Spirit-Driven Critique and World Christianity

Pneumatologically grounded hermeneutics of suspicion extend beyond the Black Sanctified church tradition. At its Web site, Pentecostals and Charismatics for Peace and Justice (PCPJ), an international, interracial, intergenerational, and ecumenical organization, celebrates the pacifism of Harvard-educated Assemblies of God (AG) theologian Stanley Horton and the hundreds of other AG members who were conscientious objectors during World War II. PCPJ invites each and every Web site visitor "to become a Jesus-shaped Spirit-empowered peacemaker, justice-seeker," listing ten reasons for joining the organization:

10. Everyone should belong to at least one organization whose very NAME will raise eyebrows and lead to questions.
9. Jesus said, "Blessed are the peacemakers" and you want to be able to name and claim that blessing.
8. This is a great chance to connect with all the radical peacemakers *and* your Pentecostal roots.
7. You get to meet and befriend a wide diversity of Christian peacemakers from all over the world whom you might otherwise never know.
6. Children deserve as peaceful a world as possible. Help work for a more peaceful world for children you love, yours, the children of your church, nieces & nephews, etc.
5. When Jesus returns, he'll expect to find us faithful to his Way.
4. Peacemaking in a world of insane and sinful violence takes miracles and the folks in PCPJ really believe in miracles.
3. Nonviolent, peacemaking Christians have a lifestyle and message that is inviting—and so aids evangelism and mission.
2. The PCPJ motto: "Jesus-shaped Spirit-empowered peace and justice" should be the guiding principle of ALL CHRISTIANS.
1. And the Number One Reason to Join/Support Pentecostals & Charismatics for Peace & Justice is: Jesus would do it.[2]

"Jesus-shaped Spirit-empowered" peacemakers and justice-seekers can also be found among people who are no longer directly affiliated with spirit-privileging churches, but whose social action was spawned in these spiritual waters. Diane Wilson is the author of *Holy Roller: Growing up in the Church of Knock Down Drag Out; or, How I Quit Loving a Blue-Eyed Jesus—A Childhood Memoir* (2008) and an environmental-justice activist who led a successful campaign against Formosa Plastics for dumping toxic waste in the waters of her hometown in Texas, where the residents have lived by fishing those waters. At a reading for her book in Raleigh, North Carolina, Wilson spoke eloquently about the ways her Pentecostal background continues to shape how she lives her life.[3] For Wilson, "being saved" lies "at the mystical end" of Christianity where the Bible is literally true, nothing is impossible, and miracles are part of routine human existence. Having had direct experiences of being filled with the Holy Ghost as a child, Wilson felt prepared to be a "warrior," in part because of the "integrity" of living in holiness and "doing the right thing."

I focus on Holy-Ghost–grounded social activism to demonstrate that a person does not have to be a liberal social gospel theologian, middle class, or privileged in order to recognize in scripture the radical call to feed the poor, pity the widowed and orphaned, welcome the stranger, protect the homeless, and dismantle the social structures that promote institutionalized sin. Despite a heinous history of complicity with tyranny, exploitation, war, and mass murder, religion has the potential to be a source of poignant social critique and divinely sanctioned radical action. Not only is religion potentially much more than an "opiate of the masses," but Christians who shout and speak in tongues have transgressed racial, ethnic, and national boundaries to pursue social justice. How does this form of social vision and activism relate to The Church? The Church's institutional emergence, nurturing of Black family and community, and practice of producing youth committed to academic excellence constitute a lived critique of social inequity in America.

This study contests the peripheralization of religious movements that cannot be readily situated near the "center" of world religions. Labeled as cults and sects, they are "othered," and their ritual and symbolic content is reduced to a mere epiphenomenon of social dislocation. Instead, this study resituates an inner-city storefront church within the discourse of World Christianity, in response to Joel Robbins's (2003a) call for the anthropological study of Christianity as an arena of intellectual knowledge in its own right. The saints have reworked Christianity in their approach to Bible study as a consensus-building communal theological reflection (Bielo 2008), but also an arena of knowledge within which literacy is achieved and presentation of the self is refined. Taking themselves out of the contemporary world of oppression, exclusion, consumerism, and moral disorder, the saints have repositioned themselves historically within the early church that predated its co-optation by empire. The saints resonate with early Christians who gathered in one another's homes, were led by women as well as men, and constituted a movement within Judaism in which there was no conflict between God's "grace" through Jesus Christ, a Jew, and the "works" of keeping the commandments. In this way, Judeo-Christian historical origins have provided The Church with a metahistorical narrative framework within which African-derived ritual and symbolic legacies have been selectively reinforced and legitimated by spirit-privileging elements in American Protestant revivalism.

·

My career as an anthropologist, including the writing of this work, is an outgrowth of The Church, in which I was imbued with spirit-grounded hermeneutical suspicion well before being introduced to the writings of Marx or Foucault. Growing up "saved and sanctified" means living on the rim of dominant culture, constantly looking at it askance. The Church has produced its own academic who, by writing this book, has documented its history, explored its sociological significance, and given voice to the saints who are too often silenced by those with the power and resources to control what is published, included in school curricula, or deemed worthy of media coverage. In telling the story of a storefront Sanctified church, this book has related one more chapter in the saga of the quest for meaning and community, one more way of being human and faithful across historical time and social space.

NOTES

Chapter 1. Call

1. The saints have cooperated with this research project on condition that I not use the real names of the church, its leaders, and its members. The saints are neither rich nor powerful in material terms; many are working poor, and many elders barely survive on Social Security. Still, they know themselves to be children of the Most High God, who deserve the good things in life, not least of which is respect for their privacy.

2. I stand within the intellectual tradition of vindicationism that arose as an intellectual critique of both the racist assumptions undergirding turn-of-the-century academic theories of social and cultural evolution and the racist caricatures of Black people that pervaded popular culture at that time (Drake 1987: xvi–xviii, 1–6, 85–86, 92, 100).

3. Enslaved Blacks escaped and established at least fifty maroon communities between 1672 and 1864 in mountainous, forested, or swampy regions of South Carolina, North Carolina, Virginia, Louisiana, Florida, Georgia, Mississippi, and Alabama (Sayers 2006; Orser 1998; Aptheker 1939: 167). Up to 100,000 slaves, about one-fifth of the population of enslaved Africans and African Americans at the outbreak of the American Revolution, were willing to be moved to Canada, the United Kingdom, and Sierra Leone after gaining their freedom in exchange for joining or assisting British troops (Sanneh 1999: 12, 33). Before the Civil War, thousands of men and women escaped slavery, fleeing north and then to Canada (Whitfield 2006: 18–20) as well as south to Spanish-controlled Florida, where they developed liaisons with native people. Still, before the Civil War most Black migration was forced, disrupting thousands of enslaved families when husbands, wives, or children were "sold down the river" or relocated west during the rapid expansion of the Cotton Kingdom (Baptist 2002: 9–11, 18–23, 30–31).

4. February 20, 2011, http://www.chicagosuperads.com/real_estate_Classifieds/C580A 826554P1/Wanted_Store_Front_for_Church_Services.

5. Since enslaved Africans represented a captive audience for Christian mission, why was this opportunity to Christianize hundreds of thousands of "pagan" souls bypassed? Slave owners feared that conversion might require manumission of their human property, even after a 1667 Maryland law guaranteed "that the conferring of baptisme doth not alter the condition of the person as to his bondage or freedom" (quoted in Scherer 1975: 30; see also Frazier 1963: 26; Raboteau 1978: 48, 80, 86–87, 96, 98–99, 113; Lewis 1996: 19). Ethical ambivalence is also exemplified by nineteenth-century Presbyterians determining that slavery was a "moral evil," but not all slave owners were guilty of a moral sin (Baer and Singer 1992: 5; Scherer 1975: 134–36). This ethical schizophrenia was bolstered by the financial dependence of clergy on slaveholding laity and their assimilation within slaveholding culture;

the complexities of church governance strategies that undermined a sustainable antislavery platform; the lure of the economic benefits that slave labor afforded post-Revolutionary America; and fear that religious literacy would fuel rebellion. For example, a minister might be sent to the colonies by British churches and arrive holding antislavery sentiments; but in time these commitments could be compromised by their financial dependence on parishioners whose profits depended on slave labor (Scherer 1975: 30). Shifting ethical footing is manifest on the institutional level: a 1784 Methodist national antislavery platform had a retroactive rule requiring all slaveholding members to set a manumission date; but twelve years later the General Conference established a new, loophole-ridden antislavery platform (Scherer 1975: 137–41). Baptists' early public opposition to slavery was difficult to sustain because of the decentralized organization of the denomination (Washington 1984: 42; Scherer 1975: 132–37). Nationalism infected clerical and secular leaders alike with the desire for wealth that unpaid slave labor provided the United States as a speedy route to economic viability for the newly independent country (Scherer 1975: 104–5). In addition, the nagging fear of slave revolt informed the ambivalence surrounding the Christianization of enslaved Africans. European Americans formulated Christianity as "a religion of the book"; Protestant Christianity requires literacy. However, Whites were convinced that "if you teach [a slave] to write, he will write himself a pass and run away" (Blassingame 1977: 689). Religious gatherings of literate slaves were feared even more after the slave revolts, led in 1800 by the politically astute and religiously motivated Gabriel Prosser (Wilmore 1983: 75), in 1822 by Denmark Vesey, an active member of an African Methodist Episcopal (AME) church in Charleston that was shut down after his execution, and in 1831 by Nat Turner, whose visions convinced him of the rightfulness of destroying slavery. Slaveholders preferred to employ preachers who taught "servants obey your master" (Colossians 3:22), used specialized catechisms, and employed patrollers to monitor Black gatherings (Levine 1977: 45, 48; Besson and Chevannes 1996: 210; Hamilton 1972: 47; Lincoln and Mamiya 1990: 24; Raboteau 1978: 152, 165, 171; Lewis 1996: 36; Olmsted 1856: 131–32).

6. Significant instances of rapprochement between White and Black Holiness and Pentecostals include the 1994 Memphis Miracle, when Charismatics and Pentecostals met to create the Pentecostal/Charismatic Church of North America (PCCNA), replacing the Pentecostal Fellowship of North America (PFNA), established in 1948 by White Pentecostals who excluded Black Pentecostals. At the 1994 gathering, White Pentecostals publicly apologized to Black participants for this racist behavior, grounding the rationale for their apology in the recollection of the interracial nature of the Azusa Street revival (Rosenior 2009). I participated in a more ecumenical expression of reconciliation with a Holiness-Pentecostal flavor at the Third International Interdisciplinary Conference of the African Christian Diaspora in Europe, held at the Hirschluch Conference Centre in Berlin, September 11–15, 2003. While clearly an academic conference, it included practitioner-scholars from various denominations and faiths. A reconciliation service was held, during which White worshippers asked Blacks to forgive them for colonization and slavery; it was proposed and initiated by a White male member of a British Holiness church.

7. Since White Holiness-Pentecostalism and the Sanctified tradition both privilege spirit, why distinguish between them? White Pentecostalism and the Black Sanctified tradition differ in their cultural roots, historical trajectories, and ontologies of worship. The cultural sources of storefront Sanctified churches extend back to West African spiritual beliefs and practices. Their historical trajectory traverses African-derived slave religion spanning two

hundred years of southern history, symbolically legitimated by initially interracial Holiness and Pentecostal outpourings and then carried from the South to the North during the Great Migration. Sources of White American Holiness spirituality have been located within ancient Christian traditions of "charismata," or signs of the Holy Ghost. These traditions survived both Roman imperial domestication and medieval institutionalization; for example, German mystic Hildegard of Bingen (1098–1179) spoke in a *lingua ignota*, an unknown tongue. Twentieth-century Pentecostalism has also been located within the Armenian evangelical stream of Orthodox Christianity, which emphasized Bible study and the piety of the early church. Additionally, although John Wesley (1703–91), the Anglican cleric and spiritual father of Methodism, cannot be described as a Charismatic or Pentecostal, his second blessing theology is important for the development of modern Pentecostalism in the British Isles and in America, where his teachings informed the Great Awakening, Methodism, and Holiness (Llewellyn 1997: 1–5). The Second Great Awakening gave rise to a short and tentative interracial milieu of Holiness and Pentecostal movements until, complying with normative racial practices, Whites chose institutional segregation over spiritual equality.

8. In the 1940s, the African Methodist Episcopal (AME) Church began ordaining women (Grant 1986: 368). The National Baptist denomination ordained its first woman minister, Dr. Olivia B. Stokes, in 1953 (Carpenter 1989–90: 12, 18; Best 1998: 153).

Chapter 2. City Tales

1. In 1794, finding segregated Sabbaths unacceptable, Philadelphia's Blacks exercised religious, institutional, and social self-determination, broke with the historically White St. George Methodist Church, and founded the African Methodist Episcopal Church (AME) and the first Black Episcopal parish, under the leadership of Richard Allen and Absalom Jones, respectively. The AME's Mother Bethel was not housed in a conventional church building but in a converted blacksmith shop. In 1816, AME became the first independent Black denomination in America (George 1973: 10–48; Gregg 1993: 2; Hopper 2008: 6–7).

2. Watson's description generally deprecates Black life, revealing the tendency of White American Protestants at that time to associate rhythmic body movement with sex, sin, and heathenism (Stuckey 1987: 24). In his 1819 book, *Methodist Error*, Watson decries the way Black Methodists were "corrupting" worship with overly enthusiastic music and dancing that, even more worrisomely, some Whites appeared to be adopting (Stuckey 1987: 22–24, 75; Nash 2006: 40–41).

3. The burning of Black churches targets the one institution that Blacks have controlled in American history because of its significance as power base and social hub of Black people. This hostility continued: between 1962 and 1965, ninety-three predominantly rural Black churches in the South were bombed or burned at a time when rural churches were encouraging voter registration (Sernett 1997: 240).

4. Providing insight into the social-psychological dynamics of White race riots, historian Gail Bederman suggests that between the end of the Civil War and the beginning of World War I, White Anglo-Saxon Protestant males experienced dramatic economic, political, sociological, and even biological assaults on their racial identity and sense of self that stimulated them to attack Black men. In the New South, White males were unable to reassert their unquestioned supremacy. Nationwide, the prevailing notion of middle-class manliness was undermined by the shift from small-scale to industrial capitalism and by several economic recessions between 1873 and 1896. European immigrant males challenged

native-born Whites' political domination when they played major roles in 37,000 strikes between 1881 and 1905. Blacks who had been concentrated in the South "voted with their feet" and migrated northward and westward in dramatic numbers, competing for jobs and social space. At the same time, middle-class White women were moving into formerly all-male professions in education, the clergy, medicine, and politics. Around this time, physicians and psychologists announced a new disease, "neurasthenia," a state of nervous prostration that was presumed to afflict middle-class men as it did middle-class women; men of "peasant stock" were believed to enjoy "primitive" manly vitality. The simultaneous popularization of Darwinism and the expansion of European colonialism conflated notions of race with culture, intensifying White men's sense of superiority and anxiety about their manhood. Relatedly, the 1890s also saw the rise of boxing as a central arena for asserting the ideal of White manliness (Bederman 1995: xi–xii, 1–4, 12–15, 17, 20, 25).

5. Major Philadelphia-area industrial employers took deliberate measures to encourage and secure Black workers. The Pennsylvania and Erie Railroad sent James H. Duckey, a Black Philadelphia clergyman and clerk in the office of the vice president of railroad operations, to Florida with an empty passenger train to recruit Black men. By 1917 the railroad had brought twelve thousand workers into the state by offering them free transportation, but fewer than two thousand actually worked for the railroad; exercising their agency, Blacks sought out better-paying jobs than the railroad offered.

6. The neighborhood's name marked its history: in 1772 business partners David Franks and Nathan Levy, who established Philadelphia's first synagogue, bought the Woodford Mansion located in this area (Meyers 1999: 16).

7. Cherry's Family Restaurant, a kosher eatery in Strawberry Mansion across from the trolley barn, was one of the very few places the saints felt free to consume hot dogs (Meyers 1999: 17). This shared diet is found today; some Muslims purchase meat at Jewish butchers because the dietary rules for *Hallal* (Arabic for permitted food) and *Kashrut* (Hebrew for the Jewish dietary code) are similar. Today I do not believe that eating pork endangers my soul, but the thought of deviating from this long-established dietary habit is discomfiting. Pork does not enter my home. I still "kosher" my chicken before cooking it, as my mother taught me, by salting down the chicken, letting it stand to draw out all the blood, and then pouring boiling water over it. I have knowingly eaten pork only twice in my life, both times in situations where food has been especially prepared for me by hosts who had gone to great lengths to offer me hospitality. Chinese students from Taiwan at the Transportation Center of Northwestern University graciously used their limited funds to prepare an elaborate banquet of foods in which pork was a major component. In Nigeria, a colleague who invited me to dinner at her home had prepared a special meal with pork entrée at great cost. On both occasions, I had failed to tell my hosts that I did not eat pork.

8. For other narratives of Black domestic workers, see Clark-Lewis 1994: vii–viii, 51–66, 195–99; Rollins 1985.

9. Hazel Carby describes the movement of women from the rural South to the urban North as generating "moral panic" expressed in the rise of institutions focused on the plight of "colored women" and in their representation as "sexually degenerated and, therefore, socially dangerous." In her 1905 article, "Southern Girls in the North," Frances A. Kellor, a Progressive reformer who directed the Inter-Municipal Committee on Household Research in New York City, observed that due to Black women's "increasing inefficiency and desire to avoid hard work" Whites were supplanting Blacks in the service sector. These

women, Kellor opined, require "preventive measures," especially "for the green helpless negro women brought up here from the South" on promises of "easy work, lots of money, and good times." Carby argues that recently arrived Black females represented a threat not only to northern White establishment notions of middle-class domesticity but also to the Black middle class, as demonstrated by representations of Black women in 1920s novels about Harlem by Claude McKay and Carl Van Vechten. Carby also notes that Jane Edna Hunter, a professional Black nurse and president of the Phyllis Wheatley Association, characterized her organization as "an instrument for the social and *moral redemption*" of young black women (Kellor and Hunter quoted in Carby 1992, emphasis added).

10. An 1881 state law had made segregation of public facilities, including schools, illegal, and by 1900 Philadelphia's Black population had an 80 percent literacy rate. Still, by 1908 the school system was segregated, by various means including the deliberate gerrymandering of the catchment areas of elementary schools and the deliberate relegation of Black students to nonacademic tracks. Only the college preparatory high schools were not segregated; because so few Black students were allowed to continue in the academic track, a separate school for them would have been too expensive for the school district. Black children who attended White schools were taught in annexes or separate classes (Ballard 1984: 52, 59; also see Levenstein 2009: 121–55).

11. United Methodist Church's Second Emancipation League endorsed women's suffrage. Child rearing and health were foci of the Mothers' Club at Zion Baptist. Banner Real Estate, designed to help blacks in property and business matters, was founded by the pastor of Holy Trinity Baptist Church, G.L.P. Taliaferro. In 1916, First African Baptist Church, under the leadership of Rev. William Credit, established the Mutual Aid Insurance Society; later it founded both the Cherry Building and Loan Association, which offered mortgages to Black home buyers, and the Downingtown Industrial School, modeled on Booker T. Washington's plan for vocational education (Hopper 2008: 30–33). Major Richard R. Wright and his son, then editor of the *Christian Recorder*, "official organ of the AME," established the Citizen and Southern Bank and Trust Company. With four AME bishops sitting on its board of directors, this company helped Black migrants secure funds to buy homes and start businesses (Gregg 1993: 59; 207–8). The Interdenominational Ministerial Alliance of Black church leaders, despite its members' limited resources, emerged in 1917 to create lodgings and jobs for new arrivals and worked hard to dispel negative stereotypes among Philadelphia residents and policy makers. The White-controlled uplift organization, Committee on Negro Migration, was a charitable arm of White-controlled industries such as Franklin Sugar Refining and the Pennsylvania Railroad, which had reaped high profits from the influx of black labor (Gregg 1993: 201–1).

12. Some of these church songs are found in *Gospel Pearls* (1921), the only songbook I recall using during devotional service in The Church. These tunes included Tindley's "We'll Understand It Better By and By" and "I'll Be Alright," which was later sung by Civil Rights activists as "I'll Overcome Someday." Eileen Southern has argued that Tindley did not intend his gospel music for use in formal worship services in his Methodist Episcopal church, but rather as "popular and religious songs for Sunday School, Prayer Meetings, Epworth League Meetings, and Social Gatherings" (Southern 1997: 457–58; Hopper 2008: 36).

13. Allen Ballard has suggested that color caste in Philadelphia was imported by free Black Charlestonians, who brought their color and status practices to the city before the Civil War. For example, T. K. Sasportas, who was reportedly the son of a Jewish merchant and a woman

of color, had been manumitted and educated, and belonged to a family of colored slaveholders, was schooled at Philadelphia's Institute for Colored Youth, established in 1837. Sasportas fought in a Black regiment during the Civil War and was a Republican Party delegate to the 1868 South Carolina Constitutional Convention (Ballard 1984: 55; 96; Marcus 1993: 208–9).

14. In addition to mentoring Frazier at the University of Chicago, Robert E. Park, a sociologist who studied race, ethnicity, and class, also taught at historically Black universities such as Tuskegee and Fiske, influencing a generation of African American scholars.

15. Mother Jones, who along with her husband had attended Corinthian Baptist Church in Philadelphia, found herself attracted to Holiness and became a member of COGIC. After attending "Prayer Meetings and Consecrations" at Mother Dabney's Garden of Prayer Church of God in Christ, she had a vision of a "community of believers which would cross denominational boundaries but remain faithful to the basic tenets of Truth." Like Mother Dabney, she fasted and prayed "for the birth of a Tabernacle where Christians could come and be healed." With her husband she co-founded the Christian Tabernacle Church, which had a distinct charter but was affiliated with COGIC. June 4, 2009, http://www.jmcogic.org/Mother%27s%20Page.htm.

16. Personal communication from Walter Wolfram, September 4, 2008.

Chapter 3. Saints Tales

1. See http://freepages.genealogy.rootsweb.ancestry.com/~ajac/scmarlboro.htm (accessed July 12, 2011).

2. Also see excerpt from "South Carolina: A Handbook" (1927), http://www.carolana.com/SC/Counties/marlboro_county_sc.html (accessed July 12, 2011).

3. Available at http://www.city-data.com/housing/houses-Blenheim-South-Carolina.html and http://www.city-data.com/city/Blenheim-South-Carolina.html and http://www.carolana.com/SC/Counties/marlboro_county_sc.html. Also see "South Carolina: A Handbook" (1927). All Web sites accessed July 12, 2011.

4. Not until I came to know members of the White side of the Crumbley family did I hear a lynching story from the perspective of a White child. James Crumbley, a successful professional now retired and living in Norfolk, extended the warm hand of friendship from the White side of the Crumbley family to the Black side. He reserved accommodations at a nearby chalet so that we might attend the first integrated Crumbley family reunion in 1997. Other interactions have grown out of that reunion, including my visit to the Alabama Crumbleys, a branch of the family that was established during the Civil War when one of three Crumbley brothers, finding slavery unsupportable, left his home and family in Georgia and went to Alabama where he fought with a New York regiment in the Union Army. His grandson, my now deceased cousin Eugene Crumbley, who had invited me to visit him in Holly Pond, Alabama, took me to his grandfather's grave site and gave me a copy of his Union Army discharge papers. The recollection of lynching was Cousin James's, who was in his eighties when he related it to me. After attending a public lecture I presented in Norfolk, he drove me to the airport, and as we waited he related his two earliest memories as a child growing up in Georgia. The first was of a Black shoeshine man whose ventriloquist puppet had terrified him with its wooden gaping mouth. The second memory began with a mob of people and loud commotion in the streets. When he asked his father what was happening, his father told him that they said a Black man had raped a White nurse. Cousin James and I sat in shared silence until I asked him if he knew whether the man was guilty. He said he

never found out. He added that no explanation was given; this lynching was part of the way it was in the only world he knew.

5. Lynching and the protracted protests against it are represented in American cultural productions, including Lin Shi Khan and Tony Perez's 1935 *Scottsboro, Alabama: A Story in Linoleum Cuts*, Jose Clement Orozco's *Negros Colgados*, and Isamu Noguchi's 1935 *Death (Lynched Figure)*. The Noguchi sculpture is a three-quarter-size burned figure made of metal suspended from a real rope, which was created in response to a photograph of African American George Hughes after he was tortured, lynched, and his body burned in Sherman, Texas, in 1930 (Apel and Smith 2008: 51–52; Apel 2004: 97; Kahn and Perez 2002: 51, 97, 99, 121). Just six months after Hughes's murder, a group of White women led by Texas native Jessie Daniel Ames started the Association of Southern Women for the Prevention of Lynching, revolting against the chivalry associated with protecting southern White women's honor (Hall 1979: 159). More recent representations of racialized lynching in America posted on the web include photographs collected by James Allen, who also provides the accompanying voiceover. See http://www.withoutsanctuary.org/movie1.html (accessed February 16, 2011).

6. "Mother" Elizabeth Juanita Dabney was a healer, teacher, "intercessor," and COGIC pioneer church woman. She is author of *Praying Through*, first published in 1954 and reprinted by Church of God in Christ Publishing House in 1987. The book chronicles her recruitment by Bishop Charles Harrison Mason, the founder of the Church of God in Christ. See http://charismamag.com/articles/index/pho/16074 (accessed February 4, 2009).

7. When Leena recounted coming to Philadelphia to marry a man whom she had not seen for some time, she added, "Always have your ticket home." I did not press the matter, for Leena, like her son, Jerald, spoke little, making these few words rare and precious gems.

8. Not all the wounds were physical. His wife Beverly recalled that when he returned from the war, she would have to hold his hands because sometimes he would simply "sit and shake," apparently suffering from what today is diagnosed as post-traumatic stress disorder.

9. Alexander Bettis founded over forty Baptist churches and several Baptist associations, including the Mount Canaan Association, made up of twenty-four Baptist churches in the vicinity that supported the academy. See "The Bettis Academy: Restoration, Preservation, Heritage Museum, and Tourist Project," American Folk Life Center, Library of Congress, http://lcweb2.loc.gov/cocoon/legacies/SC/200003514.html (accessed September 25, 2006); "Bettis Academy and Junior College: Former Private Institution for Blacks, Trenton, S.C.," Mount Canaan Association Inc., http://mtcanaanassociation.org/bahistory.html (accessed September 29, 2006); "Records, 1939–1948, of Bettis Academy (Edgefield County, S.C.)," South Carolina Library, University of South Carolina Society Manuscript Collections, available at http://www.sc.edu/library/socar/uscs/1999/bettis./html (accessed October 2, 2006).

10. Brutal violence was endemic in Edgefield (Moore 2006: 147, 150). For example, in an 1896 fight between a White man named Dorn and an unnamed Black man, Dorn dispatched the Black man by chopping off his head. The judge ruled it a justifiable homicide, after which Dorn was released (Moore 2006: 193).

11. Jacob Rubenstein (1877–1948) emigrated to the United States from Latvia and arrived in Edgefield around 1903, where he started a business that he ran until 1987. In 1911, Israel Mukashy (1882–1964), who had immigrated from the Russian Empire, purchased a business formerly owned by Goldsberg & Son and operated it until he retired in 1950. *Historical Marker Database: The Jewish Merchants of Edgefield*, http://www.hmdb.org/marker.asp?marker=12412 (accessed August 7, 2009).

12. See http://www.southcarolinagenealogy.org/south-carolina-counties/berkeley/; http://freepages.genealogy.rootsweb.ancestry.com/~ajac/sccharleston.htm; http://www.discoversouthcarolina.com/cities/127.aspx; http://www.epodunk.com/cgi-bin/genInfo.php?locIndex=13264; and http://south-carolina/plantations.com/berkeley/mepkin.html. All Web sites accessed July 1, 2009.

13. "Basket names" refers to a naming practice of the Gullah-Geechee people who assign a child a name that only family members use. I observed a similar naming practice among the Yoruba of Nigeria, where I had become close to the family of my Harvard classmate, Doyin Ashamu. "Uncle Alaji" Ashamu, a member of the family who had a business in Ibadan where I was based at the time, gave me the name "Ashabi" to accompany the Yoruba name "Funke," a shortened form of Oluwafumike, which I had adopted. He explained that Ashabi would be my special name to be used at home by the family, and he used it to address me whenever I visited him. Although more research on this matter is needed, one wonders if basket names used by the Gullah Geechee, whose West African provenance is well supported, exemplify a cultural practice common to this African region.

14. The College of Charleston's Jewish Heritage Project lists names and birthplaces of the city's Jewish residents, the majority of whom were born during the first two decades of the twentieth century. While most were born in the United States, and in Charleston in particular, the vast majority of those from abroad were born in Poland. See http://www.cofc.edu/~jhc/oha/database.html (accessed July 1, 2009).

15. See http://www.cmhpf.org/S&RR/AlexSlaveCem.html (accessed July 14, 2009).

16. See http://www.nbcphiladelphia.com/news/local-beat/Wallace_s_Love_Story_Philadelphia.html (accessed August 6, 2010).

17. See http://www.jtamec.org/church/htm (accessed July 20, 2009).

18. A very unusual thing happened after that White family moved out. In most cases, fleeing Whites were replaced by Black families; however, our new neighbors were three White women who appeared to be well past retirement age. Miss Unger, Miss Gruener, and Miss Helen were sisters, and they were quiet and pleasant neighbors. Miss Gruener took special interest in me, in part because of my piano playing, which she and her sisters enjoyed hearing. I was a teenager in the early 1960s when Miss Gruener took me, as her guest, to my first outdoor concert at Robin Hood Dell, now the Mann Center for the Performing Arts, in Fairmount Park. I recall that the guest conductor that night was Leopold Stokowski (1882–1977), who had preceded Eugene Ormandy as conductor of the Philadelphia Orchestra. That night, under a cloudless sky and a full moon, the orchestra performed Debussy's "Clair de Lune." Miss Unger, Miss Gruener, and Miss Helen were living next door to our old house when we moved to Mount Airy. They were an exception to the White flight phenomenon; these three White sisters' neighborliness and profound humanity remains an outstanding memory.

Chapter 4. Becoming Saints

1. In *Go Tell It on the Mountain*, James Baldwin writes of this song when he describes the start of worship in a Sanctified church that is very much like The Church. "Service began when Brother Elisha sat down at the piano raised a song. . . . Elisha hit the keys, beginning at once to sing and everybody joined him, clapping their hands, and singing, and beating the tambourines. The song might be: 'Down at the cross where my savior died.'" (Baldwin 1953: 14).

2. See the Civil Defense Administration's official 1951 film, http://www.archive.org/details/DuckandC1951 (accessed July 13, 2006).

3. See http://www.thesilhouettes.org/uptown-theater.html (accessed June 24, 2009).

4. "Great Change Since I Been Born," by Rev. Gary Davis, copyright © Chandos Music. The song can be heard sung by the blind street preacher and singer at the first Web site listed below. Born in Lauren, South Carolina, in 1896, Davis moved to Harlem in 1940 and died in 1972. An accomplished blues and ragtime guitarist, he seldom played these genres after his ordination in the Free Baptist Connection Church in 1933. In Harlem, he preached and played on its street corners and late in life was "discovered" by musicians and aficionados. Available at http://www.rhapsody.com/reverend-gary-davis/harlem-street-singer-2006 and http://www.reverendgarydavis.com/bio.html (both accessed July 10, 2009). (Lyrics quoted by permission of Mitch Greenhill, Folklore Productions International.) This song was a favorite of Brother Jonathan Nichols, who sang it often during song service on Sabbath. Brother Jonathan struggled his entire life with schizophrenia and was in and out of the Byberry Mental Hospital until President Reagan's policy of cutting corporate taxes at the expense of social welfare services forced many mental health institutions to close (Thomas 2008). The family and The Church were crucial in providing continuity and support for Brother Jonathan during his bouts of mental illness. He was never rejected by either his kin or The Church. Although he never rose to the office of deacon or elder, he was always a "brother" and, when able to do so, supported the deacons in their duties. In his mature years, he married Elder Hannah.

5. The indigenous church movement among the Yoruba is known as the "Aladura," or praying people; their reformulation of Christianity entails the selective wedding of Yoruba and Christian religious traditions. Christ Apostolic Church (CAC) is one of the three older and major Aladura institutions that were the focus of my fieldwork; the others were the Church of the Lord-Aladura and the Celestial Church of Christ. Although their institutional history, organizational processes, and gender practices vary, all three have reformulated Christianity by selectively incorporating features of the traditional Yoruba religion, including spirit possession, religious dance, divination prophecy, belief in witchcraft, healing through divine intervention and use of holy water, and communal spontaneous prayers rather than reading from the Anglican Book of Common Prayer. Although the founders of these three Aladura churches had been affiliated with major missionary churches, they were to varying degrees aware of and influenced by Holiness Pentecostalism. Indeed, CAC established brief institutional affiliations with a Holiness church in America, whose literature had reached its founders, and with a British Pentecostal denomination as well (Crumbley 2008a).

6. These ongoing cultural infusions may also have been reinforced by Northern slaveholders' willingness to tolerate religious gatherings, since they found the relatively small number of slaves less threatening than did slaveholders in the rural South.

Chapter 5. Family

1. See http://freepages.genealogy.rootsweb.ancestry.com/~ajac/vamecklenburg.htm and http://www.google.com/search?q=mecklenburg+virginia+history+slavery&hl=en&cleint=firefox-a&rls=org.mozilla:en-US:official&hs_TvN&tbs=tl:1&tbo=1&ei=KIpcSvicB4jsMfSauK4C&sa=X&oi=timeline_result&ct=title&resnuym=11 (both accessed August 7, 2010).

2. Also see http://zorafestival.com/ (accessed August 14, 2009).

3. I am grateful to Mrs. Minnie Wright for making the biographies of the founding saints available to me. The contributions of those who passed on before they could be interviewed for this project are central to the story of The Church.

4. Deacon Ezekiel coproduced the CD *Touch Me Lord* (2002), arranging all the songs himself; the choir, Predestined Praise, consisted of selected members of The Church as well as some members of another congregation. Grant Birchard and Ezra Williams for New Destiny Productions, MorningStar Studies, Spring House, Pa. http://www.predestinedpraise.com/body_index.html (accessed July 12, 2011).

5. I am deeply indebted to my brother Dr. Joseph Crumbley for insights into the social-psychological implications of growing up "saved and sanctified." His internationally respected career in psychological social work and his many years of conducting family counseling have made him an excellent source of strategies for exploring the subtle dynamics of such a close-knit community. For his work on kinship care and transracial adoption, see http://www.drcrumbley.com (accessed August 7, 2010).

Chapter 6. Response

1. Bishop Alonzo A. Daughtry, a former follower of Bishop Charles Manuel "Daddy" Grace, moved the congregation from a storefront into a proper church building by 1930, attracting both Blacks and Whites. He openly disobeyed local segregation laws, holding that "it is better to obey God than man." His example set the precedent for saints to blend personal sanctification with social action, a perspective that accompanied the spread of this church throughout the South and then into the North in the 1940s. When he was on his deathbed in 1952, the founder turned the national leadership of the church over to Mother Inez Conry, and when she expressed personal reservations about assuming this great responsibility, he prophesied that one of his sons would return to the church and lead it. In 1958, his son Herbert, who had been "saved" while in prison, returned to the church, trained for ordination, and became National Presiding Minister. Through Bishop Herbert's leadership, the church helped found the Coalition of Concerned Leaders and Citizens to Save Our Youth and the political action group Black United Front. Global in orientation, this faith community established anti-apartheid organizations in the 1970s when other Black churches had hardly recognized this issue. In 1989, church members played important roles in the election of David Dinkins, the first Black mayor of New York City. Uplift endeavors have continued into the twenty-first century, including affordable housing development and youth mentoring programs (Grossman and Lipton-Lubet 2009).

2. This list of reasons for joining is attributed to Michael Westmoreland White (October 2005). See http://www.pcpj.org/index.php/about-us-mainmenu-44/88-join/271-top-10-reasons-to-join-pcpf.html (accessed September 6, 2009). Also see the Web sites regarding Stanley Horton and AG pacifism and these other PCPJ Web pages: links:http://pcpj.org/blog (accessed September 6, 2009); http://www.pcpj.org/index/php/join-pcpf-mainmenu-50-join.html (accessed September 6, 2009).

3. On October 7, 2008, during a book signing at Quail Ridge Book Store in Raleigh, I heard Diane Wilson speak. Her 2005 book, *An Unreasonable Woman: A True Account of Shrimpers, Politics, Polluters, and the Fight for Seadrift, Texas*, focuses on her life as an environmental-justice activist who, despite powerful corporations, their high-priced lawyers, and their unethical "divide and conquer strategies," campaigned successfully against

Formosa Plastics' toxic waste dumping in the waters of her hometown on Lavaca Bay, Texas. She delved deeply into ways that her Pentecostal background contributed to her being labeled a "loose cannon" and a "dangerous crazy lady" by the powers that be. Her youthful experiences of being filled with the Holy Ghost enabled her to move past fear to speak the truth whenever it was necessary and regardless of the risks. Being saved was more than a creed; it was "a place where you lived . . . in a world apart." In her life, this perspective led her to acknowledge evil, first in her personal habits, then in institutional structures, and eventually in the intersection of the two.

BIBLIOGRAPHY

Abrums, Mary E. 2009. *Moving the Rock: Poverty and Faith in a Black Storefront Church.* Lanham, Md.: Altamira Press.
Adams, Walter Randolph. 1997. Introduction. In *Explorations in Anthropology and Theology*, edited by Frank A. Salamone and Walter Randolph Adams, 1–22. Lanham, Md.: University Press of America.
Adeyemi, L. E. 1979. "African Indigenous and Pentecostal Churches in Sierra Leone: Challenge or Problem?" Paper presented to the Annual Clergy and Ministers Vacation Course, Department of Theology, Fourah Bay College of Sierra Leone.
Aguilar, John L. 1981. "Insider Research: An Ethnography of a Debate." In *Anthropologists at Home in North America*, edited by Donald A. Messerschmidt, 15–26. Cambridge: Cambridge University Press.
Alexander, Estrelda Y. 2008. *Limited Liberty: The Legacy of Four Pentecostal Women Pioneers.* Cleveland, Ohio: Pilgrim Press.
Allen, James, Hilton Als, John Lewis, and Leon F. Litwack. 2000. *Without Sanctuary. Lynching Photography in America.* Santa Fe, N. Mex.: Twin Palms. Also see http://www.withoutsanctuary.org/movie1.html.
Alpers, Edward A., and Allen Roberts. 2003. "What Is African Studies? Some Reflections." *African Issues* 30, no. 3: 11–18.
Amadiume, Ifi. 1987. *Male Daughters, Female Husbands: Gender and Sex in an African Society.* London: Zed Books.
———. 1997. *Reinventing Africa: Matriarchy, Religion, and Culture.* London: Zed Books.
Anderson, Allan. 2005. "The Origins of Pentecostalism and Its Global Spread in the Early Twentieth Century." *Transformation* 22, no. 3: 175–85.
———. 2006a. "Pandita Ramabai, the Mukti Revival and Global Pentecostalism." *Transformation* 23, no. 1: 37–48.
———. 2006b. "The Azusa Street Revival and the Emergence of Pentecostal Mission in the Early Twentieth Century." *Transformation* 23, no. 2: 107–18.
Andrews, William L. 1986. *Sisters of the Spirit: Three Black Women's Autobiographies of the Nineteenth Century.* Bloomington: Indiana University Press.
Apel, Dora. 2004. *Imagery of Lynching: Black Men, White Women, and the Mob.* New Brunswick, N.J.: Rutgers University Press.
Apel, Dora, and Shawn Michelle Smith. 2008. *Lynching Photographs.* Berkeley: University of California Press.
Appadurai, Arjun. 1996. *Modernity at Large: Cultural Dimensions of Globalization.* Minneapolis: University of Minnesota Press.

Aptheker, Herbert. 1939. "Maroons within the Present Limits of the United States." *Journal of Negro History* 24, no. 2 (April): 167–84.
Austin-Broos, Diane. 1997. *Jamaica Genesis: Religion and the Politics of Moral Orders*. Chicago: University of Chicago Press.
Baer, Hans A., and Merrill Singer. 1992. *African American Religion in the Twentieth Century: Varieties of Protest and Accommodation*. Knoxville: University of Tennessee Press.
Bakalaki, Alexandra. 1997. "Students, Natives, Colleagues: Encounters in Academia and in the Field." *Cultural Anthropology* 12, no. 4: 502–26.
Baldwin, James. 1948. "The Harlem Ghetto." *Commentary*, February. In *Notes of a Native Son*. Boston: Beacon Press, 1955. Reprinted in *Listening for God: Contemporary Literature and the Life of Faith*. Vol. 4. Edited by Paula Carlson and Peter Hawkins, 29–46. Minneapolis, Minn.: Augsburg Fortress, 2002.
———. 1953. *Go Tell It on the Mountain*. New York: Knopf.
———. 1954. *The Amen Corner: A Drama in Three Acts*. New York: Dial.
Ballard, Allen B. 1984. *One More Day's Journey: The Story of a Family and a People*. New York: McGraw-Hill.
Baptist, Edward E. 2002. *Stony the Road They Trod: Forced Migration of African Americans in the Slave South*. Rare book, Manuscript and Special Collections Library, Duke University, Durham, N.C.
Bass, Jack, and Marilyn Thompson. 2005. *Strom: The Complicated Personal and Political Life of Strom Thurmond*. New York: Public Affairs.
Bederman, Gail. 1995. *Manliness and Civilization: A Cultural History of Gender and Race in the United States, 1880–1917*. Chicago: University of Chicago Press.
Besson, Jean, and Barry Chevannes. 1996. "The Continuity-Creativity Debate: The Case of Revival." *New West Indian Guide* 70: 209–28.
Best, Felton O. 1998. "Breaking the Gender Barrier: African-American Women and Leadership in Black Holiness-Pentecostal Churches, 1890–Present." In *Flames of Fire*, edited by Felton O. Best, 153–68. Lewiston, N.Y.: Edwin Mellen.
Best, Wallace D. 2004. "The South and the City: Black Southern Migrants, Storefront Churches, and the Rise of a Religious Diaspora." In *Repositioning North American Migration History: New Directions in Modern Continental Migration, Citizenship and Community*, edited by Marc S. Rodriguez, 302–27. Rochester, N.Y.: University of Rochester Press.
Bielo, James S. 2008. "On the Failure of 'Meaning': Bible Reading in the Anthropology of Christianity." *Culture and Religion* 9, no. 1: 1–21.
Blassingame, John W. 1977. *Slave Testimony*. Baton Rouge: Louisiana State University Press.
Brawley, Benjamin G. 2001 [1921]. *A Social History of the American Negro*. New York: Dover.
Braziel, Jana Evans, and Anita Mannur. 2003. "Nation, Migration, Globalization: Points of Contention in Diaspora Studies." In *Theorizing Diaspora*, edited by Jana Evans Braziel and Anita Mannur, 1–22. Malden, Mass.: Blackwell.
Brundage, Fitzhugh W. 1993. *Lynching in the New South: Georgia and Virginia, 1880–1930*. Urbana: University of Illinois Press.
Burton, Orville Vernon. 1978. "Race and Reconstruction: Edgefield County, South Carolina." *Journal of Social History* 12, no. 1 (Autumn): 31–56.
Butler, Anthea D. 2007. *Women in the Church of God in Christ: Making a Sanctified World*. Chapel Hill: University of North Carolina Press.

Butowsky, Harry. 2008. *The U.S. Constitution: Pittsylvania Courthouse.* Available from the Division of History, National Park Service, Washington, D.C. http://www.nps.gov/history/online_books/butowsky2/constitution6./htm, http://www.victorianvilla.com/sims-mitchell/local/arrest-judge_courthouse.htm (accessed October 20, 2008).

Butterfield, Fox. 1995. *All God's Children: The Bosket Family and the American Tradition of Violence.* New York: Alfred A. Knopf.

Byfield, Judith. 2000. "Introduction: Rethinking the African Diaspora." *African Studies Review* 43, no. 1: 1–9.

Caillois, Roger. 1961. *Man, Play and Games.* New York: Free Press.

Caknipe, John, Jr. 2008. *Chase City (Images of America: Virginia).* Mount Pleasant, S.C.: Arcadia Publishing.

Canton, David A. 2008. "A Dress Rehearsal for the Modern Civil Rights Movement: Raymond Pace Alexander and the Berwyn, Pennsylvania, School Desegregation Case, 1932–1934." *Pennsylvania History* 75: 260–84.

Carawan, Guy, with Candie Carawan. 1995. "Singing and Shouting in Moving Star Hall." *Black Music Research Journal* 15, no. 1: 17–28.

Carby, Hazel V. 1992. "Policing the Black Woman's Body in an Urban Context." *Critical Inquiry* 18, no. 4: 738–55.

Carpenter, Carole H. 1999. "Arthur Huff Fauset, Campaigner for Social Justice: A Symphony of Diversity." In *African American Pioneers in Anthropology,* edited by Ira E. Harrison and Faye V. Harrison, 213–42. Urbana: University of Illinois Press.

Carpenter, Delores. 1989–1990. "Black Women in Religious Institutions: A Historical Summary from Slavery to the 1960s." *Journal of Religious Thought* 46, no. 2: 7–27.

Chireau, Yvonne Patricia. 1995. "Hidden Traditions: Black Religion, Magic, and Alternative Spiritual Beliefs in Womanist Perspective." In *Perspectives on Womanist Theology,* edited by Jacquelyn Grant, 65–88. Atlanta, Ga.: Interdenominational Theological Center Press.

———. 2000. "Black Culture and Black Zion: African American Religious Encounters with Judaism, 1790–1930, an Overview." In *Black Zion: African American Religious Encounters with Judaism,* edited by Yvonne Chireau and Nathaniel Deutsch, 15–32. New York: Oxford University Press.

———. 2003. *Black Magic: Religion and the African American Conjuring Tradition.* Berkeley: University of California Press.

Church of God. 1951. *Doctrinal Points of the Church of God (7th Day Apostolic) Re-organized 1933.* Church of God Publishing House.

Clark-Lewis, Elizabeth. 1994. *Living in, Living out: African American Domestics and the Great Migration.* Washington, D.C.: Smithsonian Institution.

Clifford, James. 1986. "Introduction: Partial Truths." In *Writing Culture: The Poetics and Politics of Ethnography,"* edited by James Clifford and George E. Marcus, 1–26. Berkeley: University of California Press.

Cnaan, Ram A. 2006. *The Other Philadelphia Story: How Local Congregations Support Quality of Life in Urban America.* Philadelphia: University of Pennsylvania Press.

Cohen, William. 1991. *At Freedom's Edge: Black Mobility and the Southern White Quest for Racial Control, 1861–1915.* Baton Rouge: Louisiana State University Press.

Collier-Thomas, Betty. 1997. *Daughters of Thunder: Black Women Preachers and Their Sermons, 1850–1979.* San Francisco: Jossey Bass Publishers.

———. 2010. *Jesus, Jobs and Justice: African American Women and Religion*. New York: Alfred A. Knopf.
Collins, Herbert. 1970. "Store Front Churches." *Negro American Literature Forum* 4, no. 2: 64–68.
Collins, Patricia Hill. 1990. *Black Feminist Thought: Knowledge, Consciousness, and the Politics of Empowerment*. New York: Routledge.
Comaroff, Jean. 1985. *Body of Power, Spirit of Resistance: The Culture and History of a South African People*. Chicago: University of Chicago Press.
Comaroff, Jean, and John Comaroff. 1992. *Ethnography and the Historical Imagination*. Boulder, Colo.: Westview Press.
———. 1993. *Modernity and Its Malcontents: Ritual and Power in Postcolonial Africa*. Chicago: University of Chicago Press.
Corten, Andre, and Ruth Marshall-Fratani. 2001. *Between Babel and Pentecost: Transnational Pentecostalism in African and Latin America*. Bloomington: Indiana University Press.
Creel, Margaret Washington. 1988. *A Peculiar People: Slave Religion and Community Culture among the Gullahs*. New York: New York University Press.
Crumbley, Deidre H. 2000. "Also Chosen: Jews in the Imagination and Life of a Black Storefront Church." *Anthropology and Humanism* 25, no. 1 (June): 6–23.
———. 2006. "Power in the Blood: Menstrual Taboos and Female Power in an African Instituted Church." In *Women and Religion in the African Diaspora*, edited by R. Marie Griffith and Barbara D. Savage, 81–97. Baltimore, Md.: The Johns Hopkins University Press.
———. 2007. "Miraculous Mothers, Empowered Sons, and Dutiful Daughters: Gender, Race, and Power in an African American Sanctified Church." *Anthropology and Humanism* 32, no. 1: 30–51.
———. 2008a. *Spirit, Structure, and Flesh: Gendered Experiences in African Instituted Churches among the Yoruba of Nigeria*. Madison: University of Wisconsin Press.
———. 2008b. "The Church as a Community Asset for Intergenerational Assessment: A Storefront Church Case Study in Cross-Generational Knowledge Transference." In *Social Work Practice with African American Families: An Intergenerational Perspective*, edited by Cheryl Waites, 69–85. New York: Routledge.
———. 2008c. "Sanctified Saints—Impure Prophetesses: Gender, Purity and Power in Two Afro-Christian Spirit-Privileging Churches." In *Philip's Daughters: Women in Pentecostal-Charismatic Leadership*, edited by Amos Yong and Estrelda Alexander, 74–94. Princeton Theological Monographs Series. Eugene, Ore.: Pickwick Press.
———. 2008d. "From Holy Ground to Virtual Reality: Aladura Gender Practices in Cyberspace—an African Diaspora Perspective." In *Christianity in Africa and the African Diaspora: The Appropriation of a Scattered Heritage*, edited by Afe Adogame, Roswith Gerloff, and Klaus Hock, 126–39. London: Continuum Religious Studies.
———. 2010. "On Both Sides of the Atlantic: Independent Church Movements (ICMs) in Africa and the African Diaspora." In *Essays on World Christianity in Honor of Lamin Sanneh*, edited by Akintunde Akinade, 177–208. New York: Peter Lang.
Curtis, Edward E., and Danielle Brune Sigler. 2009. Foreword. In *The New Black Gods: Arthur Huff Fauset and the Study of African American Religions*, edited by Edward E. Curtis and Danielle Brune Sigler, 1–13. Bloomington: Indiana University Press.
Daniels, David. 2001. "A New Role for Holiness Codes?" *The Living Pulpit* 10, no. 3: 9.
———. 2003. "'Doing All the Good We Can': The Political Witness of African American Holi-

ness and Pentecostal Churches in the Post–Civil Rights Era." In *New Day Begun: African American Churches and Civic Culture in Post–Civil Rights America*, edited by R. Drew Smith, 164–82. Durham, N.C.: Duke University Press.

Davis, Dernoral. 1991. "Toward a Socio-Historical and Demographic Portrait of Twentieth-Century African Americans." In *Black Exodus: The Great Migration from the American South*, edited by Alferdteen Harrison, 1–19. Jackson: University Press of Mississippi.

Dehavneon, Anna Lou. 1995. "'First You Feed Them, Then You Clothe Them, Then You Save Them': The Hungry and Homeless and the Sunday Feast at a Pentecostal Storefront Church in East Harlem." In *Feasts and Celebrations in North American Ethnic Communities*, edited by Ramón A. Gutiérrez and Geneviève Fabre, 87–99. Albuquerque: University of New Mexico Press.

Dick, Everett N. 1970. *The Lure of the Land: A Social History of the Public Lands from the Articles of Confederation to the New Deal*. Lincoln: University of Nebraska Press.

Dill, Bonnie Thornton. 1994. *Across the Boundaries of Race and Class*. New York: Garland.

Dodson, Howard, and Sylviane Diouf. 2004. *In Motion: The African-American Migration Experience*. Washington, D.C.: National Geographic Society.

Dodson, Jualynne E., and Cheryl Townsend Gilkes. 1995. "There's Nothing Like Church Food: Food and the U.S. Afro-Christian Tradition: Re-membering Community and Feeding the Embodied S/spirit(s)." *Journal of the American Academy of Religion* 43, no. 3: 519–36.

Dorn, T. Felder. 1994. *The Tompkins School 1925–1953*. Greenwood, S.C.: The Attic Press.

——. 2006. *The Guns of Meeting Street*. Columbia: University of South Carolina Press.

Downey, Dennis B., and Raymond Hyser. 1991. *No Crooked Death: Coatesville, Pennsylvania and the Lynching of Zachariah Walker*. Urbana: University of Illinois Press.

Drake, St. Clair. 1987. *Black Folk Here and There: An Essay in History and Anthropology*. Los Angeles: Center for Afro-American Studies, University of California.

Drewal, Henry. 1989. "Art or Accident: Yoruba Body Artists and their Deity Ogun." In *Africa's Ogun: Old World and New*, edited by Sandra T. Barnes, 235–60. Bloomington: Indiana University Press.

Drewal, Margaret Thompson. 1989. "Dancing for Ogun in Yorubaland and in Brazil." In *Africa's Ogun: Old World and New*, edited by Sandra T. Barnes, 199–234. Bloomington: Indiana University Press.

Du Bois, W.E.B. 1899. *The Philadelphia Negro: A Social Study*. Philadelphia: University of Pennsylvania Press.

——. 1910. "Reconstruction and Its Benefits." *American Historical Review* 15, no. 4: 781–99.

Dupree, Sherry Sherrod, and Herbert C. Dupree. 1993. *Exposed: Federal Bureau of Investigation (FBI) Unclassified Reports on Church and Church Leaders*. Washington, D.C.: Middle Atlantic Regional Press.

Eddy, G. Norman. 1958–59. "Store-Front Religion." *Religion in Life* 28, no. 1: 68–85.

Fauset, Arthur Huff. 2002 [1944]. *Black Gods of the Metropolis: Negro Religious Cults of the Urban North*. Philadelphia: University of Pennsylvania Press.

Feleppa, Robert. 1986. "Emics, Etics, and Social Objectivity." *Current Anthropology* 27, no. 3 (June): 243–55.

Foner, Eric. 1988. *Reconstruction: America's Unfinished Revolution, 1863–1877*. New York: Harper and Row.

Fordham, Damon L. 2008. *True Stories of Black South Carolina*. Charleston, S.C.: History Press.

Foucault, Michel. 1981. "Two Lectures." Translated by Colin Gordon, Leo Marshall, John Mepham, and Kate Soper. In *Power/Knowledge: Selected Interviews and Other Writings, 1972–1977*, edited by Colin Gordon, 78–108. New York: Pantheon.
———. 2003. *Society Must Be Defended: Lectures at the Collège de France, 1975–76.* Translated by David Macey, edited by Mauro Bertani and Allesandro Fontana. New York: St. Martin's.
Fox, Richard G. 1991. "For a Nearly New Culture History." In *Recapturing Anthropology: Working in the Present*, edited by Richard G. Fox, 93–113. Santa Fe, N. Mex.: School of American Research Press.
Frankiel, Tamar. 2003. "The Cross-Cultural Study of Christianity: An Historian's View." *Religion* 33, no. 3: 281–89.
Franklin, Robert Michael. 1989. "Church and City: Black Christianity's Ministry." *The Christian Ministry* 20: 17–19.
———. 1995. "Defiant Spirituality: Care Traditions in the Black Churches." *Pastoral Psychology* 43, no. 4: 255–67.
Fraser, Ronald. 1986. *Blood of Spain: An Oral History of the Spanish Civil War*. New York: Pantheon Books.
Frazier, E. Franklin. 1963. *The Negro Church in America*. New York: Schocken Books.
Gaines, Kevin Kelly. 1996. *Uplifting the Race: Black Leadership, Politics, and Culture in the Twentieth Century*. Chapel Hill: University of North Carolina Press.
Geertz, Armin W. 2002. "As the Other Sees Us: On Reciprocity and Mutual Reflection in the Study of Native American Religion." In *Personal Knowledge and Beyond: Reshaping the Ethnography of Religion*, edited by James Spickard, J. Shawn Landres, and Meredith McGuire, 225–36. New York: New York University Press.
George, Carole V. R. 1973. *Segregated Sabbaths: Richard Allen and the Rise of Independent Black Churches 1760–1840*. New York: Oxford University Press.
Giggie, John M. 2008. *After Redemption: Jim Crow and the Transformation of African American Religion in the Delta 1875–1915*. New York: Oxford University Press.
Gilkes, Cheryl Townsend. 1986. "The Role of Women in the Sanctified Church." *Journal of Religious Thought* 43, no. 1: 24–41.
———. 1987. "Some Mother's Son and Some Father's Daughter: Gender and Biblical Language in Afro-Christian Worship Tradition." In *Shaping New Vision: Gender and Values in American Culture*, edited by Clarissa W. Atkinson, Constance H. Buchanan, and Margaret R. Miles, 73–95. Ann Arbor, Mich.: UMI Research Press.
———. 1990. "Together and in Harness: Women's Tradition in the Sanctified Church." In *Black Women in America: Social Science Perspectives*, edited by Micheline R. Malson, Elisabeth Mudimbe-Boyi, Jean F. O'Barr, and Mary Wyer, 223–44. Chicago: University of Chicago Press.
———. 1994. "The Politics of Silence: Dual-Sex Political Systems and Women's Traditions of Conflict in African-American Religion." In *African-American Christianity*, edited by Paul E. Johnson, 80–109. Berkeley: University of California Press.
———. 2002. "A Conscious Connection to All That Is: *The Color Purple* as Subversive and Critical Ethnography." In *Personal Knowledge and Beyond: Reshaping the Ethnography of Religion*, edited by James V. Spickard, J. Shawn Landres, and Meredith B. McGuire, 175–91. New York: New York University Press.

Gilroy, Paul. 1993. *The Black Atlantic: Modernity and Double Consciousness*. Cambridge: Cambridge University Press.
Glazier, Stephen D. 2001. *Encyclopedia of African and African-American Religions*. New York: Routledge.
Gomez, Michael Angelo. 2005. *Reversing Sail: A History of the African Diaspora*. Cambridge: Cambridge University Press.
Gordon, Edmund T., and Mark Anderson. 1999. "The African Diaspora: Toward an Ethnography of Diasporic Identification." *Journal of American Folklore* 112, no. 445: 282–96.
Graebner, Brooks. 2009. "The Episcopal Church and Race in Nineteenth-Century North Carolina." *Anglican and Episcopal History* 78, no. 1 (March): 94–104.
Grant, Bradford C. 2002. "The Sanctified Warehouse: An Architect Looks at Storefront Churches." *International Review of African American Art* 18, no. 3: 49–51.
Grant, Jacquelyn. 1986. "Black Women and the Church." In *All American Women: Lines That Divide, Ties That Bind*, edited by Johnnetta B. Cole, 359–69. New York: Free Press.
Gregg, Robert. 1993. *Sparks from the Anvil of Oppression: Philadelphia's African Methodists and Southern Migrants, 1890–1940*. Philadelphia: Temple University Press.
Grossman, Jonathan, and Natan Lipton-Lubet. 2009. "A History of Oberlin's Youngest Church." http://oberlin.edu/external/EOG/AfAmChurches/HouseoftheLord.htm (accessed September 4, 2009).
Gwaltney, John L. 1976. "On Going Home Again—Some Reflections of a Native Anthropologist." *Phylon* 37, no. 3: 236–42.
Hahn, Steven. 2009. *The Political Worlds of Slavery and Freedom*. Cambridge, Mass.: Harvard University Press.
Hall, Jacquelyn Dowd. 1979. *Revolt Against Chivalry: Jessie Daniel Ames and the Women's Campaign Against Lynching*. New York: Columbia University Press.
Halstead, Narmala. 2001. "Ethnographic Encounters: Positionings within and outside the Insider Frame." *Social Anthropology* 9, no. 3: 307–21.
Hamilton, Charles V. 1972. *The Black Preacher in America*. New York: William Morrow.
Haney, LaVerne J. 1995. "Praying Through: The Spiritual Narrative of Mother E. J. Dabney." *Journal of the Interdenominational Theological Center* 22: 231–40.
Harding, Rachel. 2006. "*E a senzala*: Slavery, Women, and Embodied Knowledge in Afro-Brazilian Candomblé." In *Women and Religion in the African Diaspora*, edited by R. Marie Griffith and Barbara D. Savage, 3–18. Baltimore, Md.: The Johns Hopkins University Press.
Harding, Susan F. 1987. "Convicted by the Holy Spirit: The Rhetoric of Fundamental Baptist Conversion." *American Ethnologist* 14, no. 1: 167–81.
Hardy, Clarence E. III. 2009. "Fauset's (Missing) Pentecostals: Church Mothers, Remaking Respectability, and Religious Modernism." In *The New Black Gods: Arthur Huff Fauset and the Study of African American Religions*, edited by Edward E. Curtis and Danielle Brune Sigler, 15–30. Bloomington: Indiana University Press.
Harris, Marvin. 1976. "History and Significance of the Emic/Etic Distinction." *Annual Review of Anthropology* 5: 329–50.
———. 1990. "Emics and Etics Revisited." In *Emics and Etics: The Insider/Outsider Debate*, edited by Marvin Harris, Thomas N. Headland, and Kenneth L. Pike, 48–61. Newbury Park, Calif.: Sage.

Harrison, Faye V. 2008. *Outsider Within: Reworking Anthropology in the Global Age.* Urbana: University of Illinois Press.

Harrison, Ira. 1966. "Storefront Religion as a Revitalization Movement." *Review of Religious Research* 7, no. 3: 160–65.

Harrison, Ira E., and Faye V. Harrison. 1999. *African American Pioneers in Anthropology.* Urbana: University of Illinois Press.

Harrison, Matthew. 2005. "Colorism in the Job Selection Process—Are There Preferential Differences within the Black Race?" Master's thesis, University of Georgia.

Harrison, Milmon F. 2005. *Righteous Riches: The Word of Faith Movement in Contemporary African American Religion.* New York: Oxford University Press.

Harvell, Valeria Gomez. 2010. "The Storefront Church and Hip Hop Movements: Homiez from the Hood." *Journal of Pan African Studies* 3, no. 9 (June-July): 152–87.

Haynes, Titus. 1978. *Fundamentalism in Black Inner-City Storefront Churches.* New York: Vantage Press.

Haywood, Chanta M. 2003. *Prophesying Daughters: Black Women Preachers and the Word, 1823–1913.* Columbia: University of Missouri Press.

Hershberg, Theodore, Alan N. Burstein, Eugene P. Ericksen, Stephanie W. Greenberg, and William L. Yancey. 1979. "Tale of Three Cities: Blacks and Immigrants in Philadelphia: 1850–80, 1930, and 1970." *Annals of the American Academy of Political and Social Science* 44, no. 1: 55–81.

Higginbotham, Evelyn Brooks. 1993. *Righteous Discontent: The Women's Movement in the Black Baptist Church, 1880–1920.* Cambridge, Mass.: Harvard University Press.

Hine, Darlene Clark. 1991. "Black Migration to the Urban Midwest: The Gender Dimension, 1915–1945." In *The Great Migration in Historical Perspective: New Dimensions of Race, Class, and Gender*, edited by Joe William Trotter Jr., 127–46. Bloomington: Indiana University Press.

Hollenweger, Walter J. 1970. "A Black Pentecostal Concept: A Forgotten Chapter of Black History—The Pentecostals' Contribution." Geneva: World Council of Churches.

Holt, Thomas C., and Molly Hudgens. 2009. "The Second Great Migration, 1940–1970." In *The African-American Migration Experience.* http://www.inmotionaame.org/texts/viewer.cfm?id=9_000T&page=1 (accessed March 30, 2009).

Hopkins, John B. 1978. "Music and the Pentecostal Church." *Jamaica Journal* 42: 22–40.

Hopper, Matthew S. 2008. "From Refuge to Strength: The Rise of the African American Church in Philadelphia 1787–1949." Preservation Alliance for Greater Philadelphia. http:/www.preservationalliance.com/files/aachurches.pdf (accessed October 23, 2008).

Hunter, Margaret L. 2002. "'If You're Light You're Alright': Light Skin Color as Social Capital for Women of Color." *Gender and Society* 16, no. 2 (April): 175–93.

Hurston, Zora Neale. 1981. *The Sanctified Church.* Berkeley: Turtle Island Press.

Hymes, Dell H. 1990. "Emics, Etics, and Openness: An Ecumenical Approach." In *Emics and Etics: The Insider/Outsider Debate*, edited by Marvin Harris, Thomas N. Headland, and Kenneth L. Pike, 120–25. Newbury Park, Calif.: Sage.

Jackson, Antoinette T. 2008. "Imagining Jehossee Island Rice Plantation Today." *International Journal of Heritage Studies* 14, no. 2: 131–55.

Jervis, L. Ann. 1991. *The Purpose of Romans.* Sheffield: Journal for the Study of the New Testament Supplement Series.

Jones, Delmos. 1970. "Toward a Native Anthropology." *Human Organization* 29, no. 4: 251–59.

Jules-Rosette, Benetta. 1975. *African Apostles: Ritual and Conversion in the Church of John Maranke*. Ithaca, N.Y.: Cornell University Press.
———. 1979. "Women as Ceremonial Leaders in an African Church: The Apostles of John Maranke." In *New Religions of Africa*, edited by Bennetta Jules-Rosette, 127–44. Norwood, N.J.: Ablex.
———. 1981. "Women in Indigenous African Cults and Churches." In *The Black Woman Cross-Culturally*, edited by F. C. Steady, 185–207. Cambridge, Mass.: Schenkman.
———. 1987. "Privileges without Power: Women in African Cults and Churches." In *Women in Africa and the African Diaspora*, edited by Roslyn Terborg-Penn and Andrea Benton Rushing, 99–119. Washington, D.C.: Howard University Press.
Kahn, Lin Shi, and Tony Perez. 2002 [1935]. *Scottsboro, Alabama: A Story in Linoleum Cuts*. New York: New York University Press.
Kalu, Ogbu. 2008. *African Pentecostalism: An Introduction*. Oxford: Oxford University Press.
Kantrowitz, Stephen. 1998. "White Supremacist Justice and the Rule of Law: Lynching, Honor, and the State in Ben Tillman's South Carolina." In *Men and Violence: Gender, Honor, and Rituals in Modern Europe and America*, edited by Pieter Spierenburg, 213–39. Columbus: Ohio State University Press.
Kim, Choong Soon. 1987. "Can an Anthropologist Go Home Again?" *American Anthropologist* 89, no. 4: 943–46.
Kostarelos, Frances. 1995. *Feeling the Spirit: Faith and Hope in an Evangelical Black Storefront Church*. Columbia: University of South Carolina Press.
Lander, E. M. 1953. "Slave Labor in South Carolina Cotton Mills." *Journal of Negro History* 38, no. 2: 161–73.
Landry, Timothy R. 2008. "Moving to Learn: Performance and Learning in Haitian Vodou." *Anthropology and Humanism* 33, no. 1–2: 53–65.
Levenstein, Lisa. 2009. *A Movement Without Marches: African American Women and the Politics of Poverty in Postwar Philadelphia*. Chapel Hill: University of North Carolina Press.
Levine, Lawrence W. 1977. *Black Culture and Consciousness*. New York: Oxford University Press.
Lewis, Harold T. 1996. *Yet With a Steady Beat: The African American Struggle for Recognition in the Episcopal Church*. Valley Forge, Pa.: Trinity Press International.
Lincoln, Charles Eric, and Lawrence H. Mamiya. 1990. *The Black Church in the African American Experience*. Durham, N.C.: Duke University Press.
Llewellyn, Henry Byron. 1997. "A Study of the History and Thought of the Apostolic Church in Wales, in the Context of Pentecostalism." Master of Philosophy thesis, University of Wales, Cardiff.
Macfarlane, Alan. 1977. "Historical Anthropology." http://www.alanmacfarlane.com/TEXTS/FRAZER.pdf (accessed August 2, 2010).
MacRobert, Iain. 1988. *The Black Roots and White Racism of Early Pentecostalism in the USA*. New York: St. Martin's.
———. 1997. "The Black Roots of Early Pentecostalism." In *African American Religion: Interpretive Essays in History and Culture*, edited by Timothy E. Fulop and Albert J. Raboteau, 295–309. New York: Routledge.
Marcus, George E. 1986. "Contemporary Problems of Ethnography in the Modern World System." In *Writing Culture: The Poetics and Politics of Ethnography*, edited by James Clifford and George E. Marcus, 165–93. Berkeley: University of California Press.

Marcus, Jacob Rader. 1993. *History of United States Jewry, 1776–1985*. Vol. 1, *The Germanic Period*. Detroit, Mich.: Wayne State University Press.

Marshall-Fratani, Ruth R. 2001. "Mediating the Global and Local in Nigerian Pentecostalism." In *Between Babel and Pentecost: Transnational Pentecostalism in African and Latin America*, edited by Andre Corten and Ruth R. Marshall-Fratani, 80–105. Bloomington: Indiana University Press.

Martin, Ruth. 1994. "Life Forces of African American Elderly Illustrated through Oral History Narratives." In *Qualitative Research in Social Work*, edited by Edward Sherman and William J. Reid, 190–99. New York: Columbia University Press.

Maruyama, Magoroh. 1974. "Endogenous Research vs. Delusions of Relevance and Expertise among Exogenous Academics." *Human Organization* 33, no. 3: 318–22.

Matory, James Lorand. 2005. *Black Atlantic Religion: Tradition, Transnationalism, and Matriarchy in the Afro-Brazilian Candomblé*. Princeton, N.J.: Princeton University Press.

Mbiti, John S. 1969. *African Religions and Philosophy*. London: Heineman.

Medicine, Beatrice. 2001a. "Learning to Be an Anthropologist and Remaining 'Native.'" In *Learning to Be an Anthropologist and Remaining "Native,"* edited by Beatrice Medicine with Sue-Ellen Jacobs, 3–15. Urbana: University of Illinois Press.

———. 2001b. "Ellen C. Deloria: The Emic Voice." In *Learning to Be an Anthropologist and Remaining "Native,"* edited by Beatrice Medicine with Sue-Ellen Jacobs, 269–87. Urbana: University of Illinois Press.

Meyers, Allen. 1999. *Strawberry Mansion: The Jewish Community of North Philadelphia*. Mount Pleasant, S.C.: Arcadia Publishing.

———. 2002. *The Jewish Community around North Broad Street*. Mount Pleasant, S.C.: Arcadia Publishing.

Miller, Albert G. 1996. "Pentecostalism as a Social Movement: Beyond the Theory of Deprivation." *Journal of Pentecostal Theology* 9: 97–114.

Miller, Timothy. 1995. "Black Jews and Black Muslims." In *America's Alternative Religions*, edited by Timothy Miller, 277–82. Albany: State University of New York Press.

Moore, John Hammond. 2006. *Carnival of Blood: Dueling, Lynching and Murder in South Carolina 1880–1920*. Columbia: University of South Carolina Press.

Morris, Michael W., Kwok Leung, Daniel Ames, and Brian Lickel. 1999. "Views from Inside and Outside: Integrating Emic and Etic Insights about Culture and Justice Judgment." *Academy of Management Review* 24, no. 4: 781–96.

Morrison, Toni. 1992. *Jazz*. New York: Alfred A. Knopf.

Mufwene, Salikoko S. 1997. "The Ecology of Gullah's Survival." *American Speech* 72, no. 1: 69–83.

Murphy, Joseph M. 1988. *Santeria: An African Religion in America*. Boston: Beacon Press.

Narayan, Kirin. 1993. "How Native Is a 'Native' Anthropologist?" *American Anthropologist* 95, no. 3: 671–86.

Nash, Gary B. 2006. *First City: Philadelphia and the Forging of Historical Memory*. Philadelphia: University of Pennsylvania Press.

Nason-Clark, Nancy. 2002. "From the Heart of My Laptop: Personal Passion and Research on Violence against Women." In *Personal Knowledge and Beyond: Reshaping the Ethnography of Religion*, edited by James V. Spickard, J. Shawn Landres, and Meredith B. McGuire, 27–32. New York: New York University Press.

Nathiri, N. Y., ed. 1991. *Zora! Zora Neale Hurston: A Woman and Her Community*. Chicago: Tribune Publishing.

Neitz, Mary Jo. 2002. "Walking between the Worlds: Permeable Boundaries, Ambiguous Identities." In *Personal Knowledge and Beyond: Reshaping the Ethnography of Religion*, edited by James V. Spickard, J. Shawn Landres, and Meredith B. McGuire, 33–46. New York: New York University Press.

Nelson, Timothy. 2005. *Every Time I Feel the Spirit: Religious Experience and Ritual in an African American Church*. New York: New York University Press.

Norris, Rebecca Sachs. 2001. "Embodiment and Community." *Western Folklore* 60, no. 2/3: 111–124.

———. 2005. "Examining the Structure and Role of Emotion: Contributions of Neurobiology to the Study of Embodied Religious Experience." *Zygon: The Journal of Science and Religion* 40, no. 1: 181–99.

———. 2009. "The Paradox of Healing Pain." *Religion* 39, no. 1: 22–23.

Nzegwu, Nkiru. 1994. "Gender Equality in a Dual Sex System: The Case of Onitsha." *Canadian Journal of Law and Jurisprudence*. 7: 73–95.

———. 2006. *Family Matters. Feminist Concepts in African Philosophy of Culture*. Albany: State University of New York Press.

Okely, Judith. 1992. "Anthropology and Autobiography: Participatory Experience and Embodied Knowledge." In *Anthropology and Autobiography*, edited by Judith Okely and Helen Callaway, 1–22. New York: Routledge.

Ola, C. S. 1978. "Foundations of the African Church in Nigeria." In *Christianity in West Africa: The Nigerian Story*, edited by Obgu Kalu, 337–42. Ibadan: Daystar Press.

Olmsted, Frederick Law. 1856. *A Journey in the Seaboard Slave States*. Reprint New York: Knickerbocker Press, 1904. Electronic edition 2000, http://docsouth,unc.olmsted/olmsted.html (accessed August 5, 2009).

Olupona, Jacob K. 2000. Introduction. In *African Spirituality: Forms, Meanings and Expressions*, edited by Jacob K. Olupona, xv–xxxvi. New York: Crossroad Publishing.

Omoyajowo, J. Akinyele. 1982. *Cherubim and Seraphim: The History of an African Church*. New York: Nok Publishers.

O'Neill, J. C. 1975. *Paul's Letter to the Romans*. Baltimore, Md.: Penguin Press.

Opala, Joseph. 1987. *The Gullah: Rice, Slavery, and the Sierra Leone-American Connection*. Freetown, Sierra Leone: United States Information Service.

Opoku, Kofi Asare. 1978. *West African Traditional Religion*. Accra, Ghana: FEB International.

Orser, C. E. 1998. "The Archaeology of the African Diaspora." *Annual Review of Anthropology* 27: 63–82.

O'Shea, Kathleen. 1999. *Women and the Death Penalty in the United States, 1900–1998*. New York: Praeger Publishers.

Oyewumi, Oyeronke. 1997. *The Invention of Women*. Minneapolis: University of Minnesota Press.

Painter, Nell Irvin. 1977. *Exodusters: Black Migration to Kansas after Reconstruction*. New York: Alfred A. Knopf.

Pandian, Jacob. 1985. *Anthropology and the Western Tradition: Toward an Authentic Anthropology*. Prospect Heights, Ill.: Waveland.

Parrinder, Edward Geoffrey. 1949. *West African Religion, Illustrated from the Beliefs and Practices of the Yoruba, Ewe, Akan, and Kindred Peoples*. London: Epworth.

Pike, Kenneth L. 1990. "On the Emics and Etics." In *Emics and Etics: The Insider/Outsider Debate*, edited by Marvin Harris, Thomas N. Headland, and Kenneth L. Pike, 28–47. Thousand Oaks, Calif.: Sage.

Pinn, Anthony B. 2006. *The African American Religious Experience in America*. Westport, Conn.: Greenwood Press.

Pitts, Waters F. 1993. *Old Ship of Zion: The Afro-Baptist Ritual in the African Diaspora*. New York: Oxford University Press.

Porter, Ruth Paul. 1943. "Negro Women in the Clothing, Cigar and Laundry Industries of Philadelphia, 1940." *Journal of Negro Education* 12, no. 1: 21–23.

Raboteau, Albert J. 1978. *Slave Religion: The Invisible Institution in the Antebellum South*. New York: Oxford University Press.

Ray, Benjamin C. 2000. *African Religions: Symbol, Ritual, and Community*. Upper Saddle River, N.J.: Prentice Hall.

Rigby, Peter. 1996. *African Images: Racism and the End of Anthropology*. Oxford: Berg.

Robbins, Joel. 2003a. "Introduction to the Symposium: What Is a Christian? Notes toward an Anthropology of Christianity." *Religion* 33, no. 3: 191–99.

———. 2003b. "On the Paradox of a Global Pentecostalism and the Perils of Continuity Thinking." *Religion* 33, no. 3: 221–31.

Rollins, Judith. 1985. *Between Women: Domestics and Their Employers*. Philadelphia, Pa.: Temple University Press.

Rosenior, Derrick. 2009. *Toward Racial Reconciliation: Collective Memory, Myth and Nostalgia in American Pentecostalism*. Saarbrücken: VDM Verlag.

Said, Edward. 1990. "Reflections on Exile." In *Out There: Marginalization and Contemporary Cultures*, 357–66. Cambridge, Mass.: MIT Press.

Sanders, Cheryl. 1996. *Saints in Exile: The Holiness-Pentecostal Experience in African American Religion and Culture*. Oxford: Oxford University Press.

Sanneh, Lamin. 1990. *West African Christianity: The Religious Impact*. London: C. Hurst.

———. 1999. *Abolitionists Abroad*. Cambridge, Mass.: Harvard University Press.

Savage, Barbara Dianne. 2002. Forward. In *Black Gods of the Metropolis: Negro Religious Cults of the Urban North*, by Arthur Huff Fauset, vii–xvi. Philadelphia: University of Pennsylvania Press.

Sayers, Daniel O. 2006. "Diasporan Exiles in the Great Dismal Swamp, 1630–1860." *Transforming Anthropology* 14, no. 1 (April): 10–20.

Scherer, Lester B. 1975. *Slavery and the Churches in Early America 1619–1819*. Grand Rapids, Mich.: William B. Eerdmans.

Schwalm, Leslie A. 1997. *A Hard Fight for We: Women's Transition from Slavery to Freedom in South Carolina*. Urbana: University of Illinois Press.

Sernett, Milton C. 1997. *Bound for the Promised Land: African American Religion and the Great Migration*. Durham, N.C.: Duke University Press.

Singer, Merrill. 2000. "Symbolic Identity Formation in an African American Religious Sect: The Black Hebrew Israelites." In *Black Zion: African American Religious Encounters with Judaism*, edited by Yvonne Patricia Chireau and Nathaniel Deutsch, 55–72. New York: Oxford University Press.

Smith, Jessie Carney, ed. 1996. *Notable Black American Women.* Vol. 2. Detroit: Gale Research Inc.
Smith, Raymond. 1997. Foreword. In *Jamaica Genesis: Religion and the Politics of Moral Orders*, by Diane Austin-Broos, xii–xix. Chicago: University of Chicago Press.
Smith-Brown, Tina. 2010. "Take 2 Aspirins and Become an Episcopalian: A Woman's Journey from the Charismatic Protestant Church, to the Quiet Conservative World of the Episcopalian." *Creative Nonfiction.* University of Denver Online. http://universityofdenvercreativenonfiction.blogspot/2010/09/take-2-aspirins-and-become-episcopalian.html (accessed February 19, 2011).
Soelle, Dorothee. 2006. *Dorothee Soelle, Essential Writings.* Maryknoll, N.Y.: Orbis Books.
Southern, Eileen. 1997. *The Music of Black Americans: A History.* New York: Norton.
Spector, Janet D. 1993. *What This Awl Means: Feminist Archaeology at a Wahpeton Dakota Village.* St. Paul: Minnesota Historical Society Press.
Spickard, James V. 2002. "On the Epistemology of Post-Colonial Ethnography." In *Personal Knowledge and Beyond: Reshaping the Ethnography of Religion*, edited by James V. Spickard, J. Shawn Landres, and Meredith B. McGuire, 237–52. New York: New York University Press.
Stewart, Dianne M. 2005. *Three Eyes for the Journey: African Dimensions of the Jamaican Religious Experience.* New York: Oxford University Press.
Stokes, Melvyn. 2007. *D. W. Griffith's The Birth of a Nation: A History of the Most Controversial Motion Picture of All Time.* New York: Oxford University Press.
Stuckey, Sterling. 1987. *Slave Culture: Nationalist Theory and the Foundations of Black America.* New York: Oxford University Press.
Synan, Vinson. 1971. *The Holiness Pentecostal Movement in the United States.* Grand Rapids, Mich.: William M. Eerdmans.
Szwed, John. 2002. Introduction. In *Black Gods of the Metropolis: Negro Religious Cults of the Urban North*, by Arthur Huff Fauset, vii–xxii. Philadelphia: University of Pennsylvania Press.
Thomas, Alexander R. 1998. "Ronald Reagan and the Commitment of the Mentally Ill: Capital, Interest Groups, and the Eclipse of Social Policy." *Electronic Journal of Sociology.* http://www/sociology.org/content/vol003.004/thomas.html (accessed August 7, 2010).
Tinney, James. 1971. "Black Origins of the Pentecostal Movement." *Christianity Today* 15: 4–6.
Tolnay, Stewart E., and E. M. Beck. 1991. "Rethinking the Role of Racial Violence in the Great Migration." In *Black Exodus*, edited by Alfreteen Harrison, 20–35. Jackson: University Press of Mississippi.
Trouillot, Michel-Rolph. 1995. *Silencing the Past: Power and Production of History.* Boston: Beacon Press.
Turner, Lorenzo Dow. 1973. *Africanisms in the Gullah Dialect.* Ann Arbor: University of Michigan Press.
Turner, Victor. 1969. *The Ritual Process: Structure and Anti Structure.* Chicago: Aldine.
Tweed, Thomas A. 2002. "Between the Living and the Dead: Fieldwork, History, and the Interpreter's Position." In *Personal Knowledge and Beyond: Reshaping the Ethnography of Religion*, edited by James V. Spickard, J. Shawn Landres, and Meredith B. McGuire, 63–74. New York: New York University Press.

Vergara, Camilo Jose. 2000. "Second Comings." *PRINT* (November-December): 74–79.
Washington, Joseph. 1984 [1972]. *Black Sects and Cults*. Garden City, N.Y.: University Press of America.
Washington-Williams, Essie Mae. 2005. *Dear Senator: A Memoir by the Daughter of Strom Thurmond*. New York: Regan Books.
Weber, Max. 1968. *Economy and Society*. Vols. 1 and 2. Edited by Guenther Roth and Claus Wittich. Berkeley: University of California Press.
Whitfield, Harvey Amani. 2006. *Blacks on the Border: The Black Refugees in British North America, 1815–1860*. Hanover, N.H.: University Press of New England.
Wiencek, Henry. 1999. *The Hairstons: An American Family in Black and White*. New York: St. Martin's Press.
Wiggins, David Kenneth, and Patrick B. Miller, eds. 2003. *The Unlevel Playing Field: A Documentary History of the African American Experience in Sport*. Urbana: University of Illinois Press.
Wilkerson, Isabel. 2010. *The Warmth of Other Suns: The Epic Story of America's Great Migration*. New York: Random House.
Williams, Melvin D. 1974. *Community in a Black Pentecostal Church: An Anthropological Study*. Groveland, Ill.: Waveland Press.
Willoughby, William. 1969. "Storefront Churches: Social Stabilizers." *Christianity Today* 13: 44–45.
Wilmore, Gayraud. 1983. *Black Religion and Black Radicalism*. Maryknoll, N.Y.: Orbis Books.
Wilson, Diane. 2005. *An Unreasonable Woman: A True Story of Shrimpers, Politicos, Polluters, and the Fight for Seadrift, Texas*. White River Junction, Vt.: Chelsea Green Publishing.
———. 2008. *Holy Roller: Growing up in the Church of Knock Down Drag Out; or, How I Quit Loving a Blue-Eyed Jesus—A Childhood Memoir*. White River Junction, Vt.: Chelsea Green.
Winkler, Allan M. 1972. "The Philadelphia Transit Strike of 1944." *Journal of American History* 59, no. 1 (June): 73–89.
Wolfinger, James. 2005. "'Liberty . . . That's a lot of bunk!' The Meaning of the 1944 Philadelphia Transit Strike to Black Philadelphia." *History Cooperative's Conference Proceedings Online*. http://www.historycooperative.org/proceedings/aaslh/wolfinder.html (accessed August 2, 2010).
Yelvington, Kevin A. 2001. "The Anthropology of Afro-Latin America and the Caribbean: Diasporic Dimensions." *Annual Review of Anthropology* 30: 227–60.
Yoes, Sean. 2003. "8 AFRO Reports on Strom's Black Kin." *New York Amsterdam News*. December 25–31, 2003.
Zahan, Dominique. 2000. "Some Reflections on African Spirituality." In *African Spirituality: Forms, Meanings and Expressions*, edited by Jacob K. Olupona, 3–25. New York: Crossroad Publishing.

INDEX

AFL-CIO, 78
African Americans: biased research on, 5, 10; constant movement of, 11–12, 166; ethnography and, 4–5; "flat images" of, 4, 165
African Christian Diaspora, 176n6
African Diaspora, 12–14; Black church in diasporic perspective, 134–38; nuanced notion of, 166
African Instituted Churches (AIC), 9, 112; bifocal vision of, 14, 136
African Methodist Episcopal (AME) Church, 30–31, 69, 85, 129, 177n8
African Methodist Episcopal Zion (AMEZ) church, 25
African religious practices, 137. *See also* West African culture
Afrophobia, 137–38
Aguilar, Abelardo, 68
Aladura churches, 130, 183n5; as ICMs, 137; shout-related event at, 136; witchcraft, belief in, 135
Alexander, Raymond Pace, 41
Alexander Slave Cemetery, 89
Ames, Jessie Daniel, 181n5
Anthropology: "decolonized," 10; fieldworker as observer, 133; as salvific, 9; and study of Christianity, 172
Anti-apartheid struggle, 170, 184n1
Anti-intellectualism, of Pentecostal and Holiness traditions, 168
Anti-lynching proposal and President Woodrow Wilson, 40
Asian storekeepers, relationship with Blacks in North Philadelphia, 79
Assemblies of God, 24, 170–71
Association of Southern Women for the Prevention of Lynching, 181n5
Asuza Street Mission, 24; revival movement, 24, 176n6
Authority and power, 3, 26, 113, 143–44, 155–59, 164

Baldwin, James, 11, 127, 170, 182n1
Ballard, Allen, 8, 11
Banner Real Estate, 179n11
Baptist church, 94; first Black congregations, 140; and gospel music, 41; The Church's break from, 57–58; opposition to slavery, 176n5; in Philadelphia, 179n11; 11; Seattle storefront, study, 21; in South Carolina, 50, 52; Southern schools founded by, 101; in Virginia, 57–58, 91; on women's ordination, 3; on women's role in, 104
Barrett High School, 84
"Basket names," 82, 182n13
Bettis, Alexander, 71, 181n9
Bettis Academy, 71, 101
Bible, The Church's view of, 121; Bible study, 121–22; biblical authority, 19, 59, 115, 120–25, 127–28, 135, 138, 142, 157–58, 167, 168, 170
Biddle family, 72
Birth of a Nation (film), 33–34
Black churches: burning of, 177n3; colorism in independent, 42; racial uplift ideas in independent, 42; Sanctified churches and independent, 24; as social hub, 177n3
Black Gods of the Metropolis: Negro Religious Cults of the Urban North (Fauset), 44
Black Jews, 43
Black Panther Party, 67
Black Religious Studies Group, x
Black trolley drivers, riots against in Philadelphia, 88, 98
Black United Front, 184n1
Black/White interactions: connections between women, 105, 144; Elder April Peters Nichols on, 57; Elder Beverly Nichols Cromwell on, 70–71; Elder Walter Nichols on, 94; Jewish employers/Black workers, 57, 64; media coverage of, 94; North and South compared, 102–3; northern racism, described by Elder Frank, 88; Quaker traditions and, 80; in South Carolina, 62–63, 83, 97

Black women's club movement, 42
Blenheim, North Carolina, 50
Blocker, Rev., 71
"Bloody Edgefield" (South Carolina), 60, 72–73. See also Edgefield, South Carolina; Edgefield Plan
Body: doing anthropology through, 133; discomfort over, in Sanctified tradition, 145; effects of Pentecostalism on, 145; sexualizing the Black body, 132; in study of religion, 132–33; in worship 22, 110, 127, 130–32, 136, 177n2
Bowman, Mr., 72
Brown, Mother. See Mother Brown
Brown v. Board of Education (1954), 115
Buchman, Mr., 69
Business. See Church, The: financial matters
Butler, Ann, 75
Butler, Carrie, 96
Byrd, William, 3, 140

Campbell's Soup factory, 77, 98
Candomblé religion, Brazil, 130
Cartier School of Beauty, 77
Catholicism, 137
Catto, O. V., 32
Celestial Church of Christ, 183n5
Chanukah, 125
Charismatic founder-leaders, 43–44
Cherry, F. S., 43, 44, 113, 124
Cherry Building and Loan Association, 179n11
Cherry's Family Kosher Restaurant, 112, 178n7
Chicago storefront churches, 15, 20
Children in The Church: Bible study, 122, 123; musical performances of, 110; Sunday Bible school, 155
Chosenness, 3, 25, 102, 113–14, 190n
Christ Apostolic Church, 130, 183n5
Christianity: anthropological study of, 172; The Church's reworking of, 13, 23, 134–35, 172; World Christianity, 14
Christian Tabernacle Church, 180n15
Church, The: age as organizing principle in, 167; annual fellowship day, 59, 162; author's insider position, interpretive implications of, 10; building/buildings of, 3, 141; as case study, 16, 166; catering matters, 98–99; characterized, 6; choir exchanges with other churches, 162; Christianity reworked by, 13, 23, 134–35, 172; Christmas customs, 125; "coming into," 149; Communion/Passover celebrated in, 113, 125, 128; decision-making structures of, 158–59; Dedication week, 120, 123; defined, 1; as Diaspora religion, 12–13; doctrine, 123–25; as expression of self-determination, 169; early male members, 95; Easter customs, 125;
and education, commitment to, 101–2, 115, 116, 163, 168; Education Fund, 163, 168; as family of families, 95; financial matters, 142–43, 159; as fortress and reservoir, 12; freewill offerings, 142–43; fundamentals reinterpreted, 159–60; fundraising rallies, 143, 162; gendered dynamics of, 26; governance of, 157–59, 167; grace, view of, 116–17; identity and affiliations, 2–3, 141, 142; influence in author's life, 9; institutional changes in, 155–57; interaction with nonmembers, 99; interpretive approaches to, 28; loans to church members, 143, 163; membership, 141–42; men, role in congregation, 167; offices described, 146–48; original site of, 17; printed materials and programs, 161–62; prohibitions, 119; reasons to join, 106; recruitment, 146–53; reorganization of, 157–59; as respite from White hierarchies, 16–17; scholarship fund, 163; shouting as religious expression, importance of, 128–29, 161; social responsibility/solidarity in, 21; and space, ritual use of, 159–60; testimony service, 110; underpinnings summarized, 27
-- Religious Law: centrality of, 121; dimensions of, 111–12; as duty and gift, 116–17; Jesus Christ according to, 113; legalism, 116; Levitical laws observed, 37, 103, 107, 178n7; love and, 116; sources and authority, 113; Torah and Gospels conflated, 112–13; for women, 112
Church of God and Saints of Christ, 43
Church of God and Saints of Christ of God, 113
Church of God in Christ (COGIC): Bible colleges founded by, 168; on covering women's bodies, 145; on death penalty, 170; founding and incorporation of, 24, 25; Melvin Williams' study of, 20; Mother Dabney and, 46, 180n15; performers and audience in, 128; role of women in, 46; Church of God Seventh Day, 124, 141
Church of God (Tennessee), 47
Church of Prayer Seventh Day, The, 2, 52–53
Church of the Living God Pillar and Ground of Truth for All Nations, 43, 44, 113
Church of the Living God Pillar and Ground of Truth Without Controversy (COLG), 43, 47, 48
Church of the Lord-Aladura, 183n5
Church of the Lord Jesus Christ of the Apostolic Faith, 43–44, 124
Church picnics, 119–20, 164
Cigar workers' unions, 56
Civil Rights Act of 1875, 53
Civil Rights Act of 1957, 96
Civil Rights Act of 1964, 64, 80, 101
Civil Rights Movement, 170
Cloth cutters, 77, 78; union, 104

Coalition of Concerned Leaders and Citizens to Save Our Youth, 184n1
Coffey, Lillian Brooks, 46
Cold War, 118
Coles, J. Doddridge, 53
College of Charleston's Jewish Heritage Project, 182n14
Color caste, 42, 179–80n13
Colored Methodist Episcopal (CME) Church, 31
Colorism, 85; in Black independent churches, 42; Cromwell family and, 76; as form of inhumanity, 105; Philadelphia and Virginia compared, 55. *See also* Sasportas, T. K.
Comfort Hotel, Ocean City, 68–69
"Coming into" The Church, 149. *See also* Church, The: recruitment
Committee of Negro Migration, 179n11
Congress of Industrial Organizations (CIO), 39
Conry, Inez, 184n1
Conversion experiences: of Elder Beverly, 80–81; of Elder Esther, 85–86; of Elder Frank, 88–89; of Elder Ronald, 91; of Elder Walter, 94–95; of Mother Brown, 141; overview of, 105–6, 113–14
Coro Gospel de Madrid, 152
Crack addiction, 163
Credit, William, 179n11
Cromwell, Elder Beverly Nichols, 70–81
Cromwell, Elder Jerald, 66–70
Crowdy, William S., 113
Crumbley, James, 180n4
Cuba, 48
Cult, use of term, 44
Cultural heritage tourism, 145
Cultural survivals across Diaspora, 45; Jamaican, 131; African, 22–24, 30, 131; shout, 23; root work, 134–35

Dabney, Juanita Elizabeth. *See* Mother Dabney
Dancing. *See* Church, The: prohibitions, 119
Data collection methods, 6
Daughtry, Alonzo A., 184n1
Daughtry, Herbert, 184n1
Davis, Gary, 126, 183n4
Deacons of The Church, 70, 95, 144, 146, 147; board of, 167; criteria for becoming, 157–58; power of, 159; role of, 167
Deference: importance of in The Church, 51; to Mother Brown, 143–44
Desegregation, 38, 101, 115, 116
Devil, founding saints' view of, 134
Dietary habits: Jews' and saints' practices compared, 37, 178n7; saints' identification with Jews, 114

Dinkins, David, 184n1
Displacement, 13, 175n3
Divine, Father, 43, 44
Dobbins Vocational High School, 67
Doctrinal Points of the Church of God (7th Day Apostolic) Re-organized 1933, 123–25
Domestic day labor: in Augusta, Georgia, 63; Black/White experiences compared, 38; child rearing and, 77, 102; children helping with, 78; criticisms of, 84; Great Migration and, 37–38, 56; Irish-American women and, 37–38; in Moncks Corner, 84; Mother Brown and, 141; in 1930s Philadelphia, 51; in South Carolina, 62, 71; in 1930s South Carolina, 51; southern assumptions about, 105; Strawberry Mansion and, 34–37, 51–52; street corner lines for, 34, 51, 105, 114; "Village" neighborhood and, 66; wages, 34, 98, 114; wartime, 76–77
Dorn, Fred, 74–75
Dorn, T. Felder, 61, 75, 87
Dorsey, Thomas A., 41
Dreams. *See* Gifts of the spirit
Dress codes in The Church, 113, 120, 145; changes to, 160, 168; degendered and desexualized, 145–46; as protective ritual action, 146
Drew Ali's Moorish Temple, 44
"Dual-sex" model of slavery, 26–27
Du Bois, W.E.B., 31, 99
Duckey, James H., 178n5
Dudley, Pastor, 52

Early church tradition, 116, 117, 172
Ecumenism, 142, 168
Edgefield, South Carolina, 60–63, 70–76, 92, 95–96, 97; Jewish family stores in, 76, 181n11. *See also* "Bloody Edgefield"
Edgefield Plan, 72–73
Education: achievement rates, 163; college, 102; high schools, 35–36, 116, 163; in Philadelphia, 35–36; quality and importance of neighborhood, 79, 101; race-based tracking in, 66–67, 102, 105; in rural South, 50–51, 62; segregation in, 39, 41, 60, 61, 62, 86, 179n10; southern two-room "field school," 90; Strawberry Mansion, 35–36; and Moncks Corner, 83–84; overview of, 101–2; Quaker influence, 87; salvation enhanced by, 92; "saved" view of, 51, 56, 84, 87, 90, 101–2
Egg Harbor, New Jersey, 99
Elders of The Church, 91, 146, 147; consensus-based shared leadership, 158, 164; criteria for becoming, 157–58; board of, 89; and "real work" of The Church, 158, 159; selection process for, 158; veto power of, 167

204 · Index

Emancipation: in Low Country (South Carolina), 82; in Virginia, 54
Ethnography, 4–8; of African Americans, 4, 165; and the body 133; eudemonia, 131, 132; historically embedded, 7; and neutrality, myth of, 10; and personal memory, 6; and person of the ethnographer, 5; political nature of, 5; of Sanctified churches, x, 19–22; thick description, 6; three-dimensional, nuanced approaches to, 165; veiled and peripheral spaces, 5, 165
European American religious tradition, 129–30
Exile, notion and biblical themes of, 12
Exodusters, 13

Fair Employment Practices Commission (FEPC), 38–39
Faith communities: scholarly approach to, 8–11; storefront churches as, 17. *See also individual congregations*
Faith healing, 46
Family, as model for The Church, 119, 139, 153–55
Fasting, 127–28
Fauset, Arthur Huss, 39, 40–41, 43, 44, 119
Fieldwork, in anthropology, 8–9
First African Baptist Church, 179n11
Fisher, Henry, 47
Fisk University, 78
Formosa Plastics, 171, 184–85n3
Foucault, Michel, 5
Founding saints of The Church, 2; collection of saints' narratives described, 5–6; importance of stories of, 4; experiences of agency, 16; and Great Migration, 48, 49; as institution-builders, 27; life stories of, 49–106; material difficulties experienced by, 8; and norm of academic excellence, 115–16; as peculiar (chosen) people, 116, 117; as "select and chosen few," 3; southern states of origin, 33; spiritual gifts of, 133–34. *See also* Saints of The Church
Fowler, George, 54
Frank, Joe, 61
Frazier, E. Franklin, 44–45, 180n14
Free blacks, 30, 42

Garden of Prayer. *See* Mother Dabney, Garden of Prayer
Gender: biblical authority and, 125; "dual-sex" model of, 26; practices, 25–26; intersections with race and power, as experienced by The Church's early members, 103–4. *See also* Church, The: men, role in congregation; Women
General Assembly, 123, 142, 162
Gifts of the spirit, 134,

Gilliam, Clarence, 74, 75
Glossolalia, 24. *See also* Speaking in tongues
Grace, Charles Manuel "Daddy," 43, 44, 184n1
Grace, view of in The Church, 116–17
Great Awakening(s), 23, 30, 177n7
Great Depression, 37
Great Migration: and African forms of spiritual expression, 31; Black health problems during, 39 (*see also* Tuberculosis); dearth of leisure facilities for Black migrants, 40; economic and job discrimination during, 16, 38; economic opportunity and, 7; factory work and, 37; family networks formed during, 100–101; founding saints as participants in, 48–49; housing discrimination during, 36–37; infant mortality rate during, 39; material difficulties accompanying, 8; mortgages/banking for migrants, 179n11; and Mother Bethel Church, 41; in North Philadelphia, 36; novels set in, 8; phases of, 2; in Philadelphia, 2–3, 33, 37–38; racial uplift and, 40–43; and religion, 1, 11–12, 14–17; response of migrants to, 43; significance of, 166; stage migration, 100; women in Sanctified churches during, 45–48, 144
Griffiths, D. W., 33
Griot (keepers of history), 6
Gullah-Geechee people, 81–82; "basket names," 82, 182n13; and ring shout, 129
Guyana, 48

Hair: 32, 54–55, 66, 76, 113, 135; hairdressing, 77
Haitian Vodun, 133
Hamer, Fannie Lou, 170
Harlem, musical and homiletic styles, 15
Healing: faith, 46; gift of, 65; Holy Ghost as source of, 127
Hermeneutics of suspicion, 169–70, 173
Herskovits, Melville J., 44, 45
Hispanics, 56, 94
Historical context, importance of in ethnographic studies, 7
Historical ethnography, 20
Holiness: comportment and dress codes, 120; and danger, 117–18; Holy Ghost as guide, 126; as way of life, 117; and worldly activities, 119, 154
Holiness movement: origins, 23; White American Holiness, 177n7
Holiness Pentecostalism, 25, 119, 169; influence of, 183n5; interracial rapprochement, 176n6
Holy Ghost: as antidote to root work, 109; experience of, 126–28; spiritual gifts and, 133–34
"Honor," code of southern White, 53, 73
Horn and Hardart cafeteria chain, 40

Horten, Elder Rose Nichols, 96–99
Horton, Stanley, 170–71
Hot dogs, 112, 178n7
House of Prayer for All People, 44
House of the Lord Pentecostal church, 170
Hughes, George, 181n5
Hunter, Jane Edna, 179n9

Immigration restrictions, 7
Independent church movements (ICMs), 13, 136–37, 166
Industrialization, 7
Institution-building: and charismatic leadership, 3, 167–68; The Church as successful experiment in, 164; as self-determination, 169; and survival of The Church, 1, 164
Interdenominational Ministerial Alliance, 179n11
Inter-Racial Committee's Anti-lynching Committee, 40

Jamaican Pentecostalism, 128, 129–30, 131, 145
Jefferies, James (Jack Johnson), 32
"Jesus-only" doctrine, 124
Jewish people: businesses of, remembered by Elder Beverly, 76; as employers, remembered by Elder Holly, 64; founding saints' views of, 114–115; relationships with, remembered by Elder Esther, 83, 85; saints' religious connectedness to, 103; saints' identification with, 114; "true Jews," 113
Job ("a man called"), Elder Esther's memory of, 83
Job discrimination, 16. *See also* Racial discrimination in the job market
Johnson, James Weldon, 15
Johnson, Sherrod, 43–44, 124
Jones, Mother, 180n15
Jones, Will, 61, 75, 105
Jones Tabernacle AME Church, 98

Kaufman family, 66, 115
Kellor, Frances A., 38, 178–79n9
Kelly, Frank, 32
Kirkland, James E., 41
Ku Klux Klan: Elder Holly's memory of, 62–63; film representation of, 34. *See also* Night riders

Lambert, Tony, 77
Land grabbing, 63, 87, 100
Laurens, Henry, 81
"Laying on of hands," 109, 127
Layten, Sarah Willie, 38
Lewis, Charles, 39–40
Liberia, emigration to, 73

Lived intangibles concept, 4
Logan Demonstration School, 102, 115–16, 118, 169
Logue family, 61, 74, 75, 76, 95–96, 102, 105
Lone Cane Holiness Church, 65
Lone Oak Baptist Church, 91
Lord's Prayer, 108
Lord's Supper, 112–13
Lynching, 7–8; cultural productions about, 181n5; in Edgefield County, South Carolina, 73; family memory of, 180–81n4; justifications of, 103–4; in Pennsylvania, 34; protests against, 33–34; during Reconstruction, 50; in Virginia, 53–54. *See also* White violence

Mader, Elder, 69
Maroon communities, 175n3
Martin family, 142
Maruyama, Magoroh, 10
Mason, Charles Harrison, 24, 46, 169–70
Masterman Junior High School, 116
Materialism, 169
McKay, Claude, 179n9
Mecklenburg, Virginia, 3, 140–41
Memphis Miracle (1994), 24, 176n6
Mental illness, 183n4
Mercy Hospital, 40
Methodist Church: antislavery platform, 176n5; Black, 30, 31; early Black expression in, 30
Methodist evangelicals, 23
Migration patterns, Civil War era, 12–13
Millennialism: date of, prophesied by Mother Brown, 59; described, 117–18; and Mother Brown's teachings, 143; and The Church's founding saints as "chosen few," 3
Miller, A. G., 170
Moncks Corner, South Carolina, 81–84
Morrison, Toni, 8
Moses, J., 51, 100
Mother Bethel African Methodist Episcopal Church, 30, 41, 177n1
Mother Brown: arrival in North Philly, 33; on articles of faith, 123; authority of, 143–44, 167; on Bible study, 121–22; call to preach, 29, 140; challenges to, 155–57; charisma of, 155, 157; chooser of The Church's elders, 158; conversion experience of, 141; death of, 106, 164; deference shown to, 143–44; on distancing from other Sabbath-keeping and Sanctified churches, 124–25; on dividing line between family members in The Church, 58–59; as domestic day laborer, 141; family of, 152; family rivalries, 156–57; on fasting, 128; fund-raising rallies of, 86, 143; as God's anointed, 121; guidance of, 52,

Mother Brown—*continued*
104; harshness of, 98; as head of The Church-as-family, 139; healing the sick by laying on of hands, 127; influence of services, 58, 98; institution-building of, 27, 157; "Jesus-only" doctrine of, 124; on Jewishness, 113; on lateness for Sabbath, 107; on "the law" (of a commandment-keeping church), 111; leadership skills, 144; Mecklenburg call, 140; and millennialism, 143; modesty in dress of, 146; on "open rebuke," 155–56; personal and religious background, 2–3, 140–41; Philadelphia ministry, 141–42; on police punishments, 103; power of, 159; on premarital sex, 155; and reorganization of The Church, 157–59; role during services, 108; on salvation, 121; as teacher of "Word of Truth," 109; on voting, 68; on worldliness and its dangers, 117–20
Mother Dabney, 58, 119, 181n6; Garden of Prayer, 46, 65, 94, 125, 180n15. *See also* Edgefield, South Carolina
Mother Jones, 180n15
Mount Sinai church, 43, 44; gender inclusivity of, 47–48
MOVE community, 67
Movies, 119, 120
Mukashy, Israel, family store, 181n11. *See also* Edgefield, South Carolina
Music: The Church youth band, 151; choir exchanges, 162; "Down at the Cross," 108; gospel compositions, 41, 151, 152, 179n12; *Gospel Pearls*, 179n12; "Great Change Since I Been Born," 183n4; James Baldwin on, 182n1; as life-changing experience for Elder Esther, 85; and musicians of The Church, 152–53; Predestined Praise choir, 184n4; Sabbath services and, 108; "signed praise" introduced into The Church's youth choir, 163; and storefront churches, rise of, 15; "Sweet Sabbath Home," 109; "Things I used to do I don't do no more," 126; *Touch Me Lord* (CD), 184n4; "You Can't Hide" as leveling vehicle, 156
Mutual Aid Insurance Society, 179n11

Nathiri, N.Y., 145–46
National Association for the Advancement of Colored People (NAACP), 34, 41
National League for the Protection of Colored Women, 38
Neutrality. *See* Ethnography: and neutrality, myth of
New Bethel Baptist Church (Virginia), 57–58
New Reformation Pentecostalism, 1
Nichols, Elder April Peters, 53–60
Nichols, Elder Hannah Pope, 49–53
Nichols, Elder Frank, 86–89
Nichols, Elder Walter, 92–96
Nigeria, 24, 130, 135–37, 166, 182n13
Night riders, 75–76
Noah's Ark Church, 66
Northeast Federation of Colored Women's Clubs, 40
Northeast High School for Boys, 67
Northern Black churches in Philadelphia, 13, 16, 31, 40–43
Northern Blacks' racial uplift work, 40–43
North Philadelphia: alternative economy in, 154; Black migrants to, 36; described, 154; family in, 93; gentrification of, 162–63; mixed neighborhoods in, 79; "the Village," 66

Obama, Barack, 76
Objectivity, ethnographic, 5, 133, 165–66
Observant participation, 9
Offices of The Church, 146–48
Oral histories, 4–6
Orozco, José Clemente, 181n5
Oswald, Richard, 81
Owdom, Clifford, 61

Pacifism, 48, 124, 169–70
Pan African Charismatic Evangelical Congress (PACEC), 170
Park, Robert E., 180n14
Parousia, 118
Passover/Communion, 77, 113, 125, 128
Pastor, divine protection of, 133–34
Patriarchy: Black male, 27; conventions of, 25
Payne, Daniel, 30–31
Peace Mission Movement, 43, 44
Penn Relays ("Negro Olympics"), 1, 19
Penn, William, 29–30
Pentecostal Assemblies of the World (PAW), 25
Pentecostal/Charismatic Church of North America (PCCNA), 176n6
Pentecostal Fellowship of North America (PFNA), 176n6
Pentecostalism: features of, 24; Jamaican and White American compared, 129–30; origins of modern, 177n7
Pentecostals and Charismatics for Peace and Justice (PCPJ), 170–71
Philadelphia: Black-Jewish encounters in, 34–37; Black Methodists in, 31, 177n1; Black neighborhoods of, 33, 56; Black Philadelphians' occupations in 1890s, 33; Black population of, 32, 33; Black/White interactions in, 51–52; Delancey Place, 84; Du Bois' study of Black churches in, 31; early ring shout practiced in, 136; and Great Migration,

2–3, 33, 37–38; larger religious life of, 119; mixed neighborhoods in, 35–37, 64, 79, 84–85; Old Black Philadelphians, migrants' views of, 43; Quaker-inspired antislavery activism in, 29–30; racial history of, 29–34, 177n1; segregated schools in, 179n10; wartime defense plant work for Blacks in, 38–39, 55, 56
West Mount Airy, 80; White violence in, 32, 34, 39
Philadelphia High School for Girls, 96, 116
Philadelphia Museum of Art, 120
Philadelphia Orchestra, 120
Philadelphia Transit Company (PTC) workers, 39, 64
Picnics, 88, 119–20, 164
Pihiras family, 142
Pittsylvania County Courthouse, 53
Plessy v. Ferguson (1896), 35, 54, 101
Police brutality, 39, 67, 102, 103
Polyocularity, 10, 28
Pork, avoidance of, 37, 112, 178n7
Preaching, Elder Holly's gift for, 65
"Pressing through," 127, 130
Primary group intimacy, 153
Prosser, Gabriel, 176n5
Protestantism, 23, 136, 137
PTA meetings, 119
PTC (Philadelphia Transportation Company), 39. *See also* Smith Connally Anti-Strike/War Labor Disputes Act; Transportation strike
Public housing, 36
Pullman Company, 88
Purnell, James W., 32

Quakers, 29–30

Race relations: northern and southern compared, 102–3; as recalled by Elder Holly, 60, 64; as recalled by Elder Jerald, 67; as recalled by Elder Ronald, 91
Racial discrimination in job market, 16, 26, 37–38, 50, 122, 145, 166, 170
Racial uplift, 40; critiques of, 42–43
Radio ministry: of Mother Dabney, 58; of Rev. Tindley, 41; WDAS (Philadelphia), 44
Randolph, A. Philip, 38
Rape allegations and White violence, 54, 73–74, 97, 103, 180n4
Rapid Transit Union (RTU) workers, 39
Respectability. *See* Sanctified churches and tradition: respectability norms of
Restrictive covenants. *See* Great Migration: housing discrimination during
Revenge killing. *See* Logue family

Revivalism: and African-derived religion, 13; Asuza Street revival movement, 24; different churches compared, 129–30; Great Awakenings, 23; legitimating effect of, 137; southern revival style of preaching, 41
Ring shout, 30, 129, 136. *See also* Slave religion
Rivers, Eugene, 170
Rizzo, Frank, 67
Robinson, Ida Bell, 47–48, 168; and Mount Sinai church, founding of, 43, 44; 47; pacifism of during World War I, 169; as political witness, 169–70
Roosevelt, Franklin Delano, 38, 97
Root work, 134–35
Routinization of charisma: traditional analyses of, 27; rethinking, 167–68; scholars on, 20, 165; surviving Mother Brown's death, 164
Rubenstein family store, 76, 181n11. *See also* Edgefield, South Carolina

Sabbath-keeping in The Church, 107; changes and modifications, 160–61; compared with other Christian churches, 116; dress for, 120, 145; Jewish and Christian practices compared, 37, 114; order of the service, 107–10; Sabbath afternoon service issues, 107, 109–10, 160–61; special blessings of, 112; strictures related to, 112
Said, Edward, 12
Saints of The Church: anonymity of, 175n1; as culture-bearers, 13; liberation of "subjugated knowledges" and, 5; notion of family among, 139; power of root work, belief in, 135; status on Sabbath, 16–17; support of women across race and class, 104; use of term, 1; and World Christianity, within discourse of, 172–73. *See also* Founding saints of The Church
Salvation: by works, 116; contingent on rejecting worldliness, 118–19; relationship with Jewish law, 113–14; understanding of, among The Church's founding saints (soteriology), 114
Sanctified churches and tradition: The Church as case study among, 166; COGIC study of, 20; and covering of female body, 132; in diasporic perspective 22, 25, 129–33, 134–38; as example of grassroots institution-building, 22; gendered dynamics of, 26; on material accumulation, 169; matrices of domination in, 26; message and ethos of, 12; new perspectives on, 168–69; religious and cultural legacies of, 22; respectability norms of, 48; as response to established Black independent churches, 24; and revivalism considered, 137; social justice focus of, 170–72, 184n1; spirituality of, 26; suspicion of status quo, 169–70; use of term,

Sanctified churches and tradition—*continued*
  24–25; valuing of women's needs in, 48; White
  Pentecostalism compared to, 176–77n7; women's
  leadership in, 45–48; youth in, 168
Sasportas, T. K., 179–80n13. *See also* Colorism
Schofield, Martha, 87
Schooling. *See* Education
Schurz, Carl, 99
Scripture in The Church: 120–25; elders on private
  interpretation of, 59; radical call of, 172
Segregation: Horn and Hardart restaurants and, 40,
  90; in Philadelphia neighborhoods, 36; of Phila-
  delphian recreational facilities, 40; in Northern
  neighborhoods, 166; school system and, 39, 41,
  86–87, 179n10; Strom Thurmond's support of, 96.
  See also Great Migration: housing discrimination
  during; White flight
Self-determination, 3, 12, 21, 23, 30, 71, 105, 118, 169,
  177n1
Sensorial landscapes. *See* Body: in study of religion
Sewing piecework, 77
Sexuality: and power, 104; and politics, 145–46; and
  the spirit, 132. *See also* Body
Seymour, W. J., 24
Sharecropping, in Church elders' narratives, 50, 55,
  57, 74, 97, 100
Shouting: African origins of, 23, 135–36; and Atlantic
  African Diaspora, 130; biblical reference to, 135;
  characterized, 129; in The Church service, 128–29;
  161; and high spirit, 108; James Baldwin on, 127;
  sacred aspects of, 127
Silver, Hanna, 36–37, 115
Singleton, Benjamin "Pap," 13
Slave patrollers, 23
Slave religion: African-derived 15, 23, 166, 176n7; in
  Philadelphia 30, 136, 183n6. *See also* Ring shout
Slave revolt, fear of, 176n5
Slavery, 12–13; cultural change under, 131; "dual-
  sex" model and, 26–27; literacy of slaves, 176n5;
  maroon communities, 175n3; Moncks Corner
  plantation, 81; in North Carolina, 50; northern
  and southern compared, 183n6; overview of, 102;
  in Pittsylvania tobacco country, 54–55; purchasing
  freedom, 66, 173n3; Reconstruction era considered, 99; religious ethics of, 175–76n4; reworkings
  of Christianity under, 23; ring shout and, 136;
  secret worship practices under, 60; in Virginia,
  54, 89–90
Smith-Connally Anti-Strike/War Labor Disputes Act
  (1943), 39, 64. *See also* Transportation strike
Soap making, as recalled by Elder Ronald, 89
Soul Force, 4

South: as Egyptland, 14; employment in, 90; rural
  conditions of, 50–53; segregation in, 7; as "Vale
  of Tears," 99, 106; White Supremacy in, 7–8, 100;
  White violence in, 62–63, 99. *See also* Edgefield,
  South Carolina; South Carolina; Virginia
South Carolina (Low Country and Moncks Corner),
  81–84
Southern praise legacy, 16
Southern revival style of preaching, 41
Speaking in tongues (glossolalia), 24; described, 130;
  doctrinal points and, 124; role in The Church
  service, 128; as sign of salvation, 52, 89, 92, 95; as
  sign of true followers, 126
Spirit (Holy Ghost), 126–27
Spirit possession, 130, 131, 132
Spiritual adoption, 139, 150
St. George Methodist Church, 177n1
Stables, Elder Holly Nichols, 60–65
Stadham's Chemical and Textile plant, 77–78
States Rights Democratic Party, 97
Status quo. *See* Sanctified churches: suspicion of
  status quo
Sterling, Anne Biddle, 40
Stokes, Olivia B., 177n8
Stokowski, Leopold, 182n18
Storefront churches, 17–19; academic view of, 15,
  17–19; Arthur Huff Fauset on, 44; author's experi-
  ence of, 17–18, 173; Black resistance/self-determi-
  nation expressed through, 21; characteristics of, 15;
  in Chicago (Wallace Best study), 15; and *Church
  Mother* role, 18–19; compensation interpretation
  of, 18, 169; defined, 17; ethnographies of summarized, 19–22; in Harlem (James Weldon Johnson
  critique of), 15; hostility toward, 15; as "locus of
  empowering theological reformulation" (Frances
  Kostarelos study), 20–21, 22; misconceptions
  about, 18–19; in Philadelphia, 33; as revitalization
  movement (Ira Harrison study), 19–20; sanctified
  origins of, 22–25; socioeconomic dimensions of,
  21; and transition from southern rural to northern
  urban settings, 19–20
Strawberry Mansion neighborhood (Philadelphia),
  34–37, 91, 115, 178n6; domestic day labor in, 34–37,
  51–52; education in, 35–36
Strick Trailer Corporation, 56, 88, 94
Supplee Dairy Company, 72
Syracuse, New York, 19

Taliaferro, G.L.P., 179n11
Tarrying, 127–28
Tate, Mary Magdalena, 43, 47
Teachers: Edler April's position as substitute teacher,

56; Elder Beverly's aspirations to become teacher, 78; Elder Beverly's memories of favorite, 72; Elder Esther's memories of White, 83; Elder Frank's mother as teacher, 87; Elder Ronald's mother as teacher's assistant, 90; Elder Walter's mother as teacher, 92
Temple University, 72, 78, 116
Ten Commandments in The Church, 107, 108, 110–12; Decalogue text, 111–12
Tenth Memorial Baptist Church, 65, 80, 88
Testimony. *See* Church, The: testimony service
Texas, 106
Textile mills, 50
Thurmond, Strom, 75, 96–97
Till, Emmett, 118
Tillman, "Pitchfork" Ben, 73
Timmerman, Cornelia, 71
Timmerman, Davis, 61, 76, 95
Tindley, Charles A., 40–41
Tithes and tithing in The Church, 142–43, 161, 162; Elder April and, 59; Elder Frank and, 89; Elder Ronald and, 91
Toasties. *See* Colorism
Tobacco country, 54–55
Touch Me Lord (gospel CD), 152
Transportation strike (1944), 39, 64, 79
Transport Workers Union, 39
Trolley drivers. *See* Black trolley drivers, riots against in Philadelphia
True Form corset company, 84
Tuberculosis, 39–40, 68
Turner, Nat, 176n5

United Holy Church, 47
United House of Prayer for All People, 43
United Pentecostal Church International, 25
Uptown Theater (Philadelphia), 119
Urban anonymity, and religious affiliation, 45–46
Urban employment: cigar factory work, 56; cloth cutting, 77; efforts to secure Black workers, 178n5; during Great Migration, 56; industrial, 37, 64, 77, 90; for men, 90–91, 94; at post office, 69; in public school system, 86; racialized hiring practices, 38–39; sewing piecework, 77; skilled labor and, 77; in True Form corset company, 84; in "Village" neighborhood, 66; wartime, 33, 76–77, 84, 88, 98, 104; and wartime defense plants, 38–39, 55, 56; for women, 34–37, 91, 98; and women's wages, 77

Vesey, Denmark, 176n5
Vilar, Pierre, 4
Vindicationist scholarship, 5, 10, 175n2

Virginia, 53–58; Mecklenburg County, 89–91; slavery in, 54, 89–90
Visions. *See* Gifts of the spirit
Vocational rehabilitation of Elder Walter, 94
Vocational schools, 179n11
Voting: and burning of Black churches, 177n3; Elder April's view of as duty, 59; Elder Walter's view of as civic responsibility, 95; Elder Wilson's opposition to, 92; southern White Supremacy and, 60; Mother Brown on, 168; White threats of violence related to, 72–73; women's suffrage, 40

Wages, south and north compared, 33
Wall of the Lord, 153–55; changes to, 162, 164
Washington, D.C., 55, 88, 97
Washington-Williams, Essie Mae, 96
Watson, John Fanning, 30, 177n2
Weinstein, Nathan, 35
Wesley, John, 177n7
West African culture: body as vehicle of divinity, 131; faith traditions in, 22, 30; religious survivals from, 22–23, 30; shout origins in, 135–36; spirit possession in, 130, 131; studies of, 26
White, Archibald, 47
White, Ellen G., 124
White, Marla, 148, 151, 156
White American Holiness, 177n7
White ethnic gangs, 103
White flight, 36, 91, 93; as avoidance strategy, 101; in Elder Beverly's critique of Jewish families, 114–15; exception to, 182n18; impact on Black neighborhoods, 102; impact on schools, 79
"Whitefolks" (nickname), 67, 103
White Pentecostalism, 176n6, 176–77n7
White race riots, 32, 177–78n4
White Supremacy: "Bloody Edgefield" and, 72–73; contradicting notions of, 18; literacy test and poll tax as examples of, 60; Philadelphia violence and, 32, 34; post-Reconstruction, 53, 100; practices driven by, 7–8; in Virginia, 53
White violence: "Bloody Edgefield," 72–73; dog-shooting incident described by Elder Frank, 87–88; Irish-American, 32; and Kennedy assassinations, 118; media coverage of, 94; in Philadelphia, 32, 34, 39, 88, 98; social-psychological dynamics of race riots, 177–78n4; in South, 62–63; and southern racial etiquette, 118; strikes and, 39, 88, 98. *See also* Lynching
Widener Memorial School, 163
Wilkerson, Isabel, 2, 8
Williams, Robert J., 41
Willow Springs Baptist Church, 62, 65, 75, 80, 88, 98

Wilson, Elder Esther Rogers, 81–86
Wilson, Elder L. Ronald, 89–92
Witchcraft, belief in, 135
Women: as apical figures of The Church's founding families, 153; effects of poverty and race on, 21; employment in Philadelphia, 34–37; during the Great Migration, 38, 144, 178–79n9; Levitical laws observed by, 112, 120; merit and status of, 145; and "pressing through" process, 130; sanctified female body, 131–32; titles of respect for, 144; values of, 48. *See also* Domestic day labor
Women and Religion in the African Diaspora (WRAD) project, x
Women Preacher's Night, 47
Women's leadership, 1; and bearing of spiritual gifts, 144; as bishops, 47, 48; and *Church Mother* role, 18–19; in COGIC, 46; and decision-making power, 167; as head saints, 144; among laity, 17; and ministerial opportunities, 25, 47; Mother Brown and, 144; reorganized structure of The Church and, 157, 159; as object of censure, 18–19; and preaching, 113; in Sanctified churches, 45–48; studies of, 25
Women's ordination, 125; AME church and, 177n8; Baptist church on, 3, 177n8
Women's suffrage, 40, 179n11

Woodford Mansion, 178n6
"Word of Truth," 121
World Christianity, 14, 172; The Church as case study in, 28
World War I: and Black migration to Philadelphia, 33; and pacifism of Sanctified church leaders, 169
World War II: Elder Jerald Cromwell's correspondence during, 67–68; defense plant work in Philadelphia, 38–39; Navy Yard work during, 55, 56
Worship, modes of, 15; blurring of boundaries between audience and performance, 128; changes to, in Sanctified tradition, 161–62; during slavery, 23, 60; early African cultural practices and, 30; embodied 17, 22, 110, 127, 130–133, 136, 177n2; Great Migration influences on, 16; misconceptions about, 18–19; stress-release interpretation of, 18
Wyatt, Addie, 170

Yoruba, 136, 182n13, 183n5
Youth in The Church: Bible study, 122–23; opposition to changes in church services, 160–61; comportment of, 120; enculturation of, 163–64; secular activities of, 164

Zion Baptist Church, 179n11

Deidre Helen Crumbley, author of *Spirit, Structure, and Flesh: Gendered Experiences in African Instituted Churches among the Yoruba of Nigeria*, is professor in the Africana Studies Program at North Carolina State University.

THE HISTORY OF AFRICAN AMERICAN RELIGIONS

Laborers in the Vineyard of the Lord: The Beginnings of the AME Church in Florida, 1865–1895, by Larry Eugene Rivers and Canter Brown Jr. (2001)
Between Cross and Crescent: Christian and Muslim Perspectives on Malcolm and Martin, by Lewis V. Baldwin and Amiri YaSin Al-Hadid (2002)
The Quest for the Cuban Christ: A Historical Search, by Miguel De La Torre (2002)
For a Great and Grand Purpose: The Beginnings of the AMEZ Church in Florida, 1864–1905, by Canter Brown Jr. and Larry Eugene Rivers (2004)
Afro-Cuban Religiosity, Revolution, and National Identity, by Christine Ayorinde (2004)
From Garvey to Marley: Rastafari Theology, by Noel Leo Erskine (2005)
Hell Without Fires: Slavery, Christianity, and the Antebellum Spiritual Narrative, by Yolanda Pierce (2005)
Where Men are Wives and Mothers Rule: Santería Ritual Practices and Their Gender Implications, by Mary Ann Clark (2005)
Around the Family Altar: Domesticity in the African Methodist Episcopal Church, 1865–1900, by Julius H. Bailey (2005)
Black Blood Brothers: Confraternities and Social Mobility for Afro-Mexicans, by Nicole von Germeten (2006)
African American Atheists and Political Liberation: A Study of the Sociocultural Dynamics of Faith, by Michael Lackey (2007)
The African American Religious Experience in America, by Anthony B. Pinn (paperback edition, 2008)
The Ethiopian Prophecy in Black American Letters, by Roy Kay (2011)
Saved and Sanctified: The Rise of a Storefront Church in Great Migration Philadelphia, by Deidre Helen Crumbley (2012; first paperback edition, 2013)

www.ingramcontent.com/pod-product-compliance
Lightning Source LLC
Chambersburg PA
CBHW020051170426
43199CB00009B/244